Lord Selborne

Notes on some Passages in the Liturgical History of the Reformed English Church

Lord Selborne

Notes on some Passages in the Liturgical History of the Reformed English Church

ISBN/EAN: 9783337162603

Printed in Europe, USA, Canada, Australia, Japan

Cover: Foto ©Lupo / pixelio.de

More available books at **www.hansebooks.com**

NOTES

ON SOME

PASSAGES IN THE LITURGICAL HISTORY

OF THE

REFORMED ENGLISH CHURCH.

By LORD SELBORNE.

LONDON:
JOHN MURRAY, ALBEMARLE STREET.
1878.

LONDON:
PRINTED BY WILLIAM CLOWES AND SONS,
STAMFORD STREET AND CHARING CROSS.

ECCLESIASTICAL LAW.

A correspondence has recently taken place in these columns between Lord Selborne, Mr. Parker, and one or two other gentlemen of congenial tastes, on an ecclesiastical question of great public interest, but one, nevertheless, of so complicated, and, in some respects, technical, a character, that few readers perhaps will be at the trouble of making themselves masters of it through the medium of those various communications. It is not difficult, however, to disentangle the main points at issue from the recriminations and occasional personalities in which they are involved, and to place the controversy in such a light as shall enable every one who cares about the subject to determine its merits for himself. The source of the correspondence is to be found in a leading article on the Church Congress which appeared in this journal on the 11th of October, and called forth a letter from Dr. Hayman, late Head Master of Rugby, in which he took occasion to observe that Mr. Parker's reply to Lord Selborne's "Liturgical Notes" had elicited as yet no answer from the noble and learned Lord, and that unless an answer were forthcoming, the judgment of the highest Court of Ecclesiastical Appeal in this country would in his opinion stand convicted of grave incompetency. To this challenge Lord Selborne thought it necessary to reply, and a letter appeared in *The Standard* of October 21, in which his Lordship professed to be surprised that any answer to Mr. Parker should be required of him. His own "Notes" were purely historical, whereas Mr. Parker had engaged in questions of a more or less legal nature, with which

in 1584, and that in it after the original title "Advertisements," "partly or due order," &c., by virtue of the Queen's Letter commanding the same, the xxvth day of January, in the seventh year of the reign of our Sovereign Lady, &c., those words follow "and of late agayne commaunded as well by her Majesty's Letters as also by her Proclamation.

Undoubtedly, at first sight, this is a strong fact, implying that the Queen certainly did at some time of her reign give the force of the Royal authority conferred on her by Parliament to the Advertisements of Archbishop Parker. But Mr. Parker handles this fact with much adroitness. The original title-page of the Advertisements, as we have seen, declares them to have been issued "partly for due order in the public administration of Common Prayer, and using the Holy Sacraments, and partly for the apparel of all persons ecclesiastical by virtue of the Queen's Majesty's Letters commanding the same," &c. Mr. Parker's contention is that the words "the same" refer to "the due order" above mentioned, and that the Proclamation which he supposes to have been the one issued in 1573 referred only to the same thing, without any specifications. There might be some little difficulty, perhaps, in accepting this construction of the title-page but for the light thrown upon the subject at the end of Mr. Parker's last letter; because the object is described as twofold, "partly for due order," &c., and "partly for the apparel," &c., and if the words "commanding the same" refer to due order, they must also refer to apparel. But even if they did, the Proclamation of 1573, whether the one referred to by John Day or not, leaves no room for doubt as to her Majesty's meaning. Mr. Parker quotes, he says, the

---

State of opinion, &c., as to clerical vestures from 1559 to 1664 .. 12
The Queen's Letter of 25th January, 1564-5; and the Advertisements 13

CONTENTS.

	PAGE
The Queen's **sanction to the Advertisements** asserted as a fact, in all works of reputation published before the eighteenth century ..	13
Hooker; Sparke; Lestrange; Heylyn	13, 14
Afterwards **disputed,** by writers professing to **follow Strype** ..	14
Strype's narrative, as a whole, inconsistent with **their statements** ..	15
Probable **source of** their **error, in Strype's erroneous statement, that** the Advertisements **were published, without the Queen's authority, in 1564**	15
Strype probably **misled by false date (1564) on** the title-page in Sparrow's Collection	16
As originally **published, they bore no date**	16
No publication of the Advertisements, in any form, before March 28th, 1566	16
Their correct title	17
Hearn's statement as to their scarcity in 1717	17
Copies **of the original, and** of two later editions with the **name and in the** lifetime of Wolfe, in the British Museum	17, 18
Reginald **Wolfe, printer to the Queen**	18
Contemporaneous acknowledgments of the Queen's authority ..	18, 19
Humfrey's letter to the Queen	19
Pamphlets of 1566	19, 20
Visit of Withers and Wiburn to Geneva and Zurich, in 1566 ..	20, 21
Wiburn's statement; and Gualter's **letters of September, 1566,** to Parkhurst and Beza	21, 22
Bishop **Cox's reply to Gualter**	23
Letters of Pilkington and Jewell	23, 24
Grindal's letter of 21st May, 1566, to the Dean and Chapter of St. Paul's	24
Original draft of Archbishop Whitgift's Articles of 1584, presented to the Queen **in October, 1583**	24, 25
The Queen's assent to Articles of 1584	25
Puritan objections to form in which the Advertisements appeared ..	25, 26
'Abstract' of 1584	26
'Considerations' of 1605	26
'**Survey**' of 1606	27
Cosin's 'Notes' and 'Particulars'	27
The publication of Cosin's '**Notes,**' &c., in 1710 became the source of a new tradition	28
Dr. Cardwell's supposition, that the Queen's sanction ought to have been given under the Great Seal	28, 29

4. King James the First's Prayer-Book 29–31

Cosin and others regarded King James' alterations as illegal .. 29
Their objections; and probable answers to them 29, 30
Mr. Parker's remark on the republication, in 1604, of the Ornaments Rubric of 1559 .. .. 30, 31
Illustration from a late Statute (35 & 36 Vict. cap. 35) 31

5. The Lords' Committee of 1640-1 31–42

Constitution of that Committee 31, 32
Divines summoned by Bishop Williams' letter of March 12th, 1640-1 32
Names and reputation of those Divines 32, 33
The Committee itself did nothing 33
Sources of information as to proceedings of the Sub-committee of Divines 33, 34
Fuller's narrative 34
Original memorandum, printed in 1641 .. .. 34, 35
Sylvester's imperfect reprint of that memorandum, from Baxter's papers; followed by Neal and Cardwell 35
Mr. Parker mistakes the memorandum for a Report of the Committee 35
Dr. Cardwell's account of those proceedings 35
Statements, on same subject, in 'Rejoinder' of Puritan Commissioners at Savoy Conference 36
Baxter's reference to the same memorandum 36, 37
Names appended to original print of 1641 37
First and second parts of memorandum:—a collection of alleged innovations in doctrine and discipline, of which complaint was then made 37, 38
Third part of ditto:—'Considerations upon the Book of Common-Prayer' 38
Bishop Hacket's narrative, in his Life of Williams 38–40
The memorandum does not support Dr. Cardwell's statement .. 40, 41
References to same subject in contemporaneous controversy between Bishop Hall and 'Smectymnuus' 41, 42

		PAGE
6. *The Revision of* 1661		42–54

Mr. Parker's theory as to concessions refused at the Savoy Conference, and afterwards made .. 42
'Cosin's Book;' not what Mr. Parker supposes .. 43
Lord Clarendon's statement, as to preparation made by the Bishops during the Recess of 1661 for the work of Revision .. 43, 44
Reasons for believing that 'Cosin's Book,' before its correction by Sancroft, contained the scheme of changes so prepared .. 44
Lord Clarendon's account of subsequent proceedings in Convocation .. 44, 45
Despatch of the work, by the House of Bishops, and their Committee .. 45, 46
Means by which concurrence of Convocation of York was obtained .. 46, 47
Sancroft's service to the Bishops and Convocation .. 47
Relation of 'Sancroft's Book,' and Sancroft's corrections in 'Cosin's Book,' to the work of Revision in the Upper House .. 47, 48
Those Books afford no measure of Cosin's influence over the work .. 48
Mr. Parker's estimate of that influence; at variance with contemporary evidence .. 48
Tabular List of material Alterations and Additions, prefixed to 'Convocation Book' .. 48, 49
Omission from that List of the change made in the Ornaments Rubric .. 49
Opinions on that subject of Wren and Sparrow .. 49, 50
In 'Cosin's' and 'Sancroft's' Books, some specification of Ornaments contemplated; but Convocation decided otherwise .. 50, 51
Sancroft's note of reason for the present form of Rubric .. 51
Proof from same Books, that the 25th and 26th sections of the Act of 1559 were then expected to remain operative .. 51
Cosin's Visitation Articles of 1662 .. 52
Their connexion with proceedings of Convocation, as to Visitation Articles, in 1661, 1662, and 1664–5 .. 52, 53
Analogy between case of the Ornaments Rubric, and that of the first two Rubrics in the Marriage Service .. 53, 54

7. *Proceedings of Parliament and Convocation in* 1661–2 .. 54–69

Puritan Petitions, as to 'Ornaments;' 1603 and 1660 .. 54
'Discourse of Liturgies,' against Bishop Gauden, in 1661 .. 54, 55

The King's promise in 1660	55
Toleration clauses in Bill of Uniformity, suggested by the King, introduced by House of Lords, and rejected by House of Commons	55
The text of those clauses	55–57
Reasons of House of Commons for rejecting them	57
Mr. Parker's view, that changes made by Convocation in the 'Table' and 'North-side' Rubrics were rejected by the King	57, 58
Evidence to the contrary	58
The King's own Declarations	58
No reference back to Convocation	58, 59
Parliament made no change beyond correction of clerical errors	59–62
Clerical errors noted in both Houses, and corrected by delegates, specially authorised by Convocation	62–65
Internal evidence of 'Convocation Book' and 'Annexed Book'	65
Six changes made in 'Convocation Book,' transcribed into 'Annexed Book,' and afterwards cancelled in both Books	66
No. 1. (in Prayer for Fair Weather)	66
No. 2. (in 'Table Rubric;' first cancelled in 'Convocation Book')	66, 67
No. 3. (in 'North-side' Rubric)	67
No. 4. (in First Commandment: noted for cancellation in 'Convocation Book')	67
No. 5. (in Preface to Prayer for Church Militant: noted for cancellation in 'Convocation Book')	67, 68
No. 6. (in Exhortation before General Confession, in Communion Office)	68
Reasons, on face of the two Books, for believing all these changes to have been cancelled by Convocation, in the last stage of its work, before the 'Annexed Book' was signed, or sent to the King	68, 69
Bearing of some of those changes on arguments used in prior controversies; by Heylyn, Wren, and Cosin	69, 70

8. *Changes in Communion Office in 1661* 70–73

Manual Acts and Rubric before Prayer of Consecration	70, 71
Exceptions of Puritans and Concessions of Bishops, at Savoy Conference	71

CONTENTS.

	PAGE
Suggestions in Baxter's proposed form of Liturgy	71
Cosin's 'Note,' as to 'Elevation' and 'Ostension'	71, 72
Welsh translation (1664) of words in ante-Consecration Rubric	72
Greek ditto (1665)	72
French ditto (1667)	72
Latin ditto (1670)	73
Quære: whether this is the Latin translation, made by order of Convocation (1662 and 1664)?	73

APPENDIX A.

Bishop Grindal's Letter of May 21st, 1566, to the Dean and Chapter of St. Paul's .. 74

APPENDIX B.

Articles presented by Archbishop Whitgift, and Bishop (Piers) of Salisbury, for themselves and five other Bishops, to Queen Elizabeth, in October, 1583 .. 75

APPENDIX C.

Minute of proceedings on the Bill of Uniformity in Committee of the House of Lords on February 27th, 1661-2; extracted from the Lords' Committee-Book .. 84

NOTES

ON SOME

PASSAGES IN THE LITURGICAL HISTORY

OF THE

REFORMED ENGLISH CHURCH.

THE following Notes were suggested to the writer by the perusal of Mr. James Parker's recent Liturgical publications.[*] They relate to some passages of history, which he had previously been led to investigate. It occurred to him that they might be put into a shape which might perhaps be acceptable to some of those whose studies have taken the same direction, without entering into any disputed or disputable questions of Ecclesiastical law. Those questions depend, not upon historical investigations of this kind, but upon the legal construction and effect of Statutes and other public documents. In the few references to questions of law which will be found in these pages, nothing has been advanced which the writer believes to be open to any variety of opinion.

If the modern revival of Liturgical controversies had borne no other fruit than Mr. Parker's volumes, English literature would have derived substantial gain from so elaborate a con-

---

[*] 'An Introduction to the History of the successive Revisions of the Book of Common Prayer:' and 'The First Prayer-book of Edward VI., compared with the successive Revisions of the Book of Common Prayer; also a Concordance to the Rubricks in the several Editions' (Oxford and London, 1877).

tribution towards a minute study of their subject. The author tells us, in the Preface to his 'Introduction,' that his work is not polemical; though he acknowledges that modern Ritual controversy has had a certain degree of influence over its structure. There is room for much difference of opinion as to the value and importance of the matter which he has collected, and the inferences which he has drawn from it: but there can be none as to the patience, dispassionateness, and good faith, with which he has conducted his inquiries.

The two volumes constitute together a single work. The first ninety-one and last seventy-eight pages of the 'Introduction' contain a summary of English Liturgical history, from the accession of Edward VI. to the close of the year 1661, and from the latter date to St. Bartholomew's day, 1662. The earlier parts of this history are concisely treated; but the proceedings of Convocation and of Parliament, in 1661-2, are exhibited in as full detail as Mr. Parker's researches enabled him to present them. Of the intermediate 357 pages, the primary object is to trace the history of all the alterations of the Liturgy introduced in 1661-2, as they appear, both in the book annexed to the Act of Uniformity of 1662, and in the printed book with manuscript alterations and additions, now in the Library of the House of Lords, from which the 'Annexed Book' was supposed to be transcribed; and which Mr. Parker, not improperly, calls the 'Convocation Book.' This part, however, of the volume is really devoted, in at least an equal degree, to an inquiry into the influence exercised by Bishop Cosin over the Revision of 1661. For this purpose the manuscript entries in two printed Prayer-books of 1619 and 1634, in the former by Cosin's own hand, with subsequent corrections by Sancroft, acting as a secretary, and in the latter by Sancroft, transcribing (with a few changes) those left standing in the first; and the three series of 'Notes' made or collected by Cosin at different uncertain dates before the Restoration, and his memorandum of 'Particulars to be considered, explained, and corrected in the Book of Common Prayer,'* are carefully collated with the results of the Revision, and are also compared with the 'Exceptions' of the Puritans, and the 'Answers' of the bishops at the Savoy Conference, and with some suggestions of Bishop Wren and others. Both the books, which (following Mr. Parker) it will be convenient to designate as 'Cosin's' and 'Sancroft's' books, are clearly shown to have been made use of by the bishops in 1661 for the purposes of the Revision: though their exact relation to that work may not be that which is supposed by Mr. Parker. It does not appear that the 'Notes' or 'Particulars,' &c., were then made use of, except so far as it may be presumed that they were referred to in the course of the preparation of 'Cosin's Book.'

Mr. Parker's conclusion, upon the whole matter, is, that Cosin's was the leading influence in the work of Revision:— that the proceedings at the Savoy Conference, and the other suggestions of which he takes notice, contributed little to it:— and that most of the changes actually made originated in the mind of that prelate.† And it would seem, from certain passages in the sections, entitled 'Historical Survey of Cosin's Corrections,' and 'Historical Survey of the work of Revision,'‡ and some illustrations, given in the Preface,§ of the way in which Mr. Parker would use his materials for the elucidation of controverted questions as to the meaning and effect of disputed

---

* These 'Notes' and 'Particulars,' &c., were first published by Nicholls in 1710 in a dislocated form. Archdeacon Harrison observes, that it should be borne in mind, that they 'were taken from the margin of a Prayer-book' [two Prayer-books], 'in which the Bishop had written them, and a manuscript book of notes, which probably were never intended, much less prepared, for publication.'—('Historical Inquiry,' &c., p. 22, *note*.)
† Introduction, pp. 387, 433.
‡ Ibid. pp. 322-406
§ Ibid. pp. 11, 12.

Rubrics in our present Prayer-book, that **he** considers the private 'Notes' and opinions of Bishop Cosin, and some of the events of his life, to be, under these circumstances, legitimate aids towards the solution of such questions; and also, that, for the same **purpose, he thinks regard** may properly be had to the details of what passed, during **the** process of legislation, in Convocation and in Parliament, and in committees appointed by those Assemblies.

It is impossible not to be struck by the wide difference between such an estimate of the nature of the evidence applicable to the exposition **of** authoritative public documents, and that **of the Law of** England. Every *tiro* knows, that although, within **certain** well-understood limits, our law takes into account **known extrinsic** facts and subsequent public usage, **as** admissible **aids towards the** solution of doubtful questions of interpretation, no **regard** whatever can be **paid, in** the interpretation (*e.g.*) of an Act **of** Parliament, to **the private** opinions or intentions **of** its framers, **to** the speeches **or** discussions which **took place while it** was passing **through Parliament,** or to the **adoption or rejection, in** either House, during the preparatory **stages before it became law,** of **any** amendments or alterations **tending to vary its form or effect.** The reasons **for** this state of the **law are not technical, but** are such as might be supposed to recommend themselves **to** every man's good sense. The document to be interpreted is the ultimate product of the whole process **of** legislation. The intention to be investigated is that of the collective Legislature, not of any of its members or component parts; which can only be discovered from the terms of the law as passed, read in the light of those relevant facts which the whole Legislature may be presumed to have had in contemplation. The propositions embodied in that law may have recommended **themselves for** different reasons to different minds. What was proposed, but **not** adopted, may have been either disapproved on its merits, or simply deemed superfluous. Even, therefore, if the proof of the intention of the mover of a particular proposition were direct and demonstrative, it is immaterial, unless it appears on the face of the law. Its irrelevancy is still more manifest when (like many of the matters taken into account by Mr. Parker) the proof is conjectural and imperfect.

It is possible, however, while demurring to the principle which seems to pervade some of the argumentative portions of Mr. Parker's work, to recognise the historical interest which may attach to investigations, irrelevant for the purpose of legal exposition. And it is from this point of view that it is proposed to follow him over some parts of the field which he has traversed.

The history of the Prayer-book of 1559 first invites notice. It may, perhaps, be hypercritical to except to the use of the word 'Revision,' to describe what was then done; but the performance certainly was unequal to the promise implied in that word. No doubt a larger scheme was at first contemplated. The 'Device for alteration of Religion,' &c.,[*] Cecil's instructions and queries to Guest,[†] and Guest's Replies to those queries,[‡] show distinctly that the restoration of some of the ceremonies which had been disused in 1552, and of some parts of the book of 1549 which had been then altered, would have been at that time acceptable to the Queen and her ministers. But this could not be done without a greater amount of concurrence from the Reforming party than it was found possible to obtain. Guest, in his 'Replies,' rejected all Cecil's suggestions, and defended the Order of 1552 against that of 1549; offering only to leave the posture of kneeling or standing at the reception of the Holy Communion optional—a change manifestly not in a

---

[*] Burnet's 'Reformation,' vol. ii. part ii. (Oxford, 1829), 'Collection of Records,' No. 1; also Cardwell, 'Conferences,' &c., p. 43.

[†] Strype's 'Annals,' vol. i. part i. book 3 (Oxford, 1824), pp. 119-124.

[‡] Ibid. Appendix No. 14, p. 459; also Cardw. 'Conf.' p. 48.

Catholic direction. These 'Replies' are described by Guest as setting forth 'some causes of the Order taken in the new service-book,' which he desired 'the Parliament with one voice to enact, and the realm with true heart to use.' Strype's paraphrase,* that Guest gave 'reasons for his own emendations and alterations,' is evidently erroneous. Except as to kneeling at the reception of the Sacrament, the reasons given are all against the alterations of the book of 1552 suggested by Cecil, and not in favour of any others. The 'new service-book' was, beyond doubt, the book of 1552, with only those few alterations which are mentioned in the third section of Queen Elizabeth's Act of Uniformity, and (probably) some relaxation of the Rubric as to kneeling at the Sacrament, which the Queen, or her Parliament, rejected. The alterations were only (1) some changes in the Table of Lessons (not completed till two years afterwards); (2) some additions (quite new, and of no doctrinal significance) to the Litany; (3) the omission from one of the suffrages in the Litany of the prayer against 'the Bishop of Rome and all his detestable enormities,' which had been in both King Edward's books; and (4) the combination, in the sentences used upon the delivery of the Sacrament of the Lord's Supper to the communicants, of the forms of the first with those of the second book. The 'Black Rubric,' or Declaration as to kneeling at the Holy Communion (to the omission of which at this time Burnet† and Echard‡ ascribe considerable importance), was not part of the book of 1552, as authorised by the statute of that year. It was added, without Parliamentary authority, under a subsequent proclamation of King Edward; and on the recurrence, by the Act of Uniformity of 1559, to the Statutory Book of 1552, it fell to the ground.

But, although these were the only changes in the text of the

---

* 'Annals,' vol. i. part i. pp. 120–124. † 'Ref.' (ed. 1829), vol. ii., p. 783.
‡ 'Hist. of England' (1707), p. 793.

book of 1552, its restoration **was subject to the two provisos** contained in the 25th and **26th sections of the Act of 1559 :—** that the 'Ornaments' of the first book were **to 'be retained'** and 'be in **use,'** ' until other order should be therein taken' by the Queen's authority, with the advice of the Metropolitan or Ecclesiastical Commissioners; and that the Queen, with **like** advice, might ordain and publish ' further ceremonies or rites.'

It is singular that in the editions of the Prayer-book, printed **in** 1559 and afterwards, two new Rubrics [*] were, without any apparent authority, ecclesiastical or civil, substituted for those which immediately preceded the Order of Morning **Prayer in the** book of 1552; both touching upon the battle-ground **of** controversies which agitated the Church for more than **a century** afterwards, and the ashes of which have again burst into flame within the last thirty years. **Gibson, in** his ' Codex,' [†] notices the fact that neither of those Rubrics formed part of **the Prayer-book** authorised by law, before **1662. Cosin** (notwithstanding **that** ' remarkable attention and deference to Acts of Parliament,' which, as Mr. Parker truly says,[‡] **is characteristic** of his **' Notes '** and ' Particulars,' &c.) took no **notice of it ;** though he **commented upon those Rubrics in several** places; and though **Mr. Parker conjectures that he may have** caused the second of **them to be altered in 1661, ' in** consequence **of the** illegal **character of the Rubrick, which** gave the Puritans the advantage in disregarding **it.'** §

The **change in the** first Rubric (relating to a subject **on which** the Act of 1559 was **silent)** was more than **formal. The** authorised Rubric of 1552 said, that (subject, in case of controversy, to the appointment of the Ordinary), **' the** Morning and Evening Prayer ' should **' be used in** such place of the church,

---

[*] Parker, 'First Prayer-book,' &c., p. 64.
[†] Pp. 296, 297 (ed. 1761).
[‡] Introduction, p. 343.
§ Ibid. p. 345.

chapel, or chancel, and the minister' should 'so turn himself, as the people might best hear.' The unauthorised Rubric of 1559 said, that it should '**be used** in the *accustomed* **place of** the church, chapel, or chancel, except it' should 'be otherwise deter**mined** by the Ordinary **of the place.**' This difference was not **immaterial** to the question afterwards so warmly debated between **the two** parties, headed respectively by Archbishop Laud and Bishop Williams, as to the proper position of the Communion Table at communion time; when it was directed to 'stand in the **body** of the church, **or in** the chancel, where Morning Prayer and Evening Prayer be appointed to be said.' The principle of the authorised Rubric might reasonably have been contended **to be the same** with that of Queen Elizabeth's Injunction* (afterwards embodied in the 82nd Canon of 1603-4); that the table should 'be so placed, in good sort, within the chancel, as whereby the minister may be more conveniently heard of the communicants in his prayer and ministration, and the communicants also more conveniently and in more number communicate with the said minister:' and **of** the 'Advertisement,' '**that** the common prayer be said or sung decently and distinctly **in** such place as the Ordinary shall think meet for the largeness **and** straightness of the church and quire, so that the people may be most edified.'† It must have been on this principle that Bishop Williams, in his 'Letter to the Vicar of Grantham,' ‡ admitted, that the place in the chancel where the altar stood might be '**the** most decent situation' for the table, **not** only when there was **no** communion, but 'for use too, when the quire is mounted by steps, and open, so that he that officiates may be seen and heard of all the congregation;' and that his antagonist Heylyn, in his 'Coal from **the** Altar,'§ added, 'that

---

* Cardw. '**Doc.** Ann.' vol. i. pp. 201, 202.   † Ibid. p. 291.
‡ Reprinted by Heylyn at the end of his 'Coal from the Altar,' p. 70.
§ Published in 1636 (British Museum; 1106 c., pp. 17, 50).

in all the lesser churches, such as country churches for the most part are, and in all others where the minister **standing at the** altar may be heard conveniently, the table may **stand altar-wise, in the time of ministration.'** A rule derived from custom, on the other hand, might **have been** very different; even if Cosin's argument from the custom *before* 1552* could have been maintained; which (considering that the word 'accustomed' for the first time occurred in **the** unauthorised Rubric of 1559, without any express reference to **the** practice **of any** former time), seems **hardly possible.**

With respect to the **second, or** 'Ornaments' Rubric, Strype† speaks of a 'proviso,' to that effect, as having been in the ' **new** service-book,' when finished by the **divines whom the Queen's** ministers had consulted. It **is,** however, quite certain, **from** Guest's letter,‡ that nothing **of** the kind was in the book when it was sent to Cecil to be brought before Parliament; because he there defends the use of the surplice only, on all occasions. Strype, in this passage, misstates the effect of a letter of Sandys, which he quotes in the immediate context, and from which **some** of the words **which he** uses are **taken.** Mr. Parker,§ following him, finds in the same letter proof that the 'Ornaments' Rubric of 1559 ' was deliberately inserted, in its proper **place, by the Revisers;'** his theory ‖ being, that 'the words, which Parker **or Guest, or one of the other Revisers, wrote** in the copy which was **prepared for the printers, were copied from** the rough **draft of the** clause before it was engrossed **in the**

---

* Second and Third **Series of** 'Notes;' 'Works,' vol. **v. pp. 227,** 435 (Angl. Cath. Library ed. Oxford, 1855).

† 'Annals,' vol. i. part i. pp. 121, 122.

‡ Appendix to Strype's 'Annals,' **vol. i. part i. book** 3, No. **14.** Cecil's fourth question was : ' Whether, in the celebration of **the** Holy Communion, priests should not use a cope beside a surplice?' **To which Guest** replied: 'Because **it** is sufficient to use but a surplice in baptizing, reading, preaching, and praying, therefore it is enough also for the celebrating the Holy Communion:'— adding reasons for that opinion.

§ Introduction, p. 44.

‖ Ibid. p. **344.**

Act;' and that 'this' (*i.e.* the form of the clause) 'was afterwards slightly varied.' It stands in the way of this theory, that the Act itself was printed at the beginning of the book, and the Rubric expressly referred to the Act as so printed; and even if so gratuitous a conjecture [*] could be accepted, as that this reference may have been due to a misunderstanding by the printer of some marginal direction, the printer could not well have been referred to an Act which had not passed. Ingenious, however, or not, the theory rests entirely on the letter of Sandys: the whole of which Mr. Parker can scarcely have considered, because, when it is read, it proves the exact contrary. It is to be found in the 'Parker Correspondence;'[†] and also in Burnet's 'Collection of Records,'[‡] where it is entitled, 'Dr. Sands' letter to Dr. Parker, concerning some proceedings in Parliament,'—a heading or endorsement (by whomsoever made) which accurately describes its contents. It was written by Sandys in London, to the future Archbishop at Cambridge, and is dated the 30th of April, 1559, just eight days before the close of the then Session of Parliament. After a short preamble, the writer says:—

'I trust we shall not linger here long, for the Parliament draweth towards an end. The Book of Service is gone through, with a *proviso* to retain the Ornaments which were in the Church in the first and second year of King Edward VI., until it please the Queen to take other order for them. Our gloss upon this text is, that we shall not be forced to use them, but that others in the mean time shall not convey them away, but that they may remain for the Queen. After this Book was passed, Boxall[§] and others quarrelled with it, that, according to the order of the Scripture, we had not *gratiarum actio*; for, saith he, *Dominus accepit panem, gratias agit*: but in the time of consecration, we give no thanks. This he put into the

---

[*] Introduction, p. 344.
[†] 'Correspondence of Matthew Parker,' &c. (Cambridge, 1853), p. 65.
[‡] Burnet's 'Ref.' (Oxford, 1829),

vol. ii. part 2, p. 465.
[§] Dean of Peterborough, Norwich, and Windsor under Queen Mary, to whom he had been Secretary of State.

Treasurer's head, and into Count de Feror's* head; **and he laboured to alienate the Queen's Majesty from confirming the Act; but I trust they cannot prevail. Mr. Secretary is earnest with the Book, and we have minuted reasons to maintain that part.'**

He then goes on to speak of the passing of the Bill of Supremacy, 'with a *proviso* that nothing shall be judged heresy which is not condemned by the canonical Scriptures and four General Councils;' of the Queen's refusal to take the title of 'Supreme Head;' and of her stopping the Bill concerning the marriage of the clergy. 'The Bill,' he adds, 'is in hand to restore men to their livings; how it will end, I know not. The Parliament is like to end shortly; and then we shall understand how they mind to use us.'

This letter speaks for itself. It was written after the two Bills, of Uniformity and Supremacy, had 'gone through' Parliament, and when they were waiting for the Royal Assent. Each of these is spoken of as having passed 'with a *proviso*,' the proper word to describe a clause of exception or qualification in an Act of Parliament. This (in the case with which we have to do) is further described in terms which are found in the Act of Parliament, but which were not found in the Rubric. Upon Sandys' 'gloss' (which, as Strype justly says, 'must be looked upon as a conjecture of a private man') it is unnecessary to dwell. It shows, however, that even in 1559 some of the divines of the school to which Sandys belonged were prepared (whether reasonably or otherwise) to interpret that proviso as leaving the 'Ornaments' of 1552 still in force, and as imposing no legal obligation to wear the vestments of 1549.

The true account of the *genesis* of the 'Ornaments' Rubric of 1559 seems to be this. It was thought necessary, by those who prepared the book for the press, to alter the Rubric of 1552, so as to make it agree in sense with (what they understood to be)

---

* The Spanish Ambassador, Count de Feria.

the immediate effect of the clause of the Act, which controlled its operation. They left standing its introductory words down to the verb 'use,' and drew a pen through the rest. To make the sense fit, they converted the words of the statute, 'such ornaments of the Church and of the ministers thereof,' into others which they thought equivalent, and which the nominative case and verb, 'the minister shall use,' might properly govern, viz. 'such ornaments *in* the Church;' taking the rest of the description of them from the words of the statute, and ending with a reference to the statute itself, as printed at the beginning of the book.

Passing on to the next stage in the history, we find opinion as to clerical attire in the performance of Divine offices fluctuating, from 1559 to 1564, between two extremes; the one favouring (as Cecil had done) the general use of cope as well as surplice in the celebration of the Holy Communion; the other objecting to the compulsory use of the surplice on any occasion whatever. The former view is represented in one of the suggestions for future legislation, contained in the paper said to have been drawn up by Archbishop Parker and Bishop Cox, entitled 'Interpretations' (*i.e.* of the Queen's Injunctions), 'and Further Considerations;'* the other in the proceedings of the party headed by Dean Nowell in the Convocation of 1562.† The alb and chasuble seem to have then found no advocates: there is reason to suppose that the 30th Royal Injunction of 1559 was practically interpreted as excluding them, without much inquiry into the sufficiency of that authority for such a purpose: and in many places they (and copes also) were defaced or destroyed, under pretence of executing the Queen's orders against 'monuments of superstition.'

---

* Cardw. 'Doc. Ann.,' vol. i. p. 205, note.
† Strype's 'Annals,' vol. i. part i.,

pp. 473, 474; and 501-505. Neal's 'Hist. of Puritans,' vol. i. pp. 149-151 (ed. 1822).

In 1564, the attention of the Queen was directed **to the disorder and inconsistency of practice on this subject then prevailing** in the Church:* and her determination to establish, **by** the use of all legal means, such a rule for the future as might secure uniformity, was declared in her celebrated letter to Archbishop Parker,† **of** the 25th January, 1564–5. The 'Advertisements' issued under it rather more than **a** year later, (*i.e.* soon after the 28th March, **1566**), were the result.

The interpretation and legal effect of the 'Advertisements,' **and** the recognition **which** they received from the official acts **of public authorities, belong to the** province **of law, into which it** is **not proposed to enter; but the controversy as to their** authority belongs to **history. No writer of reputation, in any** work published before **the eighteenth century, seems to have** suggested a doubt that they **were, as a matter of** *fact*, authorised by Queen Elizabeth. Hooker,‡ **in his letter to Archbishop Whitgift,** answering **the 'Supplication' made by Travers to the Privy Council in** 1586, **described them as 'a decree agreed upon by the Bishops, and confirmed by Her** Majesty's **authority.'** Sparke,§ one of the Puritan representatives at the Hampton Court Conference, who after it recommended conformity, wrote, in 1607, thus:—

'I cannot deny but that, at the first, by the statute 1 Elizabeth, ministers were to use in their ministration the same ornaments that were in use in the reign of Edward VI., and in the second year of his reign, amongst which this alb was. But her Majesty, by virtue of the said statute, with the consent of the Archbishop **and High** Commissioners, **in the seventh** year **of her** reign (as appears **by the** " Book of Advertisements," **then by** authority published), beliko of

---

* Strype's 'Life of Parker,' vol. i. p. 302. Burnet's 'Reform.' vol. iii. p. 587.

† Strype's 'Parker,' vol. iii. p. 65; Appendix, No. 24.

‡ Keble's 'Hooker,' vol. iii. p. 587 (2nd ed. Oxford, 1841).

§ 'A brotherly perswasion to unitie and uniformitie,' &c.; 'written by Thomas Sparke, D.D., and seene, allowed, and commanded by publicke authoritie to be printed' (London, 1607), p. 20.

purpose to remove the scandal taken by the Popish alb, appointed the surplice, in the **form and** manner that we wear it, to be used instead thereof.'

Lestrange, in his 'Alliance of Divine Offices,'* published in 1659, spoke of the 'Advertisements' as an exercise, by Queen Elizabeth, of the power reserved to her by the 25th section of the Act of 1559. Heylyn (who died in 1662), in his 'History of the Reformation,' † said :—

'To bring this quarrel to an end, or otherwise to render all opponents the more inexcusable, **the** Queen thought fit to make a further signification **of her royal** pleasure—not grounded only on the sovereign **power and** prerogative Royal, by **which** she published **the** "Injunctions" in the **first year of** her reign, but legally declared by her Commissioners **for causes** Ecclesiastical, according **to** the Acts and **Statutes made in that** behalf. The **Archbishop** is thereupon required **to consult together with** such Bishops **and** Commissioners as were next **at hand, upon the making** of such **rules and orders** as they thought necessary **for the peace of** the **Church, with** reference to the **present** condition and **estate** thereof; which **being** accordingly presented **to the** Queen, and **by** her approved, **the** said **rules** and orders **were set forth** and published in a certain **book** intituled "**Advertisements,**" &c. (he gives the full title); '**and that** they might be known to have the stamp of Royal **authority, a Preface** was prefixed before **them, in which it was expressed that,**' &c. (stating the Preface); 'and, finally, **that in** obedience **to her** commands, the said Metropolitan and the **rest had** agreed **upon the rules** and orders ensuing, which were by **her** thought **meet to be used** and followed.'

It is **true, that some later** ecclesiastical historians,‡ of the eighteenth **century, professing to** follow Strype, (the first volume of whose 'Annals' appeared **in** 1709,) represented the Queen **as** having never given **any sanction** to the publication of the 'Advertisements.' These **writers seem to have taken** what

---

* **P.** 104 (Angl. Cath. Library edition).

† Vol. ii. pp. **408-9** ('Eccl. Hist.' Society's edition).

‡ Collier, vol. vi. pp. 195-6 (folio paging, ed. **1845**), **first** published 1714; Neal, 'Hist. **of** the Puritans,' vol. i. pp. 156, 167, **168,** 172 (ed. 1822), first published 1732.

is said in the 'Annals,'* (where this subject is not pursued beyond the events of the year 1564–5), and in one chapter of the 'Life of Parker'† containing the events of that year only, as if Strype had said nothing more about the matter. Even, however, at the end of that chapter,‡ after having spoken of the rejection of the first draft of the 'Advertisements,' and of other difficulties encountered by the Archbishop and by Grindal, he had added, that those difficulties were finally overcome; and his narrative of the events of the next and later years, in subsequent chapters,§ traces the sequel down to the promulgation of the 'Advertisements' in their ultimate form, their enforcement by law, and the schism ‖ to which they led; ascribing all that was so done, as distinctly as possible, to the will and commandment of the Queen.¶

There is one passage in Strype,** avowedly conjectural, which, being itself erroneous, may not improbably be the principal source of the error of Collier and Neal:—that in which he suggests that when, in March 1564–5, the Articles, as first proposed by the bishops, were refused by the Queen's Council,—

'The Archbishop thought it advisable to print them, under his and the rest of the Commissioners' hands, to signify at least what their judgment and will was, and to let their authority go as far as it would, which was probable to take some effect with the greater part of the clergy, especially considering their canonical obedience they had sworn to their diocesans. But, because the book wanted

---

* Vol. i. part ii. pp. 125-130.
† Vol. i. pp. 313-319, first published in 1711.
‡ Strype, 'Parker,' vol. i. p. 319.
§ Ibid. pp. 432-452.
‖ The objection of the Puritans was to the orders for the use of the surplice, &c., which were made to be enforced. They naturally would have preferred a continuance of the former neglected and ineffective state of the law.
¶ Strype, 'Parker,' vol. i. p. 451. See also Cardw. 'Conf.' p. 38, note; Keble's 'Hooker' (2nd ed.), vol. i. p. 141, note; Cosin's Works (Angl. Cath. Lib. ed.), vol. v. p. 43, note; Archdeacon Harrison's 'Historical Inquiry,' &c. (Rivingtons, 1845), pp. 81-137; and Mr. Parker's Introduction, pp. 50, 133.
** Strype, 'Parker,' vol. i. p. 311.

the Queen's authority, they thought fit not to term the contents thereof "Articles" or "Ordinances," by which name they at first went, but, by a modester denomination, "Advertisements." This' (he adds) 'was the reason that there is some difference in the preface thereof, as we have it printed in Bishop Sparrow's Collections, **from that which is in the** manuscript copy, sent **to the Secretary.'**

And he speaks afterwards of other differences.

All this occurs in Strype's narrative of the events of the year 1564–5. He had evidently not compared with the rejected draft, or with Sparrow's reprint, the original text of the 'Advertisements,' as officially issued in 1566 ; which, perhaps, he may have never seen : and he may reasonably be supposed to have been misled by the date, 'A.D. 1564,' at the foot of Bishop Sparrow's title-pages. That date does not occur in the original of any early or authentic edition : and it is, no doubt, to be traced to the same cause, which led the 'Advertisements' to be commonly cited,* as of the seventh year of Queen Elizabeth's reign :—viz. the mention of that year in their title ; where it, in fact, relates to the Queen's letter, and not to the promulgation of the Order taken pursuant thereto. But, as the time of the first publication did not there appear, this distinction was, in a very short time, lost sight of.

That the 'Advertisements' were never published in their rejected form, (in which the preamble was different, and there were eight additional Articles, afterwards omitted), we know from Cecil's endorsement : † ' *These were not authorised, nor published.*' That they were not printed before 1566 in the form which they finally assumed, we know from Archbishop Parker's two letters, ‡ both dated the 28th of March, 1566, to Grindal and Cecil : in the former of which he speaks of the 'orders,' (enclosing them for official publication in the diocese

---

* *e.g.* in the Canons of 1603-4.
† Strype, ' Parker,' **vol.** i. p. 314, and vol. iii. Appendix ; No. **28** ; p. 84.
‡ ' Parker Correspondence,' pp. 272-**274.**

of London,) as 'agreed upon among us long ago, and yet in certain respects *not published* ;'—and, in the latter, he says to Cecil, (enclosing both the 'Advertisements' and the letter, not yet sent, to Grindal,) 'This form is *but newly printed*, and yet stayed till I may have your advice.' The reprint, in Bishop Sparrow's Collection, differs from their ultimate form only in the addition to the foot of the title-page of the false date, 'A.D. 1564' (in some editions, '*Anno* 7 *Eliz. R.*' is added), and in the omission, probably accidental, from the title, of the words italicised in the following transcript (otherwise exact) of the title in the original text :—

'Advertisments, partly for due order in the publique administration of *common prayers and usinge* the holy Sacramentes, and partly for the apparell of all persons ecclesiasticall, by vertue of the Queene's majesties letters commaunding the same the xxv day of January in the seventh yeare of the reigne of oure Soveraigne Lady ELYZABETH, by the grace of God of Englande, Fraunce, and Irelande, Queene, defender of the faith, &c.'

As early as 1717 (the date of Hearn's edition of 'Camden's Annals'), original copies of the first or any other early edition of the 'Advertisements' had become rare. Hearn, in his Preface,* reprinted them from one which he had seen in the Rawlinson Library; adding, 'Monitiones istas, seorsim editas (nam editionem in Collectione Sparroviana nihil moror), non sine summa difficultate apud bibliopolas comparari posse.' The text in Wilkins' 'Concilia,' and in Cardwell's 'Documentary Annals,' is taken from this reprint by Hearn. Dibdin † mentions two copies, as having been in Herbert's and Mr. Heber's libraries. There are in the British Museum three copies of the first edition, corresponding with Hearn's text in all respects.

---

* Camden's 'Annales,' &c. (1717), preface, p. 31.
† Herbert and Ames, 'Typographical Antiquities' (Dibdin's edition), vol. iv. pp. 30, 31.

At the foot of the title-page are the words, 'Londini cum privilegio ad imprimendum solum.' Every page, after the Preface, (except some which begin with new sub-titles,) is headed 'Articles.' At the end, after the names of the subscribing bishops, are the words, 'Imprinted at London by Reginald Wolfe.' There is also in the British Museum a later edition, corresponding with the first in absence of date, and in all other points except the spelling of some words: and a third, with other differences of spelling and of type, and with Wolfe's name at the back, instead of the foot, of the last page, followed by the date, 'Anno Dom. MDLXXI.'

Wolfe (who died in 1574) was one of the printers to the Queen, under a patent,* originally granted by Edward VI. in 1547; by which the exclusive privilege was conferred upon him of printing, publishing, and selling, all Latin, Greek, and Hebrew books, and all others which might be commanded; heavy penalties being denounced against those who should infringe that privilege. A list of his publications is given by Dibdin.

'He was employed' (says Strype)† 'in printing several of Archbishop Cranmer's books, and most of the public orders and books for religion in the times of Henry VIII., King Edward, and Queen Elizabeth. . . . He was printer to the Queen, and a citizen of great esteem and reputation. Sir William Cecil took particular notice of him and favoured him; and so did Parker, Archbishop of Canterbury.'

The Puritan leaders were kept informed by their friends at Court of the whole course of events from the beginning of 1564, as is evident from the contemporary 'Zurich Letters,' in which the question whether the orders for the use of the surplice &c., should be submitted to or not was discussed between them and the foreign Calvinistic Reformers; the foreigners advising submission, and being at the same time in correspondence with

---

* Herbert and Ames, 'Typographical Antiquities' (Dibdin's edition), vol. iv. p. 1, reprinted from Rymer's 'Foedera.'   † 'Annals,' vol. i. part ii. p. 530.

seven English Prelates, whose sympathies were **also in a Calvinistic direction**—Grindal, Cox, and Horn (who all consented to, and signed the 'Advertisements'), Parkhurst, Sandys, **Jewell**, and Pilkington. In this correspondence, and with reference to that question, the phrase, '**edictum regium,**'* several times occurs: and **it is** throughout **assumed, that the principle involved was that of obedience, in such matters, to the Queen's commandment.** The whole **Puritan interest at Court** was exerted, in vain, to prevent the execution of those orders. Laurence Humfrey, in a letter printed (No. 27) in Strype's Appendix,† thus addressed the Queen herself:—

'Rogamus **igitur** iterum **atque iterum,** Elizabetha **Princeps, ut** edictum tuum vestiarium **ac ceremoniale vel** abroges piè, **vel** proroges benignè. . . . Cur **tua, O** Regina, erga nos clausa **est misericordia,** quæ patere solet omnibus? Cedere non vis Princeps subditis; **at potes parcere clemens miseris.** Decretum publicum non **vis** rescindere; relaxare potes, et remittere. Non **potes legem tollere;** at poteris tolerare.'

The publication of the 'Advertisements' **was** followed, in the **spring** of the **same year, 1566,** by the Puritan '**Declaration,**' ‡ &c., and the '**Examination**' § in **reply to it:** two pamphlets

---

* Ibid. Append. **No.** 24 ('Bullinger to Humfrey and Sampson,' 1 May, 1566); '**Zurich Letters**' (second series), p. **142** ('**Gualter to Beza,**' 11 Sept. 1566), &c.

† The **letter is** without date: but **it** evidently belongs to the spring or **summer of 1566.**

‡ British Museum: 692, a. 22. (On the title-page, which bears **the date** 1566, it is called '**A** brief **discourse against the** outward apparel and ministering garments of the Popish Church;' but the title **on the first page is,** '**A Declaration** of the doings of those **ministers of God's** Word and Sacraments **in the** City of **London,** which have refused **to** wear the upper apparell **and** ministring garments of the **Pope's** Church.' The running title **at the head** of each page, is 'The **unfolding of the** Popish attire.')

§ British **Museum:** 702, g. 1.—'**A** briefe **Examination for the tyme of a certain Declaration lately put in print in the** name and **defence of certain ministers in** London, refusing to **weare** the apparell prescribed by the lawes and **orders of** the Realme—Imprinted **at** London in Paules Churchyarde by Richarde Jugge, printer to the Queene's Maiestie. *Cum privilegio Regiæ* **Majestatis.**'

mentioned by Strype,[*] of which the history is given in a contemporaneous letter from Abel to Bullinger, dated the 6th of June, 1566. Of the 'Declaration,' &c., it is there stated, that one of five deprived London preachers had 'caused to be printed a book against the Queen's command respecting the cap and surplice: but, as soon as the authorities heard of it, the book was prohibited, the printers cast into prison, and the copies destroyed:'—and, of the 'Examination,' that 'another book was afterwards published by order of the Commissioners, wherein is declared the judgment of master Doctor Peter Martyr, and Master Bucer: viz., that every preacher and minister ecclesiastical may wear a surplice, cap, and the other habits, without committing sin.' The whole controversy, in these pamphlets, is as to the moral obligation of obedience to orders of 'the Prince,' enjoining the use of what the one calls 'the upper apparell and ministring garments of the Pope's Church,' and the other, 'the apparell prescribed by the lawes and orders of the Realme.' The former quotes and impugns the statement in 'the Advertisements that are published in print,'[†] that the things in question were required, not as essential to the ministerial office, 'but only for decencie and comely order, uniformitie, and obedience to our Prince.' The latter justifies it, as sufficient proof that the minister 'may with discharge of conscience obey his Prince, knowing that comelynes and order edifie the Churche of Christ.'

In the summer of the same year, 1566, the chief ministers of the Puritan party sent two of their number, George Withers (as

---

[*] 'Annals,' vol. i. part ii. pp. 162-3; 213, 214.

[†] Not 'the Bishops' Advertisements,' as might be supposed from the language of Strype; though such a designation (which was used in two of the Zurich Letters, Nos. 58 and 62, Second Series, from George Withers and John Barthelot to Bullinger, and from Withers to the Prince Elector Palatine) would have been perfectly correct; and would not imply that the 'Advertisements,' which the Bishops signed and issued, wanted Royal authority.

Strype supposes), and Percival Wiburn, on a mission to Geneva, to obtain the interposition of the leading ministers there.* They took with them a letter † from Coverdale, Humfrey, and Sampson to Farel, Viret, Beza, and others, dated in July 1566; and Beza sent them on to Zurich with another ‡ from himself to Gualter (3rd September, 1566), in which he suggested, that some of the leading Zurich Reformers should personally visit England, and interpose with the Queen. At Zurich they saw Bullinger and Gualter; § and Wiburn drew up, and left with those Reformers, a paper ‖ containing thirty-nine Articles of complaint against the existing state of things in the Church of England, one of which was directed against the 'Protestation,' and others against the 'Apparel,' required by the 'Advertisements.'

'Ministers' (he said, in his 7th Article) 'now protest ¶ and promise, that they will observe the laws of their country, as being good (as they are called) and wholesome, as well in matters external and political, as in the rites and ceremonies of the Church and all things which are there customary and in use; and this too they must attest by their subscription.' And (in the 29th Article), 'In every church throughout England, during prayers, the minister must wear a linen garment, which we call a surplice. And in the larger churches, at the administration of the Lord's Supper, the chief minister must wear a silk garment, which they call a cope; and two other ministers, formerly called the deacon and sub-deacon, must assist him to read the epistle and gospel.' **

---

* Strype's 'Life of Parker,' vol. i. p. 472; and vol. iii. p. 159; Appeal, No. 54.

† See 'Zurich Letters' (first series), No. 78; and ibid., Appendix, No. 7.

‡ Ibid. (second series), No. 50.

§ Ibid., No. 53.

‖ 'Zurich Letters' (second series), Appendix, No. 4.

¶ The 'Protestation,' required by the 'Advertisements' to be subscribed by all persons who should be thereafter admitted into any ecclesiastical ministry or office, contained (*inter alia*) a promise, in these words: 'To observe, keep, and maintain such order and uniformity, in all external policy, rites, and ceremonies of the Church, as by the laws, good usages, and orders, are already well provided and established.'

** The 'Advertisement,' on this point, is: 'In the ministration of the Holy

Misled (as he afterwards* explained) by the 'calumnies and false accusations' of these messengers from the discontented ministers, Gualter addressed a letter† to Parkhurst (11th September, 1566), to be communicated by him to the other Bishops; in which he spoke of misgivings, which he had himself felt at the beginning of the controversy; adding:—

'Et certè non fefellit nos animi præsagium, siquidem vera sunt quæ audimus: nimirum, præter vestes illas multa alia obtrudi ecclesiis, et ministros ab ecclesiis ejici, quod decretis quorundam subscribere nolunt, qui vel Reginæ nomine abutuntur, vel suâ indulgentiâ illam in ejusmodi rebus audaciorem reddunt, ut quidvis ex suo arbitrio statuat.'

On the same day he also wrote to Beza; ‡ explaining, that he thought it useless to go to England; because it was very unlikely, that the Queen, 'quæ potestate suâ hucusque in multis pro suo arbitrio licenter nimis abusa est, et suorum consiliis atque admonitionibus moneri non potuit,' would accept any counsel from foreigners: adding, that he still thought the Churches ought not to be forsaken solely on account of the habits, if the question referred solely to the habits of ministers, and if 'omnes Edicti Regii§ super hac re facti verbis insisterent, quibus diserte negatur, neque eandem cum Verbo Dei auctoritatem istis legibus tribuendam esse, neque alicujus conscientiam iisdem debere

---

Communion in cathedral and collegiate churches, the principal minister shall use a cope; with gospeller and epistoller agreeably.'

* 'Zurich Letters' (first series), Appendix, No. 7.

† Ibid. (second series), No. 56.

‡ 'Zurich Letters' (second series), No. 57.

§ The 'Advertisements' are declared, in their Preface, to be 'orders and rules, which have been thought meet and convenient to be used and followed, not yet prescribing these rules as laws equivalent with the eternal Word of God, and as of necessity to bind the consciences of her' [the Queen's] 'subjects in the nature of them considered in themselves, or as they should add any efficacy or more holiness to the virtue of public prayer and to the sacraments; but as temporal orders mere ecclesiastical, without any vain superstition, and as rules in some part of discipline concerning decency, distinction, and order for the time' (Cardw. 'Doc. Ann.,' vol. i. p. 288).

obstringi:'—words, which are found in the 'Advertisements,' and there alone.

Through some accident, the letter of Gualter to Parkhurst, just quoted, was not seen by Bishop Cox till five years afterwards: when he wrote* (12th February, **1571**) to Gualter, expostulating with him for having so easily listened to the representations of the malcontents. He says:—

> 'Vanissima sunt sane, quæ a contentiosis tuis auribus insusurrantur; nimirum, præter vestes multa alia obtrudi ecclesiis, et esse qui Reginæ nomine abutantur: præterea, ministros ejici ab ecclesiis, qui decretis quorundam subscribere nolunt. Quasi vero quidam sint in Angliâ, qui privatâ auctoritate decreta condere audeant, et fratribus observanda proponere! Illud autem ut falsum, ita etiam injurium est et Reginæ et Verbi ministris, nimirum quod indulgeamus Regiæ Celsitudini, audacioremque reddamus, ut quidvis ex suo arbitrio statuat. Absit hoc, ut quisquam tale suspicetur de tam piâ et religiosâ heroinâ, cui summa semper religio est a præscriptis legibus vel tantillum quidem deflectere.'

With this reply, Gualter † expressed (9th June, 1572) his satisfaction; and explained, that his visitors in 1566 had not only made other representations which had been proved to be untrue, but had added, 'that their most grievous cause of complaint was, that most of the Bishops had become the willing executors of those things, which were daily coined at Court by superstitious and ambitious courtiers.'

Pilkington, Bishop of Durham (who sympathised with the moderate Puritans), in a letter to Gualter of the 20th of July, 1573,‡ after lamenting that 'the unhappy dispute about the affair of the habits and the dress of the clergy' had then extended itself to the whole outward regimen of the Church, and that all the blame was cast upon the bishops, proceeded thus:—

---

* 'Zurich Letters' (first series), No. 94.
† 'Zurich Letters' (first series), Appendix, No. 7.
‡ Ibid. pp. 286-288; Burnet 'Ref. vol. iii. p. 606.

'We endure, I must confess, many things against our inclinations, and groan under them; which, if we wished ever so much, no entreaty can remove. We are under authority, and cannot make any innovation without the sanction of the Queen, or abrogate anything without the authority of the laws; and the only alternative now allowed us is, whether we will bear with these things, or disturb the peace of the Church.'

Jewell had, in substance, said the same thing in a letter to Bullinger and Lavater,* dated in February, 1565–6.

There are also, in the Record Office, two unpublished State Papers, referred to in the decision of the Folkestone case, which were unknown to Strype and other later historians. The first of these is Grindal's official letter, as Bishop of London, to the Dean and Chapter of St. Paul's, dated the 21st of May, 1566;† in which he requires them to convene the clergy under their jurisdiction, and to enjoin them all, on pain of deprivation,

'to prepare forthwith, and to weare, such habit and apparell as is ordayned by the Queene's Majesties authoritie expressed in the treaty intituled the Advertism[ts], &c., which I send herein enclosed unto you; and in like to injoyne everie of them under the said payne of deprivacōn as well to observe the order of mynistracōn in the Church with surples, and in such forme as is sett forth in the saide treatie, as alsoe to require the subscription of every of them to the said Advertisem[ts]'

The other is:—'Articles presented to Her Majesty' (Queen Elizabeth) 'by the Archbishop of Canterbury' (Whitgift), 'and the Bishop of Salisbury' (Piers), 'in the names of themselves and the Bishops of London, Rochester, Lincoln, Peterborough, Gloucester, at St. James, October 1583.'‡ The fifth Article

---

* Strype's 'Annals,' vol. i. part ii.; Append. No. 36.

† 'State Papers, Domestic, Eliz.,' vol. xxxix. No. 76. See Appendix A, post, p. 74.

‡ Ibid. vol. clxiii., No. 31. See Appendix B, post, p. 75.

runs thus:—'That all preachers and others in Ecclesiasticall orders doo at all tymes weare and use such kynds of apparell as is prescribed unto them by the booke of Advertisementes, that is, cloke with sleeves, square capp, gowne, tippett, &c.' Against which there is, in the original, this marginal note:—' The last wordes, viz. cloak with sleeves, &c., may be leafte out, yf it bee thought good. But the Article is warranted, both by the Advertisementes set out by Her Maties authoritie, and also by the Q. Iniunctions, *anno primo Elizab.*'

This document is, evidently, the original draft of the celebrated Articles of 1584;* in which the Article just cited became the fourth, omitting the words, as to which it was suggested in the draft that they might be left out, and adding (after 'Advertisements') 'and her Majesty's Injunctions, anno primo.' That the Articles of 1584 were issued by the Queen's authority, appears distinctly from Archbishop Whitgift's official letter sending them to the Bishops and Ordinaries of his province; a copy of which (as sent to the Bishop of London) is printed by Strype.†

'Where of late' (he says), 'by advice, as well of your Lordship, as of certain others of my brethren the bishops of my province, I have set down certain Articles for good orders to be observed in the Church of England, the true copy whereof I have sent unto you herewith, whereunto it hath pleased Her Majesty of her princely clemency to yield her most gracious assent and allowance; to the intent that the said Articles may take the better effect throughout your diocese of London, I have thought good to will and require you, that with such care and diligence as appertaineth you cause the same Articles effectually to be put in execution throughout the same diocese of London.'

There were, indeed, Puritan writers (generally anonymous),

---

* Cardw. 'Doc. Ann.' p. 411.
† 'Life of Whitgift' (Oxford, 1822), pp. 232, 233.

who afterwards suggested **doubts as to the** legal efficacy of the
'Advertisements' **as an execution of the** statutory power of
the Crown; not (apparently) upon historical, but upon technical
and formal grounds. **Thus, a** pamphleteer* of Queen Elizabeth's
time, mentioned by Strype, and also, in terms of disparagement,
by Hearn,† objected, **that** 'the book came forth
without her Majesty's privilege, and was not printed by her
Majesty's printer, or any in his name:' an objection which
has been shewn to be false **in fact.** A tract of 1605 ‡ **is**
referred to in the 'Purchas **Judgment**,' in which (after contending
that the penalties of the Act of 1559 did not apply
to any contravention of the proviso in the 25th Section) the
authority **of the** 'Advertisements' was disputed, **on the** ground
that the Queen's **approval** ought to have unequivocally appeared
on the face of them, but did not so appear; complaint being,
at the same time, made that the penalty **of deprivation was
enforced by** the Ecclesiastical Courts against ministers who refused
to wear the surplice: and that it was the 'Advertisements'
'**whereupon they did** principally **rely, and by** authority whereof

---

* 'An Abstract of certain Acts of Parliament,' &c. (without date, or printer's name; No. 697 in the British Museum), see p. 47. Strype ('Annals,' vol. iii. part i. p. 338) attributes this pamphlet to the year 1584.

† Preface to Camden's 'Annales,' pp. 30, 31. He is speaking of the 'Advertisements:'—' monitiones quasdam, longè majoris auctoritatis quam voluit auctor libri cujusdam ipsâ Reginâ vivente excusi,' &c. The whole passage, to which he refers in a footnote to this place, is as follows:—' Though hir Maiest. most excellent name be used by the publishers of the saide Advertisements for confirmation of them, and that they affirme hir M. to have commanded them thereunto by hir Highnes Letters, yet because the book it self cometh forth without hir M. priviledge, and is not printed by hir M. printer nor any in his name, therefore it carrieth no such credit and authority with it as whereunto hir M. subjects are necessarily bound to subscribe, having other laws and other Injunctions under hir M. name, and authorized by hir M. priviledge, contrary to the same.'

‡ 'Certain considerations drawn from the canons of the last Synod, and other the King's Ecclesiastical and Statute law, *ad informandum animum Episcopi Wigorniensis*,' &c. (Brit. Mus.: 5155, a.), p. 35.

they did chiefly proceed.' The 'Survey of the Book of Common Prayer'* (frequently referred to in Cosin's 'Notes'), which was published in 1606, does not (in any place which the present writer has examined) expressly mention the 'Advertisements.' But it represents the 58th Canon, ordering the use of surplices and hoods at the Holy Communion, as contradictory to the 14th Canon, and to Queen Elizabeth's Act of Uniformity. And, putting the case hypothetically, that Queen Elizabeth did order the use of surplice and cope (which the author calls 'garments of Baal's priests'), it suggests that the condition of the Statute would have been violated, which required all such ceremonies or rites as she should ordain to be 'for the advancement of God's glory,' &c.

These arguments, or some of them, seem for a time to have made some impression upon the mind of Cosin. In one passage of his first set of 'Notes'† (not derived by him from Bishop Andrewes, as has been sometimes erroneously supposed), he referred to the 'Advertisements' as an exercise of the Queen's statutory power. In another,‡ he adopted the view which had been taken in the 'Survey,' as to the supposed discrepancy between the 14th and the 58th Canons. At some time afterwards, not ascertained, he corrected § this last passage, as having been written in forgetfulness of the statutory power. But in his later 'Notes,'‖ and 'Particulars to be considered,'¶ &c. (if they were, in fact, later than this correction), he again, in several places, represented the vestments of 1549 as still enjoined by law; apparently on the ground, that no 'other order, so qualified,'** as was required by the Act of 1559, had ever

---

* British Museum; 3406, b. See pages 41–43.
† 'Works' (A. C. L. ed.), vol. v. p. 90.
‡ Ibid. pp. 42, 43.
§ Ibid. p. 43. Nicholls, in 1710, published the 'Note,' without the correction.
‖ 'Works,' vol. v. pp. 230–233; 305, 306; 439, 440.
¶ Ibid. p. 507.
** Ibid. p. 233.

been taken. Mr. **Parker*** justly says, that 'it is not clear to what qualification Cosin **refers.**' Yet these passages in Cosin's 'Notes,' &c., when published in 1710, became the fountainhead of a new tradition, afterwards carried on by several **writers of** the eighteenth and present centuries—by Nicholls, Gibson, **Wheatley,** John Johnson, Burn, Cardwell, and others—reversing **that of** Hooker, Sparke, Lestrange, **Wren,** Heylyn, Sparrow, and every other **earlier** Churchman of views similar to Cosin's, except Cosin himself.

Dr. Cardwell suggests **a reason, which, if it had** been historical or **well-founded in law,** might have explained this opinion. He says : †—

'The Advertisements, . . . though they did **not overcome the** objections of the **violent Puritans,** moderated **the ancient Rubric** respecting vestments, **by** removing the distinction between the Eucharist and other services **in parish** churches, and retaining it **in** cathedrals only. . . . *It is true* **that these** *Advertisements were* **not** *binding in law, as they had not been sanctioned under the Great* **Seal** *;* ‡ but it is clear **they were** considered binding, as they certainly were approved by the **Queen:** *and it had not yet been ruled, that edicts issued by the Queen's commission were not binding, unless they* **were** *confirmed by the Queen officially. See Croke's Reports,* 2 **Jac., p. 37.**'

It **was,** of course, possible, that **a public** document, which for many years had been treated, not by unauthoritative writers only, but **also in Canons and constitutions** ecclesiastical, by bishops in their **official visitations, and by** Church Courts in their sentences, **as issued with the authority** of the Crown, might, by some later decision **of a temporal** court, have been proved to **be deficient** in some **necessary point of** form. But **was** there ever, **in fact, any** such decision? Dr. **Cardwell's** reference (which **is** inaccurate) seems **to be to a case of** *Keyley* v. *Manning,* §

---

* Introduction, p. 133.

† Cardw. 'Conf.,' pp. 38, 39, *note.*

‡ There is a **trace** of the same notion of the necessity **of the Great Seal, in**

Neal's 'Hist. of the Puritans,' vol. i. (ed. 1822), **p. 172.**

§ Reported in Croke 'Car.,' p. 180.

determined by the Court of King's Bench in 1630, as to the proper manner of pleading a certain Royal Proclamation by way of defence to a civil action; which, it was held, should have been alleged to be under the Great Seal. The 'Advertisements,' whatever else they might be, were not a Royal Proclamation; and the Judges, in *Keyley* v. *Manning*, decided nothing as to the proper mode of executing a statutory power given to the Crown in terms such as those of the Act of Elizabeth, which prescribed no particular formality. The authority of the Crown may be given to acts of State, the forms of which are not prescribed by custom or statute, without Seal, or Proclamation, or Order in Council. The doctrine laid down in the 'Purchas Judgment,' that, 'if the Queen's mandative letter preceded * the compilation of the "Advertisements," and if they were afterwards enforced as by her authority, her assent must be presumed,' is not, to the knowledge of the present writer, inconsistent with any previous decision, ever pronounced.

Passing now to the alterations and additions introduced into the Prayer-book after the Hampton Court Conference, we find that Cosin † (again following, in his 'Notes,' &c., the opinion previously advanced by the author of the 'Survey') regarded them all as unauthorised and illegal. The author of the 'Survey' ‡ thought that the powers given by the 25th and 26th sections of the Act of 1559 were personal to, and died with, Queen Elizabeth. But the King never dies; and in a

---

* The Queen's letter of the 22nd January, 1560-1 (under her 'Signet'), for the alteration of the Table of Lessons, also preceded the changes made under its authority; and it does not appear to have been followed by any other formal instrument, approving those changes. (See Cardw. 'Doc. Ann.,' vol. i. p. 260.)

† See Parker, 'Introduction,' pp. 139, 156, 158, 251, 267, 373.

‡ 'Survey,' &c., pp. 41–43; Nicholls and Burn (and probably Cosin, see Parker, 'Introduction,' p. 110), adopted the same view.

statute giving the King **powers for a public** purpose, not limited **as to** time, his heirs and successors are, *primâ facie*, implied. **Another** argument found favour with some of the Puritans in the next reign ; viz. that even if the King's prerogative had **extended** so far, still the efficacy of his act did not continue beyond King James's lifetime, ' all proclamations determining **with the** King's life.'* Those changes, however, were not made by Proclamation, but by Letters Patent† under the Great Seal, specifying them all in detail, as advised by the Metropolitan and the Ecclesiastical Commissioners : nor is there any law to the effect, that the exercise of a statutory power, by Royal Proclamation, may not endure beyond the life of the reigning Sovereign. An objection of more apparent weight might have been derived **from the** conditional character of the power given by the 26th section, under which those changes were **made**. But the Crown lawyers, **who must necessarily have been consulted** on that occasion, probably thought that the **King** was the proper judge whether any such ' **contempt** or **irreverence,**' as was supposed **in that section, had** happened, and that **proof** of it might be found **in the circumstances** under which the Hampton Court Conference had been assembled, as recited in the Proclamation ‡ by **which the Letters Patent** were followed. It might **still be** doubtful whether **the** power to **ordain** and publish *further* ceremonies or rites **would authorise** changes **in** the existing **rites, as** well as additions **to them.** But what was actually then done was chiefly by **way of addition ; the** rest was of small importance, and may have been **thought** sufficiently covered by **the larger power.**

Mr. Parker observes,§ **that ' the Rubrics, as to** the place of Morning Prayer, **and on Church Ornaments,** introduced in Elizabeth's reign,' were at this **time ' kept** intact, and totally un-

---

* See Neal's ' Hist. of Puritans,' vol. ii. (ed. 1822), p. 20.
† Card. ' Conf.,' pp. 217-225.
‡ Card., ' **Conf.**' pp. 225-228.
§ Int. p. 58.

influenced by the "Advertisements" of 1564.' It could **not be otherwise,** unless some unauthorised person had then taken occasion of the King's directions, to do what the King had not directed. Those Rubrics were not mentioned or referred to in any of the alterations or additions then made, or in the King's Letters Patent or Proclamation. The order to reprint the book, with the alterations and additions specifically mentioned, could not make anything not so mentioned (and as to which the King had not received the advice required by the statute), part of the Book of Common Prayer, unless it was so before. **The subsequent** republication, therefore, of those Rubrics did not alter their effect, or their relation to the law. **An illustration,** sufficiently apposite, may be derived from a recent example, in which there might have been much greater reason for changes, which, nevertheless, were not made. **In 1871 an Act of Parliament*** was passed, authorising many **deviations from the** order of Divine Service prescribed **by the present Rubrics.** But the Rubrics themselves were, and have ever since been, 'kept intact,' and ' totally uninfluenced **by ' that Act of Parliament;** and they may probably so remain until all the necessary authorities of Church and State are able to agree upon some general revision.

The year 1640–1 is the next epoch **to which Mr. Parker's work directs our attention ; and here we have another instance of the way in which, under the influence of controversy, historical** errors may **grow. On the 1st of** March, **1640–1 (the day on which Laud was committed to the** Tower), **a Committee was appointed by** the House **of Lords,† ' to take into** consideration all innovations in the **Church concerning religion ;' and a petition** from Kent, complaining **of such innovations, was**

---

* 35 & 36 Vict. cap. 35.

† The disposition of the House of Lords was not then favourable to the Puritans. See Lords' Journals, January 16, 1640, April 22, 1641 ; Clarendon's 'Rebellion' (Oxford 1826), vol. ii. pp. 7, 8; Hallam's 'Const. Hist.' (ed. 1832). vol. ii. p. 163.

referred to it. It consisted* of thirty lay Peers and ten bishops; among whom were Bishop Williams of Lincoln (Chairman); Wren of Ely (then under notice of impeachment); Hall of Exeter (afterwards of Norwich);† and Warner of Rochester. Morton, Bishop of Durham, and two more lay Peers, were afterwards‡ added. On the 10th of March the Committee was empowered, by Resolution of the House,§ 'to send for what divines they should please for their better information; as the Lord Archbishop of Armagh' (Ussher), 'Dr. Prideaux, Dr. Warde, Dr. Twiste, Dr. Hacket.' On the 12th of March, when the Committee first met, Bishop Williams addressed a letter to these and eleven ‖ other divines, summoning them 'to attend as assistants to the Committee;' informing them that the Committee intended 'to examine all innovations in doctrine or discipline, introduced into the Church without law since the Reformation,' and afterwards (if necessary) 'to examine the degrees and proportion of the Reformation itself;' and directing them 'to prepare their thoughts, studies, and meditations accordingly.'¶

Of the divines thus summoned, eleven were Churchmen, noted for learning and, generally, for moderation (though some of them were decided Calvinists); Archbishop Ussher; Brownrigg, Prideaux, Westfield, Hacket, and Sanderson, all afterwards

---

* 'Lords' Journals,' March 1, 1640. Archbishop Laud, from imperfect information, stated the numbers as 'ten Earls, ten Bishops, and ten Barons'; in which he has been followed by other writers:—*e.g.* Dr. Cardwell ('Conf.,' p. 238); Walker ('Sufferings of the Clergy,' 1714), p. 29; Neal ('Hist. Pur.,' ed. 1822), vol. ii. p. 396. There were, in fact (besides the Lord Treasurer and the Lord Chamberlain), 13 Earls, one Viscount, and 14 Barons.

† Hall was translated to Norwich, December 16, 1641, in the place of Montague, who died April 6, 1641; Dr. Cardwell ('Conf.,' p. 239) has confounded Montagne with Hall.

‡ 'Lords' Journals,' March 12, 1640.
§ Ibid. March 10, 1640.
‖ Fuller and Hacket name only those who regularly attended the meetings, which Westfield, White, and Shute did not. Those three names are from Laud's Diary, 'Works' (Ang. Cath. Libr. ed.), vol. iii. p. 438.
¶ Laud's 'Works,' vol. iii. pp. 437, 438.

bishops; Ward, Holdsworth, and Hill, then or afterwards Masters of Colleges and Professors at Cambridge; **Featly, Rector** of Lambeth; and Shute, Archdeacon of Colchester. **The rest** were strong Puritans: Marshall and Burgess, (whom Clarendon * describes as having had more influence over that Parliament than the archbishop ever had at **Court**); **Calamy, Twisse, and** White of Dorchester, called the 'patriarch **of** the Puritans,' and praised as one of the most learned and moderate of his party.

The Committee itself seems to have had four **or**, at most, five meetings; † **the** last on the 8th of April, 1641. On **the 7th** of May the House of Lords instructed the bishops who were on it to inquire **into** and report upon certain books alleged **to be** 'full of innovations of doctrine;' after which there is **no further** notice of it on the journals. Laud ‡ had feared **much, and** others § had hoped much from it; but it never made any Report, nor is there any public or other record **of its proceedings.** So little importance was attributed to it at that time, that it is not even mentioned by Clarendon ‖ or Whitlocke, in May's 'History **of** the Long **Parliament,' or** in Rushworth's **or Nalson's** 'Collections.'

There are, however, besides the Lords' Journals and Archbishop Laud's **Diary, three** other **sources of information upon this subject,** which **may** be described **as** original; **viz. Fuller's** 'Church **History,'** who says ¶ that his narrative (published in 1656) came from 'one **of the** Committee;' the statements of Baxter, and **the** other Puritan Commissioners **at the Savoy** Conference (of whom **Calamy** was one); **and Hacket's 'Life of**

---

* 'Hist. of the Rebellion' (ed. 1826), vol. ii. p. 25.
† 'Lords' Journals,' 24th **March,** 1640; 29th March, **5th** April, 8th April, 1641.
‡ 'Works,' vol. iii. pp. 437, 438.
§ **Fuller's** '**Church** History' (ed. 1656), p. 175.

‖ Though Clarendon ('Reb.' **vol. ii.** pp. 102-118) goes into much detail as to the public acts and character of Archbishop Williams, whom he judges with unsparing severity.
¶ Fuller's 'Church History' (ed. 1656), pp. 174, 175.

Archbishop Williams;'* to which may be added Hacket's own 'Life,' by his friend Archdeacon Plume, † published (before the 'Life of Williams') in 1675. Walker,‡ Collier,§ Neal,‖ and other later historians, follow, or profess to follow, the two first of these authorities.

The substance of Fuller's narrative (with which that of Plume agrees) is, that the Lords' Committee appointed a 'Sub-Committee,' consisting of their Chairman, Bishop Williams, and Bishops Morton and Hall, with the sixteen consulted divines as their assistants, 'to prepare matters for their' (the Committee's) 'cognizance.' This Sub-Committee met and debated, under the presidency of Bishop Williams, for six days, in the Jerusalem Chamber; during which time (to adopt Plume's paraphrase ¶ of Fuller's quainter words), 'many things were propounded; but in the midst of May, while in order to settlement divers things were upon the loom, the Bill, called "Root and Branch," was brought into the House of Commons; and that, like Atropos, cut off all the threads of this proceeding, so that the whole matter proved abortive and came to nullity.'

A memorandum, one of the original prints** of which is in the possession of the present writer, was drawn up (doubtless, for the consideration of this Sub-Committee) by seven of its members, and was printed in the same year (1641), though not by the Sub-Committee itself, or with its authority, as is evident from the title: 'A copie of the proceedings of some worthy and

---

* Published in 1692, after Hacket's death, under the title 'Scrinia Reserata, a Memorial offered to the great deservings of John Williams, D.D., &c.' See pp. 146-148.

† Republished by Walcott, 1865 (London: Masters), pp. 43-46. Plume was Vicar of Greenwich and Archdeacon of Rochester; and was Bishop Hacket's agent for his London business.

‡ 'Sufferings of the Clergy' (1714), p. 29.

§ 'Hist.,' vol. viii. p. 197 (ed. 1846).

‖ 'Hist. of Puritans,' vol. ii. (ed. 1822), pp. 395-399.

¶ Walcot's edition, 1865, p. 43.

** A pamphlet, of ten pages, with 'London, Printed 1641,' on the title-page—no printer's name.

learned divines, appointed by the Lords to meet at **the Bishop of Lincolnes in Westminster : touching innovations in the doctrine and discipline of the Church of England, together with** considerations upon the Prayer-book.' It was re-published, from Baxter's papers, by Sylvester,* **in** 1696, and abridged from his book by Neal;† and has been more recently reprinted at full length, from the same book, **by Dr. Cardwell.**‡ Mr. Parker § falls into the error of calling it the 'Report' of the Committee, by which **it was certainly never seen ; nor could it with** any greater propriety **have been called a Report of the** Sub-Committee. **Dr. Cardwell, however, was** led (apparently by the references **made to it at the Savoy Conference) to** suppose that its contents, generally, **were 'agreed upon' and 'advised' by** all the Churchmen **who attended the Sub-Committee ; and** he describes them ‖ as thereby making concessions,

'surrendering by implication **some of the** most solemn convictions of a great portion of the clergy, on the authority of the Church, **the** nature of the two Sacraments, and the sanctity of the priesthood. Their decision' (he says) 'became a record to be quoted as authority by future Nonconformists, and to be lamented **by** the orthodox party **as** one of the many causes that weakened the **defences** of the Church, **and** led, by certain consequence, **to** its **overthrow.** As a series of concessions which **on** previous **occasions they had** refused—which abandoned in the outset the **whole principle of** Church-government, and was so closely followed by the **violences it** dreaded, that **it might** be said **to have** invited them—it was remembered by the **Royalists,** when they **recovered** the **ascendant,** with feelings of irritation **and** resentment.'¶

---

* ' Reliquiæ **Baxterianæ**; or, Mr. Richard Baxter's **narrative of** the most memorable passages **of** his Life **and Times,** faithfully published from his own original manuscript,' by Matthew Sylvester (London, 1696), p. 369. In the memorandum, as printed by Sylvester, and reprinted by Dr. Cardwell, some words are omitted from the title, and the names at the end are **not** given. The **substance of the** document (with **a** few verbal differences) is the same as **in the** original of **1641.**

† ' Hist. **Pur.,' vol. ii.** pp. 395–397.
‡ ' Conf.,' pp. 270–277.
§ Introduction, pp. 353, 379, 381.
‖ ' Conf.,' pp. 238–241.
¶ Mr. Parker uses similar language : Introduction, p. 61.

These are strong words: and it is due to the reputations on which they seem to cast reproach, that their accuracy should be tested.

The bishops, at the Savoy Conference, refused not only all the more important demands of their opponents, but several others,* the reasonableness of which was, in the end, practically admitted by giving effect to them. The discussion of those matters, upon that occasion, ended with the 'Rejoinder' of the Puritans; in the 'Preface' to which they said:— †

'And whereas divers reverend bishops and doctors, in a paper in print before the late unhappy wars began, yielded to the laying aside of the cross, and the making many material alterations; you, after twenty years such calamities and divisions, seem unwilling to grant what they, of their own accord, then offered.'

The references to the same subject, in the body of the 'Rejoinder,' are these:— ‡

(A.) 'We beseech you, deny not the name of Protestants to the Primate of Ireland, the Archbishop of York, and the many others, that had divers meetings for the reformation of the Liturgy, and who drew up that catalogue of faults or points that needed mending, which is yet to be seen in print.'

(B.) 'Divers other unfit expressions' (*i.e.* in the Prayer-book) 'are mentioned in the exceptions of the late Archbishop of York and Primate of Ireland and others, before spoken of.'

There is nothing more in the 'Rejoinder.' Baxter § explained these allusions, by giving the text (not quite accurately copied) of the memorandum itself, with this introduction:—

'And here, because they would abate us nothing at all considerable, but made things far harder and heavier than before, I will annex the

---

* Park. Introduction, p. 406.

† 'An accompt of all the proceedings of the Commissioners,' &c. (London, 1661; Brit. Mus. 3747, aaa.), p. 2. The report is the same in 'The Grand Debate,' &c. (London, 1661; Br. Mus. 3475, b.).

‡ Ibid. pp. 27, 28 (A.); p. 39 (B.).

§ 'Reliquiæ Baxterianæ,' p. 369.

concessions of Archbishop Ussher, Archbishop Williams, Bishop Morton, Bishop Holdsworth,* and many others, in a Committee at Westminster, before mentioned, 1641.'

In the original print of the memorandum (though not in Baxter's copy, which was followed by Neal and Dr. Cardwell) the names of its known or reputed compilers, viz. 'Archbishop of Armach, Bishop of Lincolne, Dr. Prideaux, Dr. Ward, Dr. Brownrig, Dr. Featly, Dr. Hacket,' are given at the end.

It † is divided into three parts. The two first parts are headed, 'Innovations in doctrine,' and 'Innovations in discipline.' To these the Puritans at the Conference do not appear to have referred at all. It is clear, upon the face of them,' ‡ that they are nothing more than a collection of alleged innovations noted for inquiry, or (as Neal§ says), 'for the debate of the Committee;'—in accordance with Fuller's statement,|| that 'some complained' of such and such matters; or Collier's,¶ that 'the greatest part of the company, being Calvinists either in doctrine or discipline, remonstrated against certain things.' In the first, or doctrinal part, the foremost item is, 'whether, in the twentieth Article' (of Religion) 'these words are not inserted:—*Habet Ecclesia authoritatem in controversiis fidei?*'—a question, which, (as every Churchman on the Sub-Committee, however hostile to Laud, must have well known,) had been placed beyond the reach of any honest controversy by Laud's speech in 1637,** at the proceedings in the Star-Chamber against Bastwick, Burton, and Prynne. In the second, or disciplinary part, the

---

* Holdsworth died in 1649, and was never a bishop.

† See Cardw. 'Conf.,' pp. 270-277.

‡ The names of particular persons (Dove, Heylyn, Brown, Sybthorp, and others), are noted as having given 'scandal,' &c., by sermons, disputations at the Universities, and otherwise. The author of Sancta Clara's book is to 'be caused to produce Bishop Watson's book that he speaks of,' &c. &c.

§ 'Hist. Pur.,' p. 396.

|| 'Hist.,' p. 174.

¶ Vol. viii. p. 197 (ed. 1846).

** Published by Badger (London, 1637). See Laud's 'Works' (Aug. Cath. Lib. ed.), vol. vi. pp. 64, 65.

chief alleged novelties were the same as in most of the Puritan complaints, at that time current; *e.g.* in the charges against Laud, Wren,* and Cosin; and in the London and Kentish Petitions,† (the latter referred to the Committee on the day of its appointment), and others of a similar character.

What the Puritans at the Conference may be supposed really to have meant to rely upon was the third part of the memorandum, which was entitled, 'Considerations upon the Book of Common Prayer;' ‡ alleging, that (not all, but) '*divers*,' or '*many*' of the divines consulted in 1641, and particularly Ussher and Williams (Baxter adds Morton and Holdsworth), were willing, and of their own accord offered, to concede such changes in the Liturgy as were there, in the form of queries, noted for consideration. The 'Rejoinder' was the last word in that stage of the Conference; and it is worthy of note that neither Bishop Warner (who was on the Committee of 1641), nor Sanderson or Hacket (both of whom were among the divines on the Church side who attended all the proceedings of the Sub-Committee), was referred to by name; though all three of them were Savoy Commissioners: and Hacket's name is one of those appended to the printed memorandum.

Hacket had been the friend of Williams, whose biographer he afterwards became. Mr. Parker § has, through some oversight, stated that he died on the 22nd of December, 1661, the day of his consecration to the see of Lichfield.‖ He lived till 1670. His account of the matter is this:—¶

---

* Laud's 'Works,' vol. iv.; 'Parl. History,' vol. ix. p. 452; Nalson's 'Collections,' vol. ii. p. 398; Parker, Introduction, pp. 389–395.

† Nalson's 'Collections,' vol. i. p. 660. *et seqq.*

‡ Cardw. 'Conf.,' pp. 274-277.

§ Introduction, p. 448, *note*.

‖ Vacant by the translation of Archbishop Frewen to York, in October, 1660. The see had been kept open more than a year, for the acceptance of Baxter or Calamy.

¶ 'Scrinia Reserata,' pp. 146-148.

'The House of Lords appointed a Committee of their own members to give glory to God by driving profaneness out of His **temple, and** at the same time selected a sub-committee of divines **of very contrary** opinions, for indifferency sake, to prepare unto **them matters** fit for their cognisance, to prevent those clamours, odious in our land, and scandalous to other nations. . . . *The Bishop*' (Williams), '*and as many as were of his judgment,* **found** no way but **to** let them that seemed to be distasted with the Church for certain things have somewhat granted **that** they asked **for, to let** suspicions pass for proofs, and any point **of a** dubious frame **for a** kind of error ; **as** they that raise a blister where there was none before, to prepare a cure for preventing **an apoplexy.** Necessity hath **no law ;** but it **shows a** great deal of reason **to** unsettle some few things **by condescension,** for the settlement of a general peace. **Sometimes a** little loss is **a** great gain. . . . Now this theological junto had six **meetings in** Westminster College; in all which time, all passages of **discourse** were very friendly between part **and part.** The complainants noted the passages of some books that suited not in their judgment with the doctrine of the Church ; they were condemned.* Somewhat **in** ceremony and outward form **was** presented, **as** beside canon and supernumerary ; they had their asking, to bid it be restrained. *Their exceptions against our Liturgy were petty and stale, older than the old Exchange ; yet, for their contentment, the* **vote of the** *meeting did bend one way to castigate some phrases, to publish* **the next** *printed books, in all passages from the beginning* **to the end,** *with the translation of King James' Bible,* **and to furnish the Calendar** *altogether with lessons of canonical Scripture,* **dispunging** *the Apocrypha.*† The Bishop **had** undertaken a draught for regulating the government ecclesiastical, ‡

---

* In the doctrinal part of the Memorandum, after the 'Innovations,' are specified 'some dangerous and most reprovable books' (Cardw. 'Conf.,' p. 272).

† Plume, whose information may be presumed to have been obtained from Hacket, (and whose book was published **seventeen years before** the 'Scrinia Reserata,') **gives** an exactly similar account of **the** Liturgical concessions of the majority of **the Sub-Committee.**

They 'condescended' (he says) 'to print the Liturgic Psalms in King James's translation ; to expunge all Apocryphal lessons, and alter some passages in the Book of Common Prayer, which divers of the Presbyterian divines said were satisfactory, save that the furious party of them put the Commons upon the violent way,' p. **46.**

‡ Neither the Committee nor the Sub-Committee was answerable for the schemes submitted to the two **Houses of**

but did not finish it. **The sudden** and quiet despatch of all **that was** done already was attributed to the **Chairman's** dexterity,' &c. . . . **When** peace came so **near to the** birth, how it abortived, and by whose fault, comes **to be remarked.** The Presbyterians knew not what to **ask** more than was yielded to them, **before the face** of such **scholars with whom** they were matched. But when they were away, **thinking in their** own body, they **would stand to nothing.** . . . A few **weak brethren** might take these **alterations in** good **part, but the noted men of the** faction **could not** bring themselves **into fame and** name, and somewhat else, but in a greater confusion. . . . The Presbyterians understood that they should expose themselves and their **cause to the censure of wise men,** if they did adventure no further in conference **at the Sub-committee.** Therefore, **to** cut off the meeting in the heat and great **hopes of it,** they **had a** champion that brought a Bill into the House **of Commons** to take away for ever all archbishops, bishops, &c. . . . **So** you have **the first and** the last part of the Presbyterian's actings with the other **divines, whom** the Lords appointed for a Sub-committee. **There may well be a suspicion,** when their deeds do make **a confession, that they would prevail by** force, when they could not by argument.'

It is evident that Bishop Hacket, **who lived in honour** and **general** respect after the Restoration, **was** not conscious of any **reproach** attaching **to the ' concessions,'** which the majority of the Sub-Committee, (of whom he was **probably** one,) had been willing **to make.** Even if those concessions **had** extended **to every one of** the changes **in the** Liturgy **suggested** by the **' queries '** * in the third part of the memorandum (of which there is no proof),

---

Parliament by Archbishops **Williams** and Ussher in July 1641 ; **the former** of which proposed to give **each bishop** a Council ; and the latter proceeded on **the** principle of combining **synodical** with episcopal government. (See Fuller, p. 182 ; Whitlocke's 'Memorials,' p. 46, ed. 1732 ; Neal's ' Pur.' vol. ii. pp. 400-402.)

* Some of those queries had, evidently, **a Puritan origin ;** and were doubtless set down by the **members of** the Sub-Committee, who **drew up the** Memorandum, in the **terms in which** they had been **proposed, as proper for consideration.** Among the errors in the text, as given by Cardwell, are the word ' confined,' instead of ' consigned,' in **the 20th** query ; ' Communion,' instead of ' Commination,' in the 30th ; and ' Liturgy,' instead of ' Litany,' **in** the 31st.

here is nothing in them to justify or account for **Dr. Cardwell's** description :—no 'abandonment' (express or implied), **of any principle of Church-government,'**—nothing about '**the authority of the Church,'** or '**the nature of the two Sacraments,'** or '**the sanctity of the priesthood'**—**nothing** even against **the use of the** surplice, or kneeling at the Holy Communion ; nothing as to the form of ordination, or the manner **of administering the** Lord's Supper. The **most** important queries were, whether there might not be some relaxation of the Rubrics as to daily service, and as to the frequency of **communion in** cathedrals ; a change in the **form of** absolution **of the sick, from** 'I absolve thee,' to '**I pronounce** thee absolved ;' **an omission from** the **Rubric which declared** children (being baptized, and **dying before the commission of sin) to** '**have all** things **necessary for their salvation,'** of the superadded words, '**and be undoubtedly saved :'** and, as to the sign of the cross **in baptism,** '**whether it be not fit to have some discreet** rule **made to take away all scandal from signing the** cross upon infants after **baptism ; or, if it shall seem more expedient** to be quite disused, **whether this reason'** (suggesting one, derived from the **association** of that sign with **the use of** oil in ancient Liturgies) '**shall be published.'**

Further, though **less** direct, evidence of the relative attitude **of the moderate** Churchmen and **the Puritans upon the** Sub-Committee **may be** obtained **from** the controversy carried on at that **very** time **between** Bishop Hall and Calamy and Marshall (with three others) * under the name of '**Smectymnuus.'** The Bishop, in the ' Defence ' † of his ' Humble Remonstrance,' and in his subsequent Answer ‡ to the ' Vindication ' of ' Smectymnuus,' referred **to** ' that honourable and reverend

---

* **Of** whom **two,** Newcomen **and** Spurstow, were among Calamy's colleagues on the Savoy Commission.
† ' Defence **of** the **humble** Remonstrance, &c.' (1641), pp. 22, 23.
‡ ' A short Answer to the tedious **Vindication,' &c.** (1641) ; Dedication ; and **p. 55.**

Committee,' as likely to alter 'whatever should be found, in the manner of the expressions' (of the Liturgy), 'fit to be changed;' adding, 'But the main fabric of it, which your reasons drive at, my hope is we shall never see to undergo an alteration.' 'Smectymnuus' said,* with much scorn, that such language gave 'just cause to suspect a mere design to gain upon the Parliament, and, by a pretended shadow of an alteration, to prevent a real and total reformation,' and to fear, 'that, although the time would not serve to make such an alteration as that of the English Liturgy sent into Scotland, yet the alteration was like to be no better than that in Queen Elizabeth's time.'

Twenty-one of the thirty-five queries of 1641 reappeared in the Puritan 'Exceptions'† at the Savoy Conference. Four of them were, either wholly or partially, conceded at that time by the bishops: of two more the concession was promised, but the promise was not afterwards fulfilled: three others were then refused, but were afterwards conceded. These, and several other concessions, ultimately made, of points stiffly refused at first, are accounted for by Mr. Parker ‡ as in fact due to Bishop Cosin, in whose 'book' corresponding changes were made. But when, and why, were those changes made in that book? Their origin cannot be traced to Cosin's own 'Notes,' or 'Particulars to be considered,' &c. It is hardly probable that the Commissioners, of whom he was one, would have refused at the Conference, against his judgment, changes which, in deference to that judgment, were afterwards approved. No hypothesis, on the other hand, can be more reasonable, than that a careful reconsideration of the Exceptions taken at the Conference may have led to those changes. There are other changes in the same

---

* 'A Vindication of the Answer, &c.; by the same Smectymnuus' (1641), p. 32.

† Some in the 'General,' and some in the 'Particular' Exceptions.

‡ Introduction, pp. 384, 400, 401, 406. See also ibid. pp. 423-426 (as to Bishop Wren's suggestions).

book, which were opposed to Cosin's private opinions, as recorded in his 'Notes;' particularly one* as to the frequency of the communions of cathedral clergy, which had been asked for in 1641 (not at the Savoy Conference), and was not ultimately granted.

Mr. Parker evidently thinks † that the entries in 'Cosin's Book' had been accumulating for a long time before the Restoration; and that, in the state in which it stood before Sancroft's alterations, that book was the product of Cosin's individual mind, influenced, no doubt, by the authorities from which his 'Notes' had been compiled, but unaffected by anything which passed in 1661, at the Conference or elsewhere. To the present writer, on the contrary, there seems to be proof, approaching to demonstration, that (although some entries may have been made in it by Cosin long before), it was made up, and assumed the character which alone gives it importance, during the interval between the close ‡ of the Savoy Conference and the meeting of Convocation on the 21st of November in that year; and that it then represented the mind, not of Cosin only, but of others who were his fellow-labourers in the work.

Mr. Parker § takes notice of the impossibility that the work done by the Upper House of Convocation between the 21st and the 27th of November, 1661, could have been got through, in that time, without previous preparation; but he makes no reference to the positive statement of Lord Clarendon,‖ which places this point beyond the region of conjecture.

'The Bishops' (says Clarendon) 'had spent the vacation ¶ in making such alterations in the Book of Common Prayer as they thought would make it more grateful to the dissenting brethren, for so the schismatical party called themselves; and such additions as in their judgments the temper of the present time and the past mis-

---

* Introduction, pp. 230, 231.
† Ibid. pp. 385, 412.
‡ 24th July, 1661.
§ Introduction, pp. 410–412.
‖ 'Life,' vol. ii. p. 118 (ed. 1827).
¶ The Parliament was adjourned on the 30th of July, and met again on the 20th of November.

carriages required. It was necessarily to be presented to the Convocation, which is the national Synod of the Church; and that did not sit during the recess of the Parliament, and so came not together till the end of November.'

The scheme of alterations, in the preparation of which 'the bishops' (some, probably, of those who had been Savoy Commissioners) spent this considerable interval of nearly four months, must of course have been written in a book; which book must afterwards have become the text, on which the first deliberations of the Upper House of Convocation proceeded. It must necessarily have expressed, not the views of any one mind, but their collective work: and, if it was settled at meetings of bishops only, no hand would be more likely to be employed in recording their proposals than Cosin's. The book, which Mr. Parker calls 'Cosin's,' was, before its alteration by Sancroft, exactly such a record as must have been made of such a work:—it extended even to the necessary directions for printing;* which (though Mr. Parker thinks this may have been contemplated long before by Cosin) are not shown by any evidence to be of earlier date; and which might naturally be expected to be found in any complete scheme of a revised Prayer-book prepared for the purpose of being submitted to Convocation.

That 'Cosin's Book' (in its unaltered state) was, in fact, the original record of the preparation made by the bishops during those four months, seems to be proved by its ascertained relation to 'Sancroft's Book,' and the changes by which it was made (generally) to correspond with that book; and by the relation, also ascertained, of 'Sancroft's Book' to the proceedings of the bishops in the November Session of the Convocation of 1661. Here it becomes necessary to refer to those proceedings.

Lord Clarendon,† (speaking, no doubt, of what passed in both Houses of Convocation,) says, that 'the consideration' of the

---

* Introduction, pp. 94, 387, 388. † 'Life,' vol. ii. pp. 118-120.

scheme presented 'took up much time: all men offering such alterations and additions as were suitable to their own fancies, and the observations which they had made in the time of confusion.' 'The bishops' (he proceeds to say) 'were not all of one mind.' Some (whom he judges, partly by the light of subsequent events, to have been the wisest) were for changing nothing in the former Prayer-book.

'Others, equally grave, of great learning and unblemished reputation, pressed earnestly both for the alterations and additions; said, "that it was a common reproach upon the government of the Church, that it would not depart from the least unnecessary expression or word, nor explain the most insignificant ceremony, which would quiet or remove the doubts and jealousies of many conscientious men, that they did in truth signify somewhat that was not intended; and therefore, since some powerful men of that troublesome party had made it their earnest request that some such alterations and additions might be made, and professed that it would give great satisfaction to many very good men, it would be a great pity, now there was a fit opportunity for it (which had not been in former times of clamour) not to gratify them in some particulars, which did not make any important difference from what was before."'

'It may be' (he adds) 'there were some, who believed that the victory and triumph of the Church would be with the more lustre, if somewhat were inserted that might be understood to reflect upon the rude and rebellious behaviour of the late times, which had been regulated by that clergy. And so, both additions and alterations were made.'

When we turn to the official record of the Acts of Convocation, we find, that the whole Liturgy, properly so called,* passed through the Upper House in five days;† and was sent down by them to the Lower House, part on the 23rd, and the rest on the

---

* Excluding the Prefaces and Calendar; the Psalms; the Ordination Services; the General Thanksgiving; and the Prayers for use at Sea; which were afterwards added.

† Introduction, pp. 87-89; 407-409.

27th of November. To enable this to be done, a **Committee of eight Bishops was appointed on the 21st** of November, the first day of their meeting:—not merely (as Mr. Parker* appears to think) to prepare matter for the subsequent consideration of the whole Body, but really **to** continue every **day's work, at** Bishop Wren's **house, after five o'clock** in the afternoon:—the Convocation sitting only **from 8 to 10 A.M.** and from 2 to 4 P.M. on each day, and itself making progress **in the same work,** during those hours. The Committee **consisted of six** of the twelve **bishops who** had been Savoy Commissioners **(Cosin, Wren, Morley,** Henchman, **Warner, and** Sanderson), **and two (Skinner** and Nicholson) who **were not. There is no trace of their** having **ever made any** reports **or** report: † **and the terms** of their appointment show that they were entrusted with **powers** making this **unnecessary:** for the Upper House '*commisit vices suas* eisdem, aut eorum tribus ad minus, *ad procedendum in dicto negotio*; **et ordinavit eos** ad conveniendum apud palatium reverendi patris domini Episcopi Eliensis, horâ quintâ post meridiem cujuslibet diei (exceptis diebus dominicis) donec dictum negotium perficiatur.' ‡ **Nor can such a** delegation of powers (amounting really to a continuation of **the** sittings of the Upper House, by **some** of its most trusted members, after business hours) seem extraordinary **to** those who **know what was, at** nearly the same time, done **to** obtain the concurrence **of the** Convocation of York. On the 23rd **of November, the Archbishop of** York, and the Bishops of Durham (Cosin), Carlisle, **and Chester, addressed** a letter **to** their own **Lower House;** saying **that** all possible expedition **was necessary;** that **they** were themselves sitting in consultation with **the**

---

* Preface, pp. 14, 15; Introduction, pp. 97, 407, 414, &c.

† **The** House would, of course, be informed every morning of the progress made at the last evening's sitting of the Committee; **and any points reserved,** or otherwise arising for consideration, would be then discussed.

‡ Introd., p. 88; Gibson, 'Syn. Angl.' (Cardwell's ed. Oxford, 1854), p. 214.

Bishops of the Province of Canterbury;* and that the ordinary course of proceeding would be too dilatory; and, upon those grounds, asking the Clergy of their province, on behalf of their whole Lower House, to appoint the Prolocutor of Canterbury, the Deans of Westminster and St. Paul's, and some others of the Clergy of Canterbury, their proxies, 'to give your consent to such things as shall be concluded here in relation to the premisses:'—which the Lower House of York accordingly did; adding only one other name to the Prolocutor of Canterbury and the two Metropolitan Deans.† In this way, and in this only, the Convocation of York was a party to the Revision of 1661.

Now it is clear, from one of the entries made by Sancroft in 'Cosin's Book,'‡ as well as from other internal evidence, that Sancroft acted as secretary, either to Cosin, or to the Convocation, or to the Committee of Bishops;§ that his alterations of 'Cosin's Book' were made while he was so acting; and that his own Book (of which Cosin's Book, as altered, was substantially the original) represents the state into which the Book of Common prayer was brought, during that stage of the process of Revision, or some part of it, by the Upper House of Canterbury. If so, it seems necessarily to follow, that 'Cosin's Book,' in its unaltered state, must be that which (according to Clarendon) was prepared and presented for the consideration of that House. Some part of the alterations included in 'Sancroft's Book' can only have been made by the Upper House itself: for the early part of the Liturgy was proceeded with at two sittings of that House on the 21st of November, ‖ before the first meeting

---

* The Northern Bishops first sat with the Southern on the 21st June, 1661. See Gibson's 'Syn. Angl.' p. 210.

† Kennet's 'Register,' pp. 564–5.

‡ Introduction, pp. 222, 367, 412.

§ Probably to all of them; as the alterations in the 'Convocation Book' are also in Sancroft's writing (Introduction, pp. 97, 414); and Sancroft was appointed by the Upper House of Convocation on the 8th March, 1661-2, to superintend the printing of the Book of Common Prayer, as revised (Gibson's 'Syn. Angl.' p. 227).

‖ Introduction, p. 88; Gibson's 'Syn. Angl.' p. 214.

of the Committee:—and it is, therefore, far from improbable, that in 'Sancroft's Book' we have really the whole result of the Bishops' Revision, as sent down by them to the Lower House;[*] and that all variations from it, which appear in the 'Convocation Book,' belong to later stages of the work.

Under these circumstances, the influence which Cosin personally exercised over the work of Revision cannot be measured (as Mr. Parker[†] seems, in part at least, to measure it) by the number of the changes entered in his 'Book,' which were ultimately adopted. Very many of these changes (whatever may have been their origin) were verbal and trivial. Many others, of greater importance,[‡] were (in one stage or other of the work of Convocation) rejected: and of these, some of the most considerable may be inferred, from their agreement with passages in Cosin's 'Particulars,' or 'Notes,'[§] to have been suggested by him. Contemporary writers, such as Baxter[||] and Burnet,[¶] ascribed the prevailing influence to Sheldon, Morley, and Henchman; who (above all the other bishops) possessed the confidence both of the King and of Lord Clarendon.[**] Neal,[††] in the next century, wishing to note for reprobation those who were reputed by the Puritans to have been the chief authors and promoters of the Act of Uniformity, mentions the same three names, with seven others; of which Sparrow's is, but Cosin's is not one.

The Tabular List or Conspectus,[‡‡] prefixed to the 'Convocation Book,' and bound up in it when sent to the House of

---

[*] Introd. p. 96.
[†] Ibid. pp. 386–7.
[‡] Ibid. pp. 153, 200, 201, 222, 223, 224, 226, 232, 260, 264, 272, 276, 277, 278, 299, 416.
[§] Ibid. pp. 153, 201, 224, 232, 264, 277, 278, 299, 416.
[||] Calamy's Baxter, 'Life and Times,' vol. i. pp. 171, 2; and see ibid. part 2, p. 363, 4; as to Cosin.
[¶] Burnet's 'Own Times,' vol. i. pp. 177, 264.
[**] Ibid. p. 177; Neal's 'Pur.' vol. iv. p. 260.
[††] Neal's 'Pur.' vol. iv. p. 332.
[‡‡] Introduction, pp. 100–105. At the end of the 'Alterations' (p. 102) are these words:—'These are all ye materiall alterations; ye rest are onely verball, or ye changeing of some Rubricks for ye better performing of ye service, or ye new moulding some of ye collects.'

Lords,* shows all the alterations and additions, then thought material, which had been made by Convocation at the time when it was drawn up:—and it would require a theological microscope of high magnifying power, to find in these (of which some were afterwards withdrawn) any substantial change of the doctrinal balance of the former Liturgy. The alteration of the 'Ornaments Rubric' could not have been (as it was) omitted † from that list, if it had been then supposed to alter the law as it stood under the 25th section of the Act of 1559, and the 'Advertisements' and Canons, or to determine in a particular way any question as to that law which may have been then regarded as open to controversy. Mr. Parker ‡ seems to think, that Cosin had some such purpose: but it will probably appear to most people, that such a purpose would not have been creditable to the good faith of any one who was a party to the list; and there is nothing in the character of Cosin to justify such an opinion, if the fact were material. But why should the purpose of Cosin be more material, on such a point, than that of Wren, or Sparrow, or of any other considerable person among the Revisers? The Committee of Bishops met at Wren's house; and Sparrow took an active and influential part, both at the Savoy Conference,§ and on some of the most important Committees ‖ appointed by Convocation during the course of the work of Revision. Wren, according to Clarendon,¶ had the reputation of being 'very learned, and particularly versed in the old Liturgies of the Greek and Latin Churches;' he had rested part of his Defence,** when impeached in 1641, upon the 'Advertisements,' as authorised by the 25th section of the Act of Elizabeth: and, in a paper of suggestions ††

---

* Introduction, pp. 464, 468, 470.
† It is clear, from 'Cosin's' and 'Sancroft's' books, that this alteration was made before the List was drawn up.
‡ Introd. p. 346. § Ibid. p. 79.
‖ Introduction, pp. 83, 90.
¶ 'Hist. of Reb.' vol. i. p. 184.
** Wren's 'Parentalia,' p. 75.
†† Introduction, p. 421.

carefully prepared for the work of 1661, he had made this remark upon the reference to the Act of 1549 in the 'Ornaments Rubric:'—'*There is somewhat in this Act, that now may not be used.*' Sparrow had published, in 1655, a learned treatise on the Liturgy:[*] and, in 1661, he 'humbly presented to the Convocation'[†] his 'Collection of Articles,' &c. (of which the 'Advertisements' formed part), 'to vindicate the Church of England, and to promote uniformity and peace in the same.' He was made Bishop of Exeter in 1667, and translated to Norwich in 1676. In the second edition of the 'Rationale'[‡] (published in 1684, the year before his death), he referred to the 'Advertisements' as still in force, and necessary to be taken into account for a correct understanding of the law as to the 'Ornaments' of Ministers in the Church.

There is, in reality, much more reason for believing, not only that the bishops generally in 1661, but that Cosin himself, at that time and afterwards, concurred in this view, than there is for a contrary opinion. Cosin's 'Particulars to be considered,' &c., had been written when he was under the persuasion that the 'Advertisements' were invalid, and the use of the Edwardian vestments obligatory in law. He there [§] suggested that the 'Ornaments' referred to in the Rubric should be 'particularly named and set forth, that there might be no difference about them.' In his 'Book'[||] (which, as has been above shown, did not represent his views only) the precise words of the present 'Ornaments Rubric' were written, with a *videlicet* after them, and a blank partially filled up (the surplice alone being mentioned); so as to show that the bishops who prepared that book meant to recommend a specification of all legal

---

[*] 'Rationale of the Book of Common Prayer.'

[†] The words within commas are on the title-page of the first edition, published in 1661. The reference to Convocation was omitted in later editions.

[‡] P. 337

[§] Cosin's 'Works,' vol. v. p. 507; Introduction, p. 136.

[||] Introduction, pp. 129 : 343-345.

'ornaments;' or, at least, to suggest the question, whether such a specification might not be desirable. The blank so left might have been afterwards filled up (if any one had thought fit to propose it), either with the particulars mentioned in the 'Advertisements,' or with those of King Edward's First Book. But the Bishops in Convocation* (for whatever reason) decided against any specification; and their reason for putting that Rubric into its present form was thus stated by Sancroft, both in 'Cosin's' and in his own book: *'These are the words of the Act itself;'* adding a reference to the penultimate (or 25th) section of the Act of 1559, as printed '*supra*.'† It clearly was not then contemplated, that the clause of the Act of 1559, so referred to, would be repealed or become inoperative: because in 'Cosin's Book' amendments ‡ were suggested of that Act itself, which was printed at the beginning of it: among which were two amendments of the 25th and 26th sections, for the purpose of making it clear, that the powers, thereby given to Queen Elizabeth, might be exercised by the King, his heirs and successors. Those proposed amendments were neither struck out by Sancroft, nor copied into Sancroft's Book; but the Act itself remained there, and queries § were placed in it against the same clauses; probably because it was understood to be necessary, on such points, to refer to the law-officers of the Crown, by whom the Act of Uniformity was prepared.

There is no trace, in any part of Cosin's 'Notes' or 'Particulars,' of what has been sometimes called the '*maximum* and *minimum*' theory: on the contrary, he everywhere favours the principle of a strict uniformity, and of making law and usage

---

* Not in the Committee, but in Convocation itself, on the 21st November, 1661; if this Rubric was considered in its proper order in the Prayer-book. See Gibson's 'Syn. Ang.' p. 210; Introduction, p. 88; and *ante*, p. 47.

† Introduction, p. 129. The addition of the words, 'at all times of their ministration,' seems to have been thought consistent, in substance, with this note.   ‡ Ibid. pp. 109, 110.

§ Introduction, p. 110.

agree. In his Articles of Inquiry* at the Visitation of the clergy of his diocese in 1662, the law as to the use of the surplice, contained in the 'Advertisements' and the 58th Canon, was assumed to be in force, and to be consistent with a strict observance of the directions of the Book of Common Prayer. He inquired (in the very words which had just been for the first time introduced into the 'Ornaments Rubric'), whether the church wardens had provided 'a large and decent surplice for the minister to wear *at all times of his* public *ministration* in the Church;' whether there was 'a hood or tippet for the minister to wear over his surplice, if a graduate;' whether the minister 'used any other words or form than what was prescribed by the Book of Common Prayer' .... 'at the reading of the Communion service, and the administration of the two Sacraments;' whether he 'did all these without omission, addition, or alteration of any of them, using all the rites and ceremonies appointed in that book;' and, 'Doth he always, at the reading or celebrating any divine office' in the church, 'constantly wear the surplice and other ecclesiastical habit according to his degree, and doth he never omit it?'

These Articles have a history of their own. On the 21st of June, 1661,† the Upper House of Convocation had appointed a Committee, at which Cosin was desired to assist, to prepare a standard form of Articles for Episcopal Visitations. On the 22nd February, 1661-2,‡ Cosin, individually, was charged with the same duty; and on the 8th of March, 1661-2,§ Cosin, 'secundum mandatum ei datum, et curam ei commissam, introduxit et tradidit in manus Domini Præsidentis librum Articulorum Visitationem concernentium, alias per eum conceptum':—

---

* Cosin's 'Works,' vol. iv. p. 508.
† Gibson's 'Syn. Angl.' p. 210.
‡ Gibson's 'Syn. Angl.' p. 225; 'Cura concipiendi, Articulos in Visitationibus observandos domino Johanni ep° Dunelm. commissa et relata.'
§ Ibid. p. 226; Introduction, p. 463.

which was thereupon referred, for revision, to Archbishop Juxon. Mr. Parker,* with much reason, supposes the book so delivered in by Cosin to have contained his own Visitation Articles of that year: and he adds, 'Visitation Articles issued by seventeen bishops during the year 1662 are extant, and, on comparison, are found very similar to those of Bishop Cosin.' The typical form was, indeed, Bishop Morley's, administered soon afterwards to the diocese of Winchester;† which may, possibly, represent the result of the reference of Cosin's Articles to the Archbishop. The proceedings of Convocation on the 4th of March, 1664–5 ‡ (the same Convocation which had settled the form of the Revised Prayer-Book, though in a later Session) are also material to a just appreciation of the Visitation Articles of that period. The President (Sheldon, then Archbishop),

'Voluit omnes Episcopos suos confratres ad exhibendam omnem quamcunque curam et diligentiam, ut quilibet ministri, vel rectores vel vicarii, seu eorum curati, cujuslibet ecclesiæ in et per eorum respectivè diœceses, divinas preces juxta formam libri publicarum precum in eâ parte stabiliti, distinctè et plenariè, absque aliquâ omissione earundem in aliquâ parte, *superpelliceis indutis*, discreto ordine peragant.'

The 'Ornaments Rubric' did not then (and does not now) stand alone in its omission to notice other laws, by which its effect might be qualified, and with which its terms, taken literally, might seem inconsistent. The two first Rubrics of the marriage service § (the form of one of which, like that of the 'Ornaments Rubric,' was varied in 1661–2) took no notice of the power of the Ordinary to dispense, by licence or otherwise,

---

* Gibson's 'Syn. Angl.' p. 463.
† 'Appendix to Second Report of Ritual Commissioners,' p. 615. Morley was confirmed Bishop of Winchester on the 14th May, 1662: just five days before the Act of Uniformity received the Royal Assent.
‡ Gibson's 'Syn. Angl.' p. 242.
§ 'First Prayer-book,' &c. p. 333.

with the publication of banns; but, according to the natural construction of their language, seemed imperatively to require such publication in every case, and to prohibit the solemnization of matrimony in any case without it. This did not escape Cosin's observation; and he desired accordingly to alter those Rubrics. In his 'Particulars to be considered,'* &c., he suggested the addition of certain words as necessary 'to secure' ministers, celebrating matrimony under a bishop's licence without banns, 'from the penalty contained in the Act of Uniformity;' and in his 'Book'† effect was proposed to be given to that suggestion, by adding to the first ‡ of those Rubrics the words 'unless the bishop shall upon due cause dispense therewith.' But the bishops in Convocation rejected this, as in their judgment unnecessary. It does not appear to have been supposed, after this was done, that the Act of 1662, by confirming these Matrimonial Rubrics, took away from the clergy the power of solemnizing marriages by licence without banns, or relieved them from the obligation to do so.

What the Puritans of the seventeenth century really believed to be the law as to 'ornaments,' it might be difficult to determine. In their 'Millenary Petition'§ of 1603, they only asked 'that the cap and surplice might not be urged,' and in their 'First Address and Proposals' of 1660,‖ that 'the use of the surplice might be abolished.' One of their most elaborate pamphlets of 1661 ('A Discourse of Liturgies,' &c.) says expressly: ''Tis true, the number of ceremonies retained in our Church, pre-

---

* Cosin's 'Works,' vol. v. pp. 522-3; Introduction, p. 277.

† Introduction, p. 277.

‡ This Rubric has, since 1662, been altered in the printed Prayer-books (without any apparent authority), to make it conformable to a later statute (26 Geo. II. cap. 33); just as the 'Ornaments' Rubric of 1552 was altered in 1559. But it still says nothing about dispensations or licences.

§ Cardw. 'Conf.' p. 131.

‖ Ibid. p. 284. The Long Parliament having (de facto, though not de jure,) abolished Deans and Chapters, there were then no Cathedral Preferments in Non-Conformist hands.

tending to any legal authority, is **but small**:—The **Surplis**, the **Cross**, and kneeling at Sacrament, are (we think) **all.'***

The King† in 1660 (not without the concurrence of **the leading bishops‡**) promised toleration **to those** who would **not use the surplice, except in the Royal Chapel**, cathedral **and collegiate** churches, and **colleges in the universities.** To give effect to this promise, his **Majesty, on the 17th March**, 1661-2,§ sent a message to the **House of Lords by the Lord Chancellor, with** the form of a **' proviso'** which he desired to have introduced into the **Act of Uniformity.** This, and other clauses connected with it, which **the Lords accordingly introduced, were rejected** by the House **of Commons**; and Mr. **Parker** ‖ appears to have been unsuccessful **in his** endeavour **to discover the text of** them, which (as far **as the present writer knows) has never** yet been published. They are, however, preserved¶ in the House of Lords among other papers connected with that Act; and they seem to **show conclusively, that** the King, and the House of Lords, **and** the eminent **lawyers by whom they were** advised, understood the surplice **to be** the only ministerial garment prescribed for the parochial clergy **under the Revised Prayer-book of 1661-2, from the** use **of which any** dispensation could be required.

The principal **proviso was** as follows:—

'Provided always, **that,** notwithstanding anything in this Act (in regard **to the** gratious offers and promises, **made by his Majesty**

---

* 'A sober and temperate discourse concerning the interest of Words in Prayer, the just antiquity and pedigree of Liturgies or Forms of Prayer in Churches, &c.' (in answer, particularly, to Bishop Gauden). 'By H. D. M. A. London, 1661.' (In the present writer's possession.) See page 91.

† Ibid. pp. 296-297. Mr. Parker (Introduction, p. 475) says, that this was 'the **result of the Conference,'** which it preceded. The **Conference arose** from the King's Declaration.

‡ **Neal's** 'Hist. **Pur.'** vol. iv. pp. 257-259.

§ Introduction, **p. 466.**

‖ Introduction, **pp.** 467, 475, 482, note.

¶ Not in the 'Journals,' but on separate slips of paper.

before his happy **Restoration, of** liberty to **tender** consciences, **the intention of** which must be **best known to** his Majesty, as likewise the several services **of those who** contributed **thereunto,** for all whom he hath in his princely heart as gratious **a desire of** indulgence as **may consist** with the good **and** peace **of the** kingdom, and would **not have a** greater severity exercised **towards them** than what is **necessary** for the public benefit and welfare thereof), **it be Enacted, and be** it therefore **Enacted, that it shall and may** be lawful **for the** King's Majesty, **by any** writing, **and in such** manner as **to his** wisdom shall **seem fit,** *so far* to dispense with any **such ministers as upon the 29th day of May,** 1660 was, **and at present is, seised** of any benefice **or spiritual promotion, and of** whose merit **toward** his Majesty **and of** whose peaceable and pious disposition **his** Majesty shall be **sufficiently** informed and satisfied, **that no such** minister **shall be deprived or lose his benefice or** other **spiritual promotion** *for not wearing the surplice,* or **for not signing** with the sign **of the cross in baptism, and so as** he **permit and be at** the charge of **some** other **licensed minister to perform that office towards such children whose parents shall desire the same, and so as** such ministers **shall not defame** the Liturgy, **rites, or ceremonies** established in the **Church of** England, **or any person for using them, by** preaching, **writing, speaking,** or otherwise, **upon pain** of forfeiting the benefit of **the dispensation.** And be it further **Enacted** that such dispensation as **aforesaid, being** granted by his Majesty, shall be a sufficient exemption **from such deprivation,** *in the cases aforesaid:* Always understood, that **this indulgence be not thought or interpreted to** be an argument of his Majesty's **indifference in the use of those** ceremonies when enjoined, though indifferent in their own nature; but of his compassion towards the weakness of the Dissenters, which he hopes will in time prevail with them **for** a full submission **to** the Church, and to the **example of** the rest of their brethren.'

There was also added **a further saving clause to** that part of the Bill, by which **a declaration of assent and** consent to the **Book of Common Prayer was required from** the clergy, in these words:—

'**Nevertheless, for such** persons only, **with** whom his Majesty, before **the Feast of St.** Bartholomew, which shall be in the year of our Lord God, 1662, shall dispense according to the intent of the proviso in that behalf hereinafter in this present Act contained, there may be a clause added to the end of the said declaration of assent in the words following, viz.: "Other than as to *such things only*, contained and prescribed in the said book, for which the King's most excellent Majesty hath dispensed with me according to a proviso contained in the Act of Uniformity, and according to the intent of the same proviso."'

Among the reasons* of the House of Commons for rejecting these provisoes the following seem noteworthy.

'That it would unavoidably establish schism; all persons of different inclinations would apply to such as should have this liberty, and that necessarily make parties, especially in great cities;' that 'these two ceremonies of the cross and surplice were long in use in the Church;' and that it was 'better to impose no ceremonies than to dispense with any,' and 'very incongruous, at the same time, when you are settling uniformity, to establish schism.'

The controversy as to what is called 'the Eastward position,' has involved in its scope not only the Rubric before the Prayer of Consecration (which first assumed its present form in 1661, and apparently was then regarded only as a 'change in a Rubric for the better performing of the service,' in consequence of the directions then introduced as to the 'manual acts'),† but also the two last‡ of the series of Rubrics prefixed to the Communion service, which Mr. Parker designates the 'Table' and the 'North-side' Rubrics. Neither of these was at that time altered; but alterations in both of them had been contemplated until a stage in the process of

---

* Introduction, pp. 482, 483.

† It is not mentioned in the List of Material Alterations and Additions; though it must have been framed when that List was made out; in which the 'manual acts' are mentioned.

‡ Introduction, p. 182.

Revision, later than the completion of the fair transcript of the whole Prayer-book intended to be subscribed by the bishops and clergy, and the List of Alterations and Additions prefixed to the 'Convocation Book.' In the text of the latter book, and of the book annexed to the Act of Uniformity, those alterations now appear cancelled, but they still remain uncancelled in the List.*

A theory, at variance with all the evidence which exists on this subject, has found favour with Mr. Parker,† and with some other writers; viz. that these particular alterations were in the book subscribed by the bishops and clergy, when it left the Convocation, and was presented to the King; but that they were afterwards objected to and struck out, either by the King, or during the passage of the Bill of Uniformity through Parliament. Mr. Parker‡ inclines to the opinion that this was done while the book was in the hands of the King, and that the responsibility of the corrections so made elsewhere was assumed by the Committee of the House of Lords, and was attributed to them by Convocation.

The evidence applicable to the time when the book was in the King's hands consists of the King's own public declarations, and of the Acts of Convocation during the same period. The former show affirmatively, and the latter negatively, that the book was sent by the King to the House of Lords in exactly the same state in which he had received it from Convocation. He said so himself expressly, both in his message§ to the House of Lords accompanying the book on the 25th of February, and in his speech ‖ to the House of Commons on the 3rd of March, 1661-2. The Convocation ¶ continued sitting throughout January and February. If any part of the book had been then dis-

---

* Introduction, p. 100.
† Ibid. pp. 449, 452, 454, 455.
‡ Ibid. p. 455.   § Ibid. pp. 459, 460.
‖ Ibid. p. 461.
¶ Ibid. pp. 461-2. Gibson's 'Syn. Angl.,' pp. 221-226.

approved, the natural course would have been to send it back for review; for which there was ample time.* But nothing of the kind was done.

The Journals of the two **Houses** of Parliament, and the Committee-Book of the House **of Lords, enable us to trace** with exactness everything **that was done after the book left the hands** of the King.

The House **of Lords did not take up the Bill of Uniformity** (which had been sent to them from the Commons, with the old Prayer-Book annexed, in the July preceding †) till January 1661–2.‡ On the 17th of that month they referred it to a Select Committee,§ who **did nothing till they had before them the** Revised Book, which was received **from the King on the 25th of** February.∥ Having, on **that day,¶ considered the King's** message, they met again on the 27th;** when their first act was to **note** for correction certain clerical omissions (to **which there will be** occasion to recur) in the **titles of** four Psalms **and in one** Rubric—omissions probably pointed out by some member of the Committee (which included eight **bishops) who had found** an opportunity of carefully examining the book. **Bishop** Morley **(who** was on the Committee) then made **this motion :—**

'That the Committee may **read the** book, not with intent to make alterations, but, **if any reasonable matter shall be objected to, that**

---

* Two months, however, was not, as Mr. Parker seems to think (Introduction, p. 450), an extraordinary time for the King's advisers to take for consideration of the book. Mr. Parker (ibid.) suggests, that 'questions as to some of the emendations had probably arisen,' and that the revised book 'may not have been found to give general satisfaction outside.' But the 'outside' world could have no knowledge of it till it had left the King's hands.

† Commons' 'Journals,' 9th July, 1661. Introduction, p. 85. Lords' 'Journals,' 10th July, 1661.

‡ Lords' 'Journals,' 14th January, 1661. Introduction, p. 457. (All these dates, from January 1 to March 25, are in the Old Style: in New Style, they would belong to 1662.)

§ Lords' 'Journals,' 17th January, 1661. Introduction, p. 457.

∥ Introduction, p. 459.

¶ Lords' MS. Committee Book, 25th February, 1661.

** Ibid. 27th February, 1661. Introduction, p. 451.

it may be referred back to the same authority which first altered it, to remedy what shall be thought fit to be amended." '

After debating that motion, the Committee decided *not to read the book at all*, but to confine themselves to the *Bill*; and they proceeded to pass resolutions * as to the frame of the Bill, and to instruct Mr. Justice Hyde and the Attorney-General (who attended them under an order of the House made on the same day †), to carry these resolutions into effect. They sat on four subsequent days; on two‡ of which it was proposed to read the alterations in and additions to the Book; but that proposition, on the first occasion, was not put, and on the second was rejected. They reported the Bill to the House on the 13th of March,§ saying that 'they had made amendments and alterations in the *Bill*; and had, in their amendments and alterations, made the Bill relate to *the Book recommended by the King to the House*, and not to the Book brought with the Bill from the House of Commons.'

The House of Lords, on receiving this Report, immediately resolved ‖ 'that the alterations and additions in the Book of Common Prayer, *as it came recommended by his Majesty*, might be read, before the alterations and amendments in the Bill were read.' This was accordingly done; ¶ and when it was finished **

---

* Mr. Parker (Introduction, p. 453) says, that 'the last sentence of that day's proceedings breaks off unfinished.' This is a mistake. The 'next page,' which he immediately notices, is a continuation of the same day's proceedings. The unfinished sentence, at the foot of the first page of the Minutes, was evidently interrupted by a change in the form of the resolution or proposition, which the clerk had begun to take down. See the full copy of the whole Minutes of that day, as they now stand in the Committee-Book, in Appendix C,

post, p. 84.

† Lords' 'Journals,' 27th February, 1661; Introduction, p. 460.

‡ MS. Committee Book; Introduction, p. 451. The four days were the 3rd, 5th, 7th, and 10th of March, 1661.

§ Lords' 'Journals,' 13th March, 1661; Introduction, p. 463.

‖ Ibid. pp. 463-4.

¶ From the 'Convocation Book.' See Introduction, p. 464, note (ᵉ).

** Lords' 'Journals,' 15th March, 1661; Introduction, p. 464.

the House passed a vote of thanks to the bishops and clergy for their work. On the 17th of March* it was resolved unanimously, 'that the Book *that hath been transmitted to this House from the King* shall be the Book to which the Act of Uniformity shall relate.' All the subsequent proceedings of the Lords on that and seven later days † (including a recommitment, consequent on the King's message as to the Toleration clauses,) related exclusively to the preamble and clauses of the Bill, which was read a third time and sent back to the House of Commons on the 9th of April.‡

The House of Commons on the 14th of April read through § 'the amendments in the Book of Common Prayer sent down from the Lords'—evidently from the 'Convocation Book;' and on the next day ‖ appointed a Select Committee to collate the Annexed Book with the book of 1604, and see whether there was any difference between them besides those amendments. It may be assumed, from what followed,¶ that this Committee (which reported the next day) found no such difference. Their Report has not been preserved, but it is not unlikely that they may have taken notice of the error, afterwards corrected, in the Rubric as to the salvation of baptized children dying before the commission of actual sin. Whether this was so or not, the House on the 16th of April ** voted, by a majority of 96 to 90, that 'debate should not be admitted' to '*the amendments made by the Convocation in the Book of Common Prayer, and sent down by the Lords to this House;*' at the same time voting unanimously that those amendments '*might*, by order of this House, have been

---

* Lords' 'Journals,' p. 466.
† Ibid. pp. 466–468; and MS. Committee Book; 20th, 22nd, and 24th March, 1661.
‡ Lords' 'Journals,' 9th April, 1662; Introduction, p. 468.
§ See Lords' 'Journals,' 10th April, 1662; (Introduction, p. 468); and Commons' 'Journals,' 10th April and 14th April, 1662 (Ibid. pp. 469, 470).
‖ Commons' 'Journals,' 15th April, 1662; Introduction, p. 470.
¶ Ibid. p. 470 (16th April, 1662).
** Ibid. p. 471.

debated.' The rest of the proceedings in the House of Commons* were strictly confined to the clauses of the Bill; which was returned to the House of Lords on the 30th of April,† with reasons for disagreeing to some of the Lords' amendments to the Bill, of which the Toleration clauses were the chief.

At the end of the Conference which followed, the manager for the House of Commons pointed out the change of the word 'children' to 'persons' (in what had been the Pre-Confirmation, but had now become the Post-Baptismal Rubric), as (what he conceived to be) 'a mistake of the writer;' and it is added in the Journals of the House of Commons, that 'they desired the Lords would take a way to consider how it might be amended.'‡ The Lords § agreed to all that the Commons had done; and Bishop Cosin informed them that he, with the Bishops of St. Asaph and Carlisle, 'had authority from the Convocation to mend the said word; averring it was only a mistake of the scribe. ‖ And accordingly they came to the clerks' table and amended the same.' ¶ No communication to the House of Commons of that amendment was thought necessary, and on the 19th of May the Act of Uniformity received the Royal Assent.

It is strange that, in the face of proofs so complete as these to the contrary, it should still be asserted, that 'changes, some trifling, some of the utmost importance, were made in the House of Lords.' **

---

* Introduction, pp. 472–477

† Ibid. pp. 477, 479–484.

‡ Introduction, pp. 484, 485, note (¹).

§ Ibid. pp. 484, 485. Lords' Journals, 8th May, 1662.

‖ Ibid. p. 485. Whoever else was responsible for it, the 'scribe' of the 'Annexed Book' was not. He had copied, correctly, what he found in the 'Convocation Book,' where the printed word 'children' was, in one place, altered to 'persons,' and the Rubric, with the word 'persons' (not 'children') was written at full length in another place, and also in the List of Alterations and Additions. (The word had been 'children,' in 'Cosin's' and 'Sancroft's' books).

¶ Introduction, p. 485.

** See 'Edinburgh Review,' July 1877, p. 247.

Mr. Parker * finds a difficulty in the proceedings of Convocation on the 5th of March and the 25th of April, 1661-2, where there is really none. The Committee of the House of Lords had (as has been seen) on the 27th of February noted for correction certain clerical omissions in the Annexed Book. Their minute † was as follows:—

The 56th, 57th, and 58th Psalm, and the number of them to be made like the rest, 60th also.—249 p. In the Rubric after the Communion, the words 'for the good estate,' &c., to be made as in the   page, ' the whole state,' &c.

The explanation of this is, that the numbers of all the other Psalms, from the 1st to the 68th inclusive, having been originally written in words, had been altered in the 'Annexed Book' to Roman numerals; but these four had been left unaltered. And the Preface to the Prayer for the Church militant, as well as its title in the Post-Communion Rubric in which that Prayer is mentioned, had been at one time altered :‡ which alteration, having been cancelled in the Preface, was left uncancelled in the Post-Communion Rubric, at page 249 of the 'Annexed Book.'

On the 5th of March,§ the attention of the Upper House of Convocation was called to *these* corrections— for Parliament had neither made, nor directed, any others—as 'nonnullas emendationes sive alterationes alias in libro publicarum precum per domum Parliamenti ∥ factas:' and the Bishops of St. Asaph, Carlisle, and Chester, were then (by the assent of both Houses) charged with the duty 'revisionis earundem alterationum,' and invested with full powers ' ad emendandas et corrigendas easdem alterationes.' Mr. Parker ¶ thinks this could not have been

---

* Introduction, pp. 452, 453, 456, 462.
† Introduction, p. 451, and *post*, Appendix C. p. 84.
‡ See *post*, pp. 67, 68.
§ Ibid. p. 462; Gibson's 'Syn. Angl.'
p. 226.
∥ 'Domus Parliamenti' must, necessarily, here mean the House of Lords, acting by its Committee.
¶ Introduction, p. 453.

necessary 'for the alteration of Roman numerals, or repeating a correction which had been made in one part, in another where it had accidentally not been made.' 'It seems' (he proceeds to say) 'only reasonable to suppose that there must have been much more important changes made *after* Convocation had signed the book; viz., after December 20th. And, if so, what were they?'

This, however, is a very gratuitous hypothesis. The book, as it stood, had been subscribed by the two Convocations.* To make that subscription applicable to it in a different state, the same authority was necessary, however trivial the corrections might seem. That it was, in fact, considered to be so, seems plain, from the terms of Bishop Morley's motion in the Committee of the House of Lords, made immediately after those particular errors had been noted. The words of delegation, 'ad emendandas et corrigendas easdem alterationes,' were exactly suitable for such a purpose. If changes of substance had been in question, the judgment of Convocation upon them would, doubtless, have been more directly expressed; though a delegation of powers might still have been necessary for the manual operation of embodying those changes in the book, so as to preserve the integrity of the subscription.

The proceedings in Convocation on the 21st of April † were the natural sequel of those on the 5th of March. The Bishop of Chester had died: and the error in the Post-Baptismal Rubric had then been discovered. It was suggested that the Lord Chancellor's advice should be taken, as to some way in which that error might be corrected, 'per Domum Communitatis Par-

---

* The Convocation of York subscribed by the Archbishop, and the Bishops of Durham and Carlisle, and by six proxies for the Lower House (not the same as those appointed in the preceding November). See Introduction, p. 448.

† Introduction, p. 478; Gibson's 'Syn. Angl.' p. 229; Mr. Parker leaves a blank for the name, which in Gibson is 'dominus episcopus *Dunelmen.*'

liamenti.' But it was thought better to appoint Bishop Cosin to the vacant place on the delegacy which had been constituted on the 5th of March: obviously, with a view to deal with this newly-discovered error, as the errors discovered on the 27th of February had been dealt with. The result was, the correction recorded in the Lords' Journals of the 8th of May; and it cannot be doubted that the oversights noted on the 27th of February had also been corrected by the hand of one or more of the delegates of Convocation, though in a less public way.*

The extrinsic evidence being thus opposed to the hypothesis of any changes (except these corrections of clerical errors) having been made in the 'Annexed Book' after the 20th of December, 1661, it remains to consider the internal evidence; for which purpose some general view of the other alterations which were made in the 'Annexed Book,' after it was first transcribed, seems necessary.

Those alterations were of two kinds:—first, such as were found requisite to make those parts of the 'Annexed Book' which had been transcribed from some other copy correspond with the 'Convocation Book,' of which it was represented to be a fair transcript (though it, in fact, only became so by collation and correction); and, secondly, those which were made both in the 'Annexed Book' and in the 'Convocation Book,' after the two had been compared together, and had been found, in those places, to correspond.

Of the former kind it is necessary here to speak only to distinguish them from the latter. It had been unavoidable (as Mr. Parker† shows), from pressure of time, to put the Tran-

---

* The numbers of the 58th and 60th Psalms, and the Post-Baptismal Rubric, are corrected, in the 'Annexed Book,' in different ways, unlike any of the other corrections in the same book. The latter correction was also made in the 'Convocation Book' (in the Psalms it was unnecessary, the numbers being there throughout in figures); but that in the Post-Communion Rubric was not.

† Introduction, p. 440.

script in hand before the changes in the 'Convocation-Book' were completed: and, for this purpose, one or more copies were used, in some parts of which variations of the text, not accidental, and certainly not authorised by Convocation, occurred. Of these (which passed into the Transcript, but were corrected on its comparison with the 'Convocation Book') Mr. Parker* gives examples; to which more might be added.

Of the second class, some were additions (in Sancroft's handwriting) which Mr. Parker † himself does not doubt to have been made in the 'Annexed Book' before it received the signatures of the bishops and clergy, and one of which, at least, was of no little importance.‡ The rest (including those in the 'Table-Rubric' and the 'North-side Rubric') were, altogether, six in number. To ascertain the stage of the Revision to which they belong, nothing more seems necessary than to pay regard, not to some only, but to *all* of them; for which purpose, it is convenient to describe them, following the order of the book.

1. In the ' Prayer for Fair Weather,' § the adjective '*kindly*' was added before 'weather,' in the margin of the 'Convocation Book,' and was copied into the Transcript. In both it was afterwards struck out.

2. The 'Table-Rubric' ‖ was altered, in both books, so as to stand:—'The Table at the Communion-time having a fair white linen cloth upon it shall stand *in the most convenient place in the upper end of the chancel (or of the body of the church, where*

---

* Introduction, pp. 437–440. Among other things, all the Psalms before the 69th, and four later, were copied from a book, in which titles, and musical and other additions, taken from the Bible version, had been joined to the Prayer-book text.

† Introduction, p. 443.

‡ The 'Black Rubric,' or Declaration as to kneeling at the reception of the Sacrament (Ibid. p. 443). It was added, evidently, after the List of Alterations and Additions was made out, in which it does not appear.

§ Introduction, p. 157. The same word was in 'Cosin's' and 'Sancroft's' books.

‖ Ibid. p. 182. The same alteration, with some differences of wording, was in 'Cosin's' and 'Sancroft's' books.

there is no chancel).' This alteration was afterwards **cancelled**, restoring the Rubric (with two trivial verbal changes) as **it stood** before. But those trivial verbal changes show that the cancellation was first made in the 'Convocation Book,' in which the old words were written back exactly as Mr. Parker* gives them, viz. with '*Prayer*' repeated after '*Morning*,' as well as '*Evening*,' and the **verb '*be*,'** not '*are*.' The first '*Prayer*' (*i.e.* after '*Morning*') **was then struck out, and '*be*'** was changed to '*are*.'† The restoration in the '**Annexed** Book' **follows**, without any intermediate **change, the latter form :—viz.** '**where Morning and Evening Prayer are appointed to be said.**'

3. The '**North-side Rubric**'‡ **was altered, by substituting the** words, '*on the North part*,' for '**at the North-side.**' This alteration was cancelled **in both books, and the old words were restored.**

4. **In the First Commandment** § (**Communion Office), after** the words, '**I am the Lord thy God**,' there was added, **in both books**, '*who brought thee out **of** the land of Egypt,* **and out of** *the house of bondage.*' In both books this addition was cancelled; the word '*delendum*,' ‖ (**afterwards itself** obliterated) being written against it **in the margin of the** 'Convocation Book' only. (Mr. **Parker ¶ erroneously reads** this word '*debate*,' and founds a note upon that error.)

5. The Preface to the '**Prayer for the Church Militant**'** **was** altered **in both books to** '*Let us pray for the good estate of the*

---

* Introduction, p. 182. Mr. Parker, in this place, does not correctly **exhibit** the present state of the book.

† See the 'Convocation Book' itself, in the Library of the House of Lords; and the 'Photo-zincographic' **copies**, printed for the Ritual Commission.

‡ Introduction, p. 182. In 'Cosin's Book,' the **word** '**side**' was altered to 'end.' **In the same** book as altered by **Sancroft, and in** 'Sancroft's Book,' both those words were used: viz. 'side or end.'

§ Introduction, p. 190. The same addition was made in 'Cosin's' and 'Sancroft's' **books**.

‖ See the 'Convocation Book' itself; and the 'Photo-zincographic' copies.

¶ Introduction, p. 190.

** Ibid. p. 200. The same alteration is in 'Cosin's' and 'Sancroft's' books.

Catholic Church of Christ.' This alteration was cancelled, and the original form was restored, in both books, agreeably to a marginal direction in the 'Convocation Book' only, thus:— '☞ *The Title stand just as it was before.*' * The minute of the Lords' Committee of the 27th of February, 1661-2 (taking notice that a corresponding restoration had not been made in the first post-Communion Rubric) clearly shows that this cancellation was made before the two books were sent to the House of Lords.†

6. In the short Exhortation‡ before the general Confession in the Communion Office, the words, 'Draw near,' were immediately followed, in the former Prayer-book, by these: 'and take this holy Sacrament,' &c. On the Revision, the words, '*in full assurance of faith,* were introduced, in both the 'Convocation' and the 'Annexed' books, after 'Draw near;' but '*with*' was afterwards substituted in both, for '*in full assurance of;*' which was cancelled.

In these six places great pains have been taken to make almost all the cancelled words illegible: and the similarity of the way in which the manual operation has been performed in all of them might alone justify the conclusion that all the cancellations were made at the same time. The inference seems irresistible, that they were, in fact, all made before the signature of the book; three of them (Nos. 1, 4, and 6) being of such a nature, that no reasonable man could seriously imagine that they originated with the King's advisers, or with either House of Parliament; and three (Nos. 2, 4, and 5,) appearing to have been first made, or ordered to be made, in the 'Convocation Book.'

The revocation of all these alterations must have been later than the preparation of the List of Alterations and Additions prefixed to the 'Convocation Book;' and the List itself cannot have been afterwards revised; because all of them (except No. 1

---

* Introd., p. 449.   † Ibid. p. 452.   ‡ Ibid. p. 208. The same words are introduced, in the same place, in 'Cosin's' and 'Sancroft's' books.

which was too trivial to be mentioned in it) now appear uncancelled in that List.* They were all, therefore, reconsidered, and cancelled, in the latest stage of the work of Convocation.

If probabilities are considered, nothing can be more likely than that those 'second thoughts,' which are, proverbially, often best, should have led Convocation to this change of purpose, as to the 'Table' and the 'North-side' Rubrics. As to the latter, some fluctuation of mind is at once seen on a comparison of 'Cosin's,' 'Sancroft's,' and the 'Convocation' books.† We know from Clarendon that the more conservative bishops were against unnecessary change. The proposed alterations of both these Rubrics must have appeared unnecessary to those who thought the arguments sound, by which Heylyn, Laud, Wren, and Cosin himself, had formerly defended the practice on those points of the higher school of Churchmen; and, if unnecessary, objectionable, because appearing to surrender, by implication, the ground so formerly taken.

Heylyn ‡ thought he had triumphantly answered Bishop Williams in 1637, as to the 'North-side Rubric,' when he appealed to the Latin translation, authorised by Queen Elizabeth under the Great Seal in 1560§ for use in all the Colleges of the Universities; in which the rendering was, '*ad cujus mensæ septentrionalem partem:*'—and when he said:—

'There is no difference, in this case, between the North end and the North side, which both come to one. For in all quadrilateral and quadrangular figures, whether they be a perfect square, which geometricians call *quadratum*, or a long square (as commonly our communion-tables are), which they call *oblongum*, it is plain that, if

---

* Introduction, pp. 100, 104. It has been already mentioned that the 'Black' Rubric, added in the latest stage of the work, is not among the Additions in the List.

† Ibid. p. 182.

‡ 'A Coal from the Altar,' &c. (1636), p. 23; and 'Antidotum Lincolniense,' &c. (1637), pp. 51–58.

§ Cardw. 'Doc. Ann.' vol. i. p. 247; and see ibid. p. 263.

wo speak according to the rules of art, every part of it is a side, however custom hath prevailed to call the narrower sides by the name of ends.'

Wren used similar arguments in his 'Defence'* in 1641, concluding, that 'North part, North side, and North end, were all one.' And Cosin,† in his own 'Defence' in the same year said, that ' he did not ever officiate with face purposely towards the East; but he constantly stood at the North side or end of the table to read and perform all parts of the Communion Service there.'

It may be added, that the change of the 'Table-Rubric' to the form which was ultimately cancelled would have done both more and less than place beyond controversy the lawfulness of the position of the table favoured by the High-Church party, and which, under the book of 1661-2 (as it was actually settled), before long found general acceptance. It would have made any other position than that at the upper end of the chancel (where there was any chancel) unlawful; and might, by so doing, have increased the risk, which the bishops and clergy manifestly sought to avoid, of raising inconvenient discussions upon the text of the Revised book in Parliament. On the other hand, it would not, by itself, have decided the question which was chiefly raised in Bishop Williams's letter to the Vicar of Grantham; viz., whether, assuming the table to stand at the upper end of the chancel, its longer sides ought, or ought not, to be placed at right angles to the east wall of the church.

The changes introduced into the 'Prayer of Consecration,' and the Rubrical direction preceding it with reference to the 'Manual Acts,' do not appear to have been, in 1661-2, the subject of any contention. If that Rubric had been then understood to enjoin the 'Eastward position,' this might probably

---

* 'Parentalia,' p. 75.　　　　† Introduction, p. 216.

have been otherwise; but if it was in that respect neutral (so long as what it expressly directed was done), it might honestly be regarded as introducing no important change. The 'Manual Acts' themselves (to which it was evidently meant to be subsidiary,) were then practised* and approved by all parties in the Church, though they had not been, in or since 1552, expressly enjoined. One of the Puritan exceptions to the book of 1604 at the Savoy Conference was, that 'the manner of consecrating the elements was not explicit and distinct enough; and the minister's breaking the bread was not so much as mentioned.'† To this the bishops agreed;‡ consenting, 'that the manner of consecrating the elements may be made more explicit and express: and, to that purpose, these words be put into the Rubric:—"Then shall he put his hand upon the Bread and break it;"—"Then shall he put his hand unto the cup."' In Baxter's form of Liturgy, presented to the Conference, § (in which the elements, after consecration, were spoken of as 'now no common bread and wine, but Sacramentally the Body and Blood of Christ') there was this direction:—' Then let the minister take the bread, and break it in the sight of the people, saying,' &c.; and, 'in like manner let him take the cup, and pour out the wine in the sight of the congregation, saying,' &c.

There is a commentary in the second series of Cosin's 'Notes'‖ upon the words, '*Took bread* . . . . *took the cup*;' from which light may be derived as to that Bishop's views on the same subject. Speaking of the Roman practice of elevation, he there said:—

'In the ancient Fathers we do not read of any such custom: and, when afterwards this rite of elevation came into the Church, it was

---

* See Cosin's 'Notes' ('Works,' vol. v.), pp. 109, 340. The note at p. 109 is from Bishop Andrewes.
† Cardw. 'Conf.' p. 321.
‡ Ibid. p. 365.
§ Baxter's 'Works' (Orme's ed. 1830), vol. xv. p. 451, &c.
‖ Cosin's 'Works,' vol. v. pp. 340, 341; partially quoted in Introduction, p. 215.

not a lifting up of the bread and wine (as soon as they were sacramentally hallowed) over the priest's head; nor were the people then appointed to fall down and adore them, as the very Body and Blood of Christ held up between the priest's fingers and set down again upon the table, which is more than any priest of them all can do; but this only was the order or custom of the Church: after the elements were consecrated, the priest and the deacon together held them in their hands, and showed them to the people. (In the order of Sarum, heretofore used in the Church of England, the priest is appointed only to elevate the consecrated elements, *usque ad frontem, ut a populo videri possint;* * no mention of the people adoring is at that time made.) And other elevation or ostension than this they had none.'

Then (after quoting two passages from 'Nicolaus Cabasilas,' of which the last is '*ostensis sanctis, vocat illos qui participare voluerint,*') he added: 'Which order and custom, *in effect,* is by us still observed.'

The early translations † of the book of 1661-2 may in some degree help to show how the phrases, 'before the table,' and 'before the people,' in the Rubric prefixed to the 'Prayer of Consecration,' were then commonly understood. In the Welsh version of 1664 (which is of high authority, having been made under the 27th clause of the Act of Uniformity ‡), the rendering is, '*yn sefyll wrth y bwrdd,*' and '*yngwydd y Bobl;*' the preposition in the former place being (as has been stated to the writer by competent Welsh scholars) equivalent to '*at*' and that in the latter to '*in the sight of.*' The Greek translation of 1665, by Duport, Dean of Peterborough and Greek Professor at Cambridge, dedicated to Archbishop Sheldon, is ἔμπροσθεν τῆς τραπέζης, and ἐνώπιον τοῦ λαοῦ. The French of 1667, by John Durel (which, by a Royal order of the 6th October,

---

* This kind of 'ostension' had been prohibited by King Edward the Sixth's Injunctions, in 1549. (Cardw. 'Doc. Ann.' vol. i. p. 64; and see ibid. p. 81.)
† Introduction, p. 509.
‡ Ibid. p. 499.

1662,* was directed to be used, as soon as it should be printed, at the Savoy and in all the parish churches of the Channel Islands) is, '*à la table*,' and '*devant le peuple.*' The Latin, 'edited' in 1670 by the same John Durel, and dedicated † to the King, as if translated by public authority, is, '*ante mensam Domini,*' and '*coram populo.*' There seems to be some reason to believe, that this may be the same Latin translation which was made under the direction of Convocation, as recorded in its Acts of the 26th April, 1662,‡ and the 18th May, 1664: § because it can hardly be supposed, that a version made under such auspices would have been entirely suppressed, and the work of a private translator preferred.

These 'Notes' have, of course, no value, beyond that of the sources of information from which they are taken; to which references have been throughout given; so that they may easily be verified, and (if in any point erroneous) corrected. All such inquiries will probably appear to many to be '*labor ineptiarum.*' Nothing, however, which seriously interests considerable bodies of educated men, particularly clergymen, of more than one school of thought, can justly be regarded as without some practical importance.

---

* Ibid. p. 509.

† The Dedication (signed ' J. D. Editor ') says, 'præstantissimam hanc Liturgiam . . . redditam voluisti; unde merito Augustissimo Nomini Tuo nuncupatur hæc Latina illius versio.'

‡ Introduction, p. 509; Gibson's 'Syn. Angl.' p. 230.

§ Gibson's 'Syn. Angl.' p. 239.

APPENDIX A. (See page 24.)

STATE PAPERS, DOMESTIC, ELIZABETH, Vol. 39. No. 76.
21 May, 1566.

Bishop Grindall to the Dean and Chapter of St. Paul's.

AFTER my hartie comendacyons these are to require and to give yo^u in especyall charge that wth all convenyent speed, yo^u call before yo^u all & singuler the mynisters and Eccliasticall psons wthin yo^9 Deanry of Poules and office, and to p̃scribe & enioyne everie of them vpon payne of deprivacõn to prepare forthwth and to weare such habit and apparell as is ordeyned by the Queenes Maiesties authoritie expressed in the treaty intituled the advertisem^{ts} &c. which I send heerein inclosed vnto yo^u, and in like to inioyne everie of them vnder the said payne of deprivacõn as well to observe the order of mynistracõn in the Church with surples, and in such forme as is sett forth in the saide treatie, as alsoe to require the subscription of every of them to the said advertisem^{ts} And yf yo^u shall pceave any of them to be disobedient, wch shall refuse to comforme themselves heerein, that then wthout any delay yo^u certifie me the names of all such before Trynitie Sundaie next ensuinge to the intent I maie pceed to the reformacõn and deprivacõn of everie of them as apperteyneth in this case with a certificate allsoe of the names of such as pmiseth conformytie And thus I bidd yo^u farwell from my Howse in London this xxjth of Maie 1566

Yo^9 in Christ

Edm : Londõn

Indorsed   To the right worshippfull the Deane and Chapter of Powles (geue theise).

APPENDIX B. (See page 24.)

N.B. The parts of this document, printed in italics, are those which are found in the Articles of 1584: the rest being omitted in those Articles.

STATE PAPERS, DOMESTIC, ELIZABETH, Vol. 163. No. 31.

October, 1583.

[Articles presented to Her Majesty by the Archbishop of Canterbury & the Bp. of Salisbury.]

Howe this may bee executed so-farre fourth as concerneth Ordinaries, I have declared in a schedule, wch I haue sent to yor Lo:

That it may please yo⁹ Ma^{ty} *to geue* strayte order *that the Lawes late made against the Recusantes may bee putt in more due execution: considering the benefite that hath* growen *vnto the Churche thereby* Where *they* haue *bene so executed and the encouragem^t wch they and others do receaue* by *remisse executing thereof.* *

That no bookes be printed beeing not before perused and allowed vnder the hande *of the Archebishopp of* Canterbury *or Bishopp of* London *for the tyme being.* And *that Printers* bee restrayned from *setting fourthe other editions or Translations* of the *Byble or newe Testament then that* w^{ch} *is*

---

* **Art. 1** of 1584.

* Allowed : viz : by the sayd Archebishopp or Bishopp of London.

*allowed : Nor to add annotations to the same till they be seen and perused by the Archebishopp of Canterbury and Synode of Bishopps And that like order bee taken for such Treatises as any way touch the state of the Realme or the churche †

This article onely forbiddeth the resorting of Straungers to priuate houses to the entent to heare those exercises. Because it withdraweth them from their ordinary Pastor and Parish, sheweth a myslike in them of the publike ministery & seruice, & geueth suspicion of schism. In consideration whereof suche priuate exercises haue bene restrayned by Prouinciall & generall Counciles (as the Council of Laödicea, & the sixth generall Councile): and by Christian Emperors, as namely Constantyne the great & Justinian. Neither is it suffered (as I thinke) at this day in any reformed Churche, in Christendom, where the Gospell is by publike authority

That all preaching, reading, catechizing, and other suche lyke exercises in priuate places and families, wherevntoo others doo resorte being not of the same familie, bee vtterly inhibited: Seing the same was neuer permitted as lawfull vnder any Christian Magistrate, but is a manifest signe of Schisme, and a cause of contention in the churche.‡

---

† Omitted in 1584 from this series of Articles; but, according to Strype ('Life of Whitgift,' p. 232), promulgated at the same time, as one of 'three more,' which he states to have been added.

‡ Art. 2 of 1584.

established. Besides that, it smelleth of Donatisme & Anabaptisme.

This is most necessary, & according to the doctrine of those that are most precise, whiche haue sett it downe for a principle, that, Idem debet esse minister verbj & sacramentorū. Besides the Counselles letters directed to all Bishoppes in Januarÿ anno. 1579. commaunding, that they should suffer none to preache but suche as ministred the Sacramentes also.

The last wordes, viz. Cloak with Sleeues &c. may be leafte out, yf it bee thought good. But the article is warranted both by the Aduertisementes sett out by her Maties authoritie, & also by the Q. Iniunctions, anno primo Elizab.

That none be permitted to preache, reade or catechise in the Churche or ellswhere, vnlesse he doo fower tymes in the yere at the least, say seruice and minister the Sacramentes according to the Booke of Common-prayre.*

That all preachers and others in Ecclesiasticall Orders doo at all tymes weare and vse suche kynde of apparell, as is prescribed vnto them by the booke of Aduertisementes.† *That is Cloke with sleeues, Square capp, gowne, tippett, &c.*

That none be permitted to interprete the Scriptures, or preache, vnlesse he bee a Preist or Deacon at the least, admitted therevntoo accordinge to the Lawes of this Realme.‡

---

* Art. 3 of 1584.
† Art. 4 of 1584: in which, after 'Advertisements,' are added the words, 'and her Majesty's Injunctions, "anno primo."'
‡ Art. 5 of 1584.

That* none *be permitted to* preache,** *reade, catechize, minis-tre the** *Sacraments, or to exe-**cute* **any other** *Ecclesiasticall**function by what authoritie* **so****eure** *he bee admytted therevnto,**vnlesse he first consent and sub-**scribe to theis Articles following,**before the* **Ordinary** *of the**diocese wherein he preachethe,**readeth, catechizeth or* **minis-***treth the Sacram^{ts} viz.*

1. *That Her Ma^{tu} vnder* **god***hath and ought to* **haue***the soueraignetee and***rule over** *all maner per-**sons* **borne** *within her***Realmes,** *dominions and***contrees, of** *what estate**either Ecclesiasticall or**Temporall* **so** *euer they**bee. And* **that** *none**other forren power, Pre-**late, State, or Potentate**hath* **or** *ought to* **haue***any Jurisdiction, power,**superioritie, præemi-**nence or authoritee,* **Ec-***clesiasticall or Spirituall,****within* Her** *Ma^{ts} sayd***Realmes,** *Dominions, or**contrees.*

Theis bookes are warranted by Acte of Parliament & euerie **one** in the ministerie is brought

2. *That the booke of Common**prayer; and of ordering**Bishopps, Preistes, and*

to bee ordered accordinge to the tenor thereof.

This booke of Articles by Acte of Parliament must bee publikely readd by euery beneficed person in the Church whereof hee hath cure: who must also then geue his vnfayned consent therevnto & subscrybe to the same before the Ordinary, vpon payne of losse of his benefice.

Deacons *conteyneth in it nothing contrarie to the worde of God: and that* **the same** *may lawfully* **be** *vsed: and that he himself* **will vse the forme in the sayd** *booke* **prescribed in** *publike* **prayer, and** *administration of the Sacram^{ts} and none other.*

3. *That he allowethe the booke of Articles of Religion agreed* **vpon** *by the Archebishoppes* **and** *Bishoppes of both Provinces* **and the** *whole Clergie* **in the** *Convocation* **holden at** *London in the yere* **of our Lorde** *God* 1562 **and sett fourth** *by her* Ma^{ts} **authoritie**
And that he $\begin{cases} \text{believeth} \\ \text{thinketh} \end{cases}$
all the Articles **therein** *conteyned, to bee agreeable to the Worde of God.**

That *from hencefourth none* **bee** *admitted* **to any** *orders eccliasticall vnlesse* **he doo** *then* **presently shewe to the** *Bishopp* **a true presentation** *of himself to a benefyce then voyde within the* **diocese or** *jurisdiction of the*

---
* Art. 6 of 1584.

sayd Bishopp: Or vnlesse hee shewe vnto the sayd Bishopp a true certificat where presently he may be placed to serue some cure within the same Diocese or Jurisdiction: Or vnlesse he bee placed in some cathedrall or collegiat churche or college in Cambridge or Oxford. Or vnlesse the sayd Bishopp shall then fourthwith place him in some vacant benefice or cure.*

And that no Bishopp hencefourth admitt any into orders, but suche as shall bee of his owne Diocese, vnlesse he bee of one of the Vniuersities, or bringe his Letters Demissaries from the Bishopp of the Diocese, and bee of age fvll $xxiiij^{ti}$ yeres and a graduate of the Vniuersitie: or at the least able in the Latin tounge to yelde an account of his fayth according to the articles of Religion agreed vpon in Convocation and that in suche sorte, as that he can note the sentences of scripture, whereupon the trueth of the sayd Articles is grounded: and bring a sufficient testimoniall with him of his honest lyfe and conversation, either vnder the Seale of some college in the Vniuersitees where he hath remayned, or

---

* Art. 7 of 1584.

*from some Justice of the Peace, with other honest men of that parish where he hath made **his** abode for three yeres before And that the Bishopp wch shall admytt any into Orders being not in this maner qualified, bee by **the** Archebishopp with the assistance of some **one** other Bishopp suspended from admitting any into Orders for the space of two yeres.**

*And that no Bishopp **insti**tute any into **a** Benefice, but suche as bee of the habilitee before described And if the Arches by Double Quarrell **or** otherwise proceede against the sayd Bishopp for refusall of suche as be **not of** that habilitee, That the Archebishopp of Canterbury either by his owne Authoritee or by meanes procured from yor Ma^{tv} may stay suche processe, that the endeauo^r of the Bishopp may take place.*†

Varietée **of translations** especially in publike seruice doth geue great offence, & ministreth occasion of quarrell to the Aduersary.

*That one kynde of the Translation of the **Bible** bee onely vsed in publike seruice, as well in Churche as Chappell: And **that to** bee the **same**, wch is **nowe** authorized by consent of the Bishoppes.*‡

---

* Art. 8 of 1584.   † Art. 9 of 1584.   ‡ Art. 10 of 1584.

That no dispensations be graunted vnto persons absent to take the benefite of great Residence, especially in Cathedrall Churches of the old foundation: the same being the onely or principall cause, why suche Churches are not furnished with learned and graue men, to the great hurte and sclander thereof.*

That from hencefourth there bee no Commutation of Pennaunce, but in rare respectes, and vpon great consideration, and when it shall appeere to the Bishopp himself that that shall bee the best way for the wynninge and reforminge of the offendo^r. And that the penaltie bee employed either to the relieffe of the poore of that parish, or to other godly vses, and the same well witnessed and made manifest to the Congregation. And yet if the fault be notorious that the Offendo^r make some satisfaction either in his owne person with declaration of his repentãce openly in the churche or ells that the ministre of the churche openly in the pulpitt signifie to the people his submission and declaration of his Repentãce done before the Ordynarie; and also in token of his repentãce, what portion of money he hath geuen to bee employed to the vses aboue-named.†

As psons of honest worshipfull and honorable calling may necessarily & reasonably haue occasions sometymes to solemnize mariage by license for the banes asking, or for once or twyce, without any great harme: so for avoidinge generally of Inconveniences noted in this behalf, it is thought expedient, that no dispensations bee graunted for mariage without banes, but vnder sufficient and large bondes, wth theis conditions followinge First that there shall not afterwards appeere any lawfull lett or impediment by reason of any præcontract, consanguinitee, affinitee, or any other lawfull meanes whatsoever. Secondly, that there be not at that present tyme of graunting suche dispensation, any suite, playnte, quarrell or demaunde moved or depending before any Judge Ecclesiasticall or Temporall for and concerning any suche

---

* Omitted in 1584 from this series: but stated by Strype (*ubi supra*), to have been one of the three others issued at the same time.   † Art. 11 of 1584.

lawfull impediment betwene suche the parties. Thirdly that they proceed not to the solemnization of the mariage without consent of Parentes or Gouerno^rs. And lastly that the mariage be openly solemnized in the Churche. (The copie of w^h bond is to be sett downe and geuen in charge for every Bishopp in his Diœcese to followe.) Provided that whosoeuer offend agaynst this order bee suspended ab executione officij for one half yere.*

That when Excommunication doth proceed vpon some cause or contempt of some original matter specified in a Statute made in the fyfte yere of yo^9 Ma^{ts} reigne, entituled An Acte for the due execution of the writt de Excommunicato capiendo: that then the said writts may goe fourth vpon the Significauit from the Ordinary without any charge of the sayd Ordinarie: the same to be deducted out of the fynes and amercements growing thereby to yo^9 Ma^{ty} wch will both encourage Ordinaries so too proceed against obstinat persons, and also encrease yo^9 Ma^{ts} commoditie by reason of the great nombre that shall be certified.†

That Sheriffes at the taking of their oathes may haue an earnest and speciall charge geuen them in yo^9 Ma^{ts} name as well for the straite emprisoning of suche as are comitted by vertue of the sayd Writtes, as also for the carefull execution of the whole Statute de Excommunicato capiendo, so farre fourth, as it concerneth them.†

[Endorsed:] Octob 1583. Articles p̃sented to hir Ma^{ty} by ye Archb. of Cant^{r}b. and ye Bish. of Sals. in the names of thẽ selues and ye BB. of Lũdon Rochester Lỹcoln, Peterb. Glocester.‡ at St. James.

---

* This is the last Art. of 1584.

† Both these were omitted from the twelve Articles of 1584: but the former is stated by Strype (*ubi supra*) to have been one of the three others also then issued.

‡ The names subscribed to the Articles of 1584 were those of the Archbishop of Canterbury, and the Bishops of London, Sarum, Peterborough, Lincoln, Norwich, Rochester, Exeter, and St. David's. (See Strype's 'Life of Whitgift,' ed. 1822: pp. 228-230.)

APPENDIX C. (See page 60.)

MINUTE IN LORDS' COMMITTEE-BOOK.
27 February, 1661-2.

Die Jovis 27 *Feb.* 1661.

[*On page* 152.]
E. Bridgwater
Uniformity.

The 56 57 & 58 psa^s **the number** of them to be made like **the** rest—the 60th also.

249 p.

In the Rubric **after** com̄on **the words ' for the** good estate' &c. to be made as in the ⎵ page ' the whole estate' &c.

Bp. Wig:

That the Committee may read **the** booke, not wth intent **to make** altera͞cons, **but if** any reasonable **matter** shalbe objected, that it may be referred back to the same authority wch first altered it to remedy w^t shalbe thought fit to be amended.

After long debate, **The Bill now before the Committee is read, & the booke not read.**

Moved, That Mr. Justice Hide & Mr. Atturney prepare a **preamble suitable to the** booke **and message of the** King **now sent to the H. of** Peeres **and** th^t **the Act** for confirming the Act concerning **ministers may be here at the** next meeting that w^t was lately p͞rmissed$_\wedge$ to H.C. to be p͞rvided **for by way** of conformity **may be done** accordingly.*

Ordered, That Mr. Justice **Hyde &c. shall** prepare &c. & to **provide** for Ordina͞con by Bishops &c.

The Tytle & **preamble** to relate to the booke of Ordina͞con and other Rites & ceremonyes &c.

[*here* page 152 *ends: the rest is in page* 153.]

Whether the booke or altera͞cons **sent by** t

Ordered &c. That **Mr.** Justice **Hyde & Mr.** Atturney shall **prepare & suite the tytle & preamble of** the$_\wedge^{sd}$ Bill **to the booke**

---

* 'May be done accordingly,' seems to have been added after the next line was written.

sent~by the King~ to the H. of Peeres useing **so much of the King's** message sent therewith as shalbe **proper & taking** notice of the Ordinaçon of Bps preists **& Deacons** and the office of Prayer to be used at Sea, **and** to provide that all [*] psons who **are** possessed **of** any spirituall promoçons w͞thin this Kingd: and have **been** ordeyned **ministers** according to the Rites of the Ch: of **England** or shall not be so ordeyned within shalbe deprived **of all** [†] **their** spirituall promoçons & be made incapable of enjoying **any** spirituall promoçons **for the future** untill they shalbe **so** ordeyned.

That a copy of the Bill [‡] for restoring & confirming ministers be **provided ag**^{t} **meeting.**

Adjo: to **Munday 3º.**

---

[*] Before '*persons*' the word '*ecclesiasticall*' had been written, and is now obliterated.

[†] After '*all*,' the words '*his or*' had been written, and are now obliterated.

[‡] After '*Bill*,' the words '*be provided*' had been written, twice over, and twice obliterated.

DID QUEEN ELIZABETH
TAKE "OTHER ORDER"
IN THE
"ADVERTISEMENTS" OF 1566?

A Letter
TO
LORD SELBORNE,
IN REPLY TO HIS LORDSHIP'S CRITICISMS ON THE

"Introduction to the Revisions of the
Book of Common Prayer,"

BY

JAMES PARKER,
Hon. M.A. Oxon.

Oxford and London:
JAMES PARKER AND CO.
1878.

5

CONTENTS.

INTRODUCTORY.

	PAGE
Reasons for writing the Letter and for the course pursued	1
Lord Selborne's "NOTES" supplementary to the late Ridsdale Judgement	2
Query whether the influence of Cosin is exaggerated	3
Argument justified by the reference to Committees, &c., in the Purchas Case	ib.

I. THE RESTORATION OF THE PRAYER-BOOK IN 1559 AND CLAUSE XXV. OF THE ACT OF UNIFORMITY.

The difficulties in reconciling the Act of Uniformity with the rubrick	4
The note of reference to the Act at the end of that rubrick	ib.
The rubrick probably printed before the Act passed	5
The two Clauses of the Act of Uniformity only one proviso	7
Not necessarily of a provisional character	8
Meaning and intention of that proviso	9

II. QUEEN ELIZABETH'S "FURTHER ORDER" TAKEN 1561.

Jan. 22, 1561, Letters issued under the Great Seal to her Commissioners	10
The exact agreement of the manner of this "further order" with the Act	11
The details of the "taking of this further order"	ib.

III. ARCHBISHOP PARKER'S ADVERTISEMENTS OF 1566 CONTRASTED WITH QUEEN ELIZABETH'S "FURTHER ORDER" OF 1561.

Formal proceedings of the same nature would be similar in style	12
A summary of the Advertisements of 1566	13
The contrast between the preamble, &c., of the "further order" of 1561, which affirms all the conditions of the Act, and that of the Advertisements of 1566, which affirms none	14
The internal evidence of the Advertisements shewing they were for the enforcement of "established order," not for creating "other order"	15
Examples from some of the Articles, to shew that they enforced existing law as far as was considered expedient, viz. as to Preaching, as to receiving the Holy Communion, and as to the Vestments	17
Example shewing an explanation of established law	21
Example shewing they were issued to the Province of Canterbury only	ib.

IV. The History of the Queen's Letter of January, 1565, and why Archbishop Parker issued his Advertisements in 1566.

	PAGE
Lawlessness in Church Discipline, and the difficulties with which Elizabeth had to deal on coming to the throne	23
The Prayer-Book of 1552 chosen and ordered by Parliament . .	24
The alterations made in the Book, and the Proviso added to the Act .	25
The Queen's Injunctions, Proclamations, &c., to restrain lawlessness .	27
Jan. 25, 1565, Queen Elizabeth's Letter ordering uniformity to be enforced	28
Misinterpretation of this letter in the "NOTES," p. 13 . . .	30
Summary of the letter shewing its purport	32
Elizabeth's letter does *not* command the Abp. to prepare the Advertisements	33
Jan. 30, 1565, Abp. Parker informs Bp. Grindal of Queen Elizabeth's letter	34
Upon which letter Abp. Parker attempts to enforce Uniformity . .	35
March 3, 1565, Abp. Parker sends to Secretary Cecil a rough copy of the Articles which he had drawn up of "varieties requiring repression"	ib.
March 8, 1565, Abp. Parker sends to Secretary Cecil a fair copy of the same Articles, subscribed by five Bishops of his Province . .	ib.
Abp. Parker is anxious to obtain the Queen's authorization for his "book of Articles"	36
Abp. Parker has his book returned to him by Cecil, *unauthorized* .	38
1566, Abp. Parker therefore modifies his "Ordinances," and changes them into Advertisements	39
Differences in the preamble of the "Ordinances" compared with that of the Advertisements	40
Other differences between the "Ordinances" and the Advertisements .	41
March 12, 1566, Abp. Parker again asks Cecil to obtain for him the Queen's authority, if not to the whole, at least to the last section, viz., on the ordinary apparel of the clergy	43
March 20, 1566, Abp. Parker and Bp. Grindal explain to Cecil what they propose to do to enforce authority, viz., to summon the London clergy on March 26, to appear at Lambeth, and to threaten them with sequestration	44
March 28, 1566, Abp. Parker again asks Cecil to look at his Advertisements, which he has now printed. He has inserted nothing but what is already lawful, and he proposes to "essay with his own authority," and hopes therefore he will meet with no interference .	45
Abp. Parker's letter quite inconsistent with the theory of the Advertisements being "other order." Misinterpreted also in the Ridsdale Judgement	46
March 28, 1566, Abp. Parker issues his Advertisements by sending copies to Bp. Grindal	47
March 28, 1566, the Publication of the Advertisements, copies being sent to the Dean of Bockinge, and to others . . .	49
How then could the Queen have taken "other order?" when could she have done so? or could Abp. Parker have taken "other order?" .	51

V. THE LIGHT IN WHICH THE ADVERTISEMENTS WERE REGARDED, AS SHEWN BY OFFICIAL DOCUMENTS, 1566—1576.

	PAGE
Result of the Proceedings at Lambeth, March 26, 1566	54
Were these Proceedings under the "Injunctions," or under the Advertisements?	55
May 21, 1566, Bp. Grindal enjoins the apparel as expressed in the Advertisements	56
Misinterpretation of Grindal's Letter in the Ridsdale Judgement	57
Testimony of Abp. Parker's Visitation Articles, 1567 and 1569	58
Distinction between the Authority of the Queen and Public Authority	59
Other Visitation Articles, 1569 to 1571	62
Abp. Parker's reference, in Articles of 1575, to unknown "Advertisements"	64
The Advertisements gradually supplant the Injunctions, and more frequently referred to	66
The errors as to the date 1564, and as to Elizabeth's Authority, both arise from the title of the Advertisements	68

VI. THE LIGHT IN WHICH THE ADVERTISEMENTS WERE REGARDED, AS SHEWN BY THE OFFICIAL WRITINGS.

The Zurich Letters of 1565 and 1566, containing the words *Edictum Regium*	69
The Controversy as to the Habits	73
The disuse of Surplices and destruction of Copes, at St. John's College, Cambridge, in 1565	75
An account of the "Habit" Controversy in 1566	77
Mention of the use of Copes and Surplices being still the law, long after the Advertisements were issued	83

VII. OBITER DICTA.

The name "Advertisements" as a title	93
Reginald Wolfe, the Printer of the Advertisements, prints Abp. Parker's "Articles," &c., but not Royal Injunctions	95
Were Albes and Chasubles ordered, or only Surplices and Copes?	96
The mention of Copes in the Prayer-Book of 1549	97
The Resolutions of the Bishops probably led to the Cope wholly superseding the Chasuble	98
But the ordering of the Surplice does not exclude the Cope	99
Need Ornaments "authorized" be imperative?	100
Were Copes in common use?	102
Copes and Church Ornaments of value often stolen, and Copes therefore became very scarce	103

VIII. THE REVISION BY JAMES I., AND THE RESTORATION BY CHARLES II.

	PAGE
Why did not James I. alter the Ornaments rubrick?	106
No analogy between the supposed "other order" taken in the Advertisements and the permissive clauses of Act of 1872	107
The [Sub-]Committee of 1641	109
The Corrections in Cosin's Book by Cosin himself	110
Cosin does not return to London until October 31, and could not therefore have worked with the Bishops during the Vacation	111
The attempt to fix *exactly* the Ornaments naturally failed	112
Two parties in the Committee rendered a definite settlement impossible	113
What I profess to have done	114
Conclusion	116

ERRATUM.

A confusion as to dates occurs on pp. 54, 55, though not affecting the argument. The Summons was issued on March **22, not** 20; and the Ministers appeared March 26, not 25.

A LETTER, &c.

My Lord,

While acknowledging the honour done to my "INTRODUCTION TO THE PRAYER-BOOK" by the special criticism which, in the "NOTES ON THE LITURGY OF THE ENGLISH CHURCH," your Lordship has bestowed upon those portions pertaining to present controversies; while acknowledging also the courtesy with which, at the commencement of that criticism, you have spoken of my labours; I am constrained to venture upon a reply. For I feel that it is not the credit of my book which is at stake; that is a small matter; but I number amongst my friends many whose good opinion I value highly, and if I left the matter for which I have contended in the Preface to my "Introduction," and in other places, as it is left by your Lordship, I fear that they might fairly convict me of deserting without an effort a position which I have, on more than one occasion, made pretensions to hold.

I propose, therefore, to consider some of those arguments by which your Lordship would prove that the lines which are there laid down are so readily to be broken through; and incidentally I shall venture to examine, on the other hand, how far those which have been adopted by your Lordship are so impregnable as they are represented.

First of all, however, I must offer an explanation as to the ground which I propose to traverse. My "Introduction to the Prayer-Book," which is the subject of your Lordship's criticism, was intended to be prefixed to a copy of the First Prayer-Book of Edward VI., with the variations occurring in the five subsequent revisions arranged rubrick for rubrick. The object of this Introduction was to sketch in the briefest manner possible, by references to, and condensed extracts from, Acts of Parliament and other authoritative documents, with exact dates, an outline of the circumstances attending each revision.

In the course of the work, however, from reasons which I need not now explain, I saw fit to change the plan, and the eight or ten pages within which I had intended to comprise the notes of the Revision of 1661 became expanded into a volume; while all that related to the reign of Elizabeth remained comprised within a few pages, as at first printed. My work, therefore, touches most imperfectly on the question of the Advertisements, which in your Lordship's book receive such prominent attention. Still, the few points on which I there laid stress, are in a manner involved in your Lordship's argument, and I therefore do not hesitate to discuss in the following pages many matters quite untouched by my "Introduction." I have also to add, that I do not hesitate to couple your Lordship's remarks with the "Judgement as delivered by the Lords of the Judicial Committee of the Privy Council," in what is known as the "Ridsdale Judgement," delivered May 12, 1877, and to which your Lordship's name appears second amongst the signatures. The two arguments run *pari passu*. The Judgement illustrates your Lordship's Book, and the Book illustrates the Judgement in several instances, as will appear hereafter.

What I have written in my "Introduction to the Prayer-Book," plays, as I have said, a very secondary part in the arguments derived from the Elizabethan Advertisements. In a word, the history of the Ornaments Rubrick (to which a very large proportion of your Lordship's "Notes" are directed) may be roughly said to centre around the persons of Archbishop Parker and Bishop Cosin. So far as your Lordship's review concerns the events surrounding the former, it is a comment on, if not a justification of, the historical arguments relied upon in the Ridsdale Judgement; so far as the review deals with the events surrounding the latter, I look upon it as a criticism on, and disapproval of, what I have written on the subject in my book.

Your Lordship begins by implying that I attach too great a value to Cosin's influence amongst the Revisers of 1661. I will not stop now to point out the grounds on which I have made certain statements as to the part which he appeared to play in the work of the Revision; but so far as your Lordship's charge (pp. 3—5) extends to my magnifying that influence so as to interpret, or to expect others to interpret, the legal bearing of a rubrick from Cosin's known opinions, I plead not guilty. I can nowhere find that I have gone beyond surveying the surrounding facts and circumstances which seem to explain what might otherwise be obscure, and here and there by illustration bringing into prominence details which might otherwise escape attention. It is included also in your charge, "that I think regard may properly be had to the details of what passed during the process of legislation, in Convocation and in Parliament, and in Committees appointed by those assemblies" (p. 4). Whether I am in error or not—whether, or not, I do not know what "every *tiro* knows"—I simply plead that I was writing with the Report of the Privy Council Judgement of the case of Hebbert *v.* Purchas[a] before me, in which points such as the following were introduced as relevant:—

"The learned Judge in the Court below assumes that the Puritan party at the Savoy Conference objected to this Rubrick, whereas it was the Rubrick of James that they were *discussing*.

"The Bishops in their Answer [i.e. at the Savoy Conference] show that they *understand* the Surplice to be in question, and not the Vestments.

"The Bishops [i.e. the Committee appointed by Convocation] *determined* that the Rubrick should continue as it is."

and such like; and so far as I could not reconcile the conclusions which the judges in that case drew from the premises, so far I discussed such proceedings, and so far may have thought them relevant to the argument.

[a] Brookes' "Six Privy Council Judgments" (London, 1874), Hebbert *v.* Purchas, p. 174.

I. THE RESTORATION OF THE PRAYER-BOOK IN 1559, AND CLAUSE XXV. OF THE ACT.

THE circumstances attending the Restoration of the Prayer-Book in 1559, to which your Lordship next turns (p. 5), present some difficulties. The Act of Uniformity ordered certain changes to be made in the Prayer-Book of 1552, and *none other or otherwise*, and hence it might be argued that the insertion of one, or rather two, new rubricks, one of which was diametrically opposed to its representative in the previous book, was illegal. Still, the illegality of the rubrick, from its having been inserted without authority, or rather against the authority of the Act of Parliament, might be said to be condoned by the direct reference in itself to the very Act of Parliament against which it offended, and which was set in the beginning of the book in which it appears. The reference (usually) runs thus :—

"According to the Act of Parliament set in the beginning of this book."

In reading the rubrick, it struck me that this line was redundant, so I wrote "*it is just possible*" that it was a "notice to the printers. If not, the words must have been added as an explanation of, or justification for, the insertion then of the new rubrick."

Your Lordship's criticism is as follows (p. 9) :—

"Mr. Parker following [Strype] finds ['Introduction,' p. 44] in the same letter [of Sandys, of which Strype mistakes the effect] proof that the Ornaments rubrick of 1559 was deliberately inserted in its proper place by the Revisers; his theory being ['Introduction,' p. 344] that the words which Parker or Guest, or one of the other revisers, wrote in the copy which was prepared for the printers, were copied from the rough draft of the clause before it was engrossed in the Act; and that this form of the clause was afterwards slightly varied."

In your Lordship's table of contents I find,—

"Error of Mr. Parker (following Strype) as to Ornaments rubrick."

It is true that on page 44 of my "Introduction" I quoted from Strype, but where I was writing (p. 344) of the character of the Ornaments rubrick with which Cosin had to deal, I neither made any reference to Strype or to Sandys; nor were either, I think I can safely say, in my mind.

I am really not concerned to fight for a theory which I put forward as "just possible," but I will take leave to make a remark upon the argument which your Lordship adduces to disprove it (p. 10).

"It stands in the way of this theory that the Act itself was printed at the beginning of the book."

This appears to me to be based upon the assumption that because the title and prefatory leaves are found bound up in the Prayer-Books before the Morning Prayer, they were printed before it. But of this there is no evidence; on the contrary, the prefatory matter in books is printed *last*, and in this case especially I would call your Lordship's attention to the *signatures* at the foot of the page, since in all the three editions we have of 1559, both by Grafton as well as by Jugge and Cawood, the signatures A i, A ij, A iij, &c., begin at the Morning Prayer (on the top of the first page of which occurs the rubrick), shewing that these pages were printed the first of all, while the eighteen preliminary pages, with separate series of signatures, and containing the Act of Uniformity, were, there is little doubt, printed the last of all. The Act was not brought up to the Lords till April 25, and copies of the book were in use in her Majesty's Chapel on Sunday, May 12, and at St. Paul's on Wednesday, May 15; while they were to be in use all over England by June 24. But if the revisers had waited till the Act was passed before they began printing the sheet which contained the rubrick, the book could not have been ready, I believe, by the time named. I conclude, therefore, that the rubrick must have been printed before the Act passed. It must be remembered that the Prayer-Book of the 5th and 6th Edward VI., which was to serve as "copy," had the Act of Uniformity of 1552 printed at the commencement; that in the nature of things would have been erased, and a note to say that a new Act would have to be put in its place. I saw no *à priori* impossibility in a similar note being added to the rubrick; and I gave several similar illustrations from the way in which the "copy" was prepared for the printer in the revision of 1661.

It was these, or similar considerations, and not Sandys' letter of April 30, which led me to throw out the suggestion that the printing the line, directing reference to the Act, was possibly accidental.

The Judges in the Ridsdale case make the following remark [b] upon this rubrick :—

> "That note or rubrick, as is pointed out by Bishop Gibson, was not inserted by any authority of Parliament. It was meant to be a compendious and convenient *summary* of the enactment on this subject. If it was an accurate summary, it was merely a repetition of this Act. If it was inaccurate or imperfect, the Act, and not the note, would be the governing rule."

But this leaves the difficulty where it was. Why should it be *inaccurate*, if the clause was there to copy? By using the word "*summary*," it is implied that the clause was shortened [e]; but the term raises a false issue, and begs the question. Would it be argued that the words, "according to the Act," referred only to the words "until further order," and therefore gave to the *rubrick*, as well as to the clause, a provisional character? To have stated this would have provoked the contrast between the rubrick then and the rubrick of 1661, when the words of reference were definitely expunged.

Your Lordship further remarks upon what is termed my "*gratuitous* conjecture :"—

> "Ingenious, however, or not, the theory rests *entirely on the letter of* Sandys, the whole of which Mr. Parker can scarcely have considered, because, when it is read, it proves the exact *contrary*."

I do not see that Sandys' letter throws any light one way or the other upon the details of the actual correction of the Prayer-Book. It is a question whether Sandys refers to the Prayer-Book

---

[b] Ridsdale Judgement, official copy, p. 7.

[e] From the words, "Provided that," down to "Edward the Sixth," the original counts 47 words; from "And here is," down to "Edward the VI.," the so-called *summary* counts 50 words.

at all, though I see Strype, in the line I quoted in the early pages of my "Introduction," thought he did. Sandys may by the words, "The last boke of service is gone thorowe," be referring only to the passing of the Act.

Had the original copy prepared for the printers been preserved, the probability is the whole process would have been clear. We should have learnt how far *any* of the suggestions of the so-called Revisers were accepted, or whether their revision, based upon the First Book of Edward VI., was wholly discarded, and the Second Book adopted as being less revolutionary than what the new Revisers contemplated: as it is, there is no evidence that these Revisers had any share whatever in making the alterations in this Second Book.

The real point of interest from which we have to start is the undoubted *legality* to wear the Vestments of 1549, from the day of the coming into operation of the Act in 1559, until that Act, or rather that clause of the Act, should be repealed.

In ordinary cases, I presume, an Act can only be repealed by another Act; but it is contended, as I understand your Lordship's argument, as explained more fully in that laid down in the Ridsdale Judgement, that the clause contains within itself certain elements of repeal, which under certain conditions can effect the same result as a definite action of the Legislature.

The words which contain these elements are—

"[XXV.] . . . until *other Order* shall be therein taken by the Authority of the Queen's Majesty, with the advice of her Commissioners, appointed and authorized under the Great Seal of England, for Causes Ecclesiastical, or of the Metropolitan of this realm."

This Clause, however, it must be remembered, is followed by—

"[XXVI.] and also, that if there shall happen any Contempt or Irreverence to be used in the Ceremonies or Rites of the Church, by the Misusing of the Orders appointed in this book, the Queen's Majesty may, by the like advice of the said Commissioners or Metropolitan, *ordain and publish such further Ceremonies or Rites*, as may be most for the advancement of God's Glory, the Edifying of His Church, and the due Reverence of Christ's Holy Mysteries and Sacraments [d]."

[d] Act, 1 Elizabeth, cap. ii.

Of the former Clause, the following gloss, and argument from it, is given in the Ridsdale Judgement :—

> "The Statute, by its 25th section, had enacted that the Ornaments of 1549 should **be retained, and be in** use, *but only** until other Order should be therein taken by the Authority of the Queen, with the advice **therein mentioned.**
>
> "The enactment was *therefore** in its nature provisional, and prepared **the way for the subsequent** exercise of a power **reserved to** the Queen."—*Ridsdale Judgement, p.* 8.

It appears to me, my Lord, that the two clauses should be taken together, in order to form a just view of the import of the words, "*until other order*," &c. If the XXVth Proviso is taken by itself, they perhaps appear to give a *provisional* character to the enactment, though not necessarily so. Taken with the next proviso, the desire to have the authority of the Crown directly acknowledged stands out as the prominent feature. The meaning of the two is that the Queen reserves the right to take further Order in the use of ornaments, and ordain and publish further ceremonies.

I may point out also that, although the sentences are numbered as separate paragraphs in the edition of the "Statutes at large," to which I have referred, I am by no means sure that they are so in the original, to which, however, I have no means of access. Certain it is, that the second does not **constitute a** distinct proviso, **so as to be read** without the first. There is no **repetition of** "Provided always, and **be it enacted;"** but the paragraph **runs on,** "and also." The two paragraphs, in fact, **are** *one proviso.*

Let me also point out to **your Lordship's attention that** this Act follows on immediately **after the Act** entitled, "*An Act to restore to the Crown the Ancient Jurisdiction over the estate Ecclesiastical and Spiritual,*" &c. Since, however, by the **Act of**

---

* The **Italics are mine, in** order to shew the gloss and the argument. Throughout the extracts, in the following pages, I have freely made use of italics, to draw attention to the sentences upon which I comment in the text, or upon passages which are specially relevant to the argument.

Uniformity the appointment of a Book of Common Prayer was vested in Parliament, it would be but natural that the Queen, jealous of the rights asserted by her father, should declare and affirm her power to control the ritual, and to add to the rites and ceremonies; and hence this declaration with which the Act of Uniformity practically¹ ends.

In fact, the clause, read with the whole context, points directly and clearly to the assertion of the rights of the Crown; it is only when separated, and by itself, that it admits of being glossed with the words "*but only*," and it is these words alone which give it the *provisional* character upon which stress is laid. But however this may be, it seems to me unwarrantable to apply the provisional character to one Clause of the Proviso specially, which is practically done by those who adopt your Lordship's argument.

The meaning, or intention of this Proviso, might by itself be of little importance, but in an investigation avowedly for the purpose of discovering whether the Queen did ever take "*other order*" on this *one point*, it cannot be right to start with the foregone conclusion that she intended to do so, which the special gloss here of *provisional* implies.

I do not for a moment deny that Queen Elizabeth *did* take some "other order." On the contrary, I distinctly affirm she did, and that, both in the matter of rites and ornaments *of the Church*, though in comparatively unimportant details; but for the very reason that this "other order" which she took in 1561 is so definitely recorded, I contend, from the absence of such a record as to the ornaments *of the ministers*, she took none at all, neither then nor later. Of this "other order," to which I am about now to refer, as far as I can see, your Lordship makes no mention, nor do I find any mention of it in the Ridsdale Judgement; but the omission is important, and I shall shew why.

¹ A usual concluding Clause, repealing former laws, is in reality the last.

II. QUEEN ELIZABETH'S "FURTHER ORDER" TAKEN 1561.

On January 22, 1561 *n. s.*, the Queen issued "Letters under the Great Seal" to her Commissioners[g], of which the following extracts present the chief points on which I would insist.

"(*a*) *BY THE QUEEN.*

"(*b*) ELIZABETH.

"(*c*) **Most** reverend father in God ; Right trusty and right well beloved ; Right **reverend ;** Right reverend father in God ; Right trusty and well beloved ; Trusty and right well beloved ; and Trusty and well beloved ; We greet you well.

"(*d*) Letting you to understand that where it is provided by act of parliament, holden in the first year of our reign, that whensoever (*e*) we *shall see cause to take FURTHER ORDER in any rite or ceremony* appointed in the book of Common Prayer, and our pleasure known therein, either to our *Commissioners for causes ecclesiastical,* **or** to the *Metropolitan,* that then eftsoons consideration should be **had** therein.

"(*f*) We *therefore,* understanding that there be in the said book certain *chapters for Lessons* . . . . which **might be supplied** with *other* chapters . . . . more to their edification.

"(*g*) [And that furthermore in sundry Churches and Chapels . . . . there is such negligence and lack of convenient reverence used towards the comely **keeping** and order of the said *Churches ;*

"(*h*) and especially of the *upper part* called the *Chancels* . . . .]

"(*i*) Have thought good to require you our said Commissioners *so authorized by our great seal,* for causes ecclesiastical . . . .

"(*k*) to peruse the order of the said lessons throughout the whole year, and **to cause** some new Kalendars to be imprinted whereby such chapters . . . . may be removed, and *other* more profitable may supply their rooms.

"(*l*) [and further also **to** consider as becometh the foresaid great disorders in the decays of *Churches,* and in the unseemly *keeping and order of the Chancels.*

"(*m*) and amongst other things to *order that the tables of the Commandments* may be comely set or hung up in the east end of the Chancel, to be *not only* read for edification, **but also to give** some comely *ornament* and demonstration that the same is a **place** of religion. . . . .]

"(*n*) And these our letters shall **be your sufficient warrant in this behalf.**

"(*o*) Given under **our signet, at our Palace of Westminster, the 22nd day of** January, in the 3rd year **of our** reign (= 1561.)

"(*p*) *To the Most Reverend father in God our right trusty and right well beloved Matthew, Archbishop of Canterbury ; the right reverend father in God,* **our** *right trusty and well beloved Edmund, Bishop of London, and to the rest* **of our Commissioners for Causes** *ecclesiastical.*"

[g] From Parker's Register at Lambeth, **fol. 215 a,** as printed by Cardwell, Documentary Annals, No. LV., vol. i. p. 294 ; and in Strype's Parker, Appendix, No. XV. Compared with the MS. in C.C.C., C., vol. cxxi. art. 31.

Now there can be no question that this document represents a taking "other" or "further" order within the meaning of the Act. It fulfils, as will be seen, every requirement, and answers in every particular to the apparent object of the particular clause of the Act under which it is evidently issued.

It is to be observed of it especially how it is the Queen's personal Act (*a, b*); how it is addressed to the Metropolitan and Commissioners for Causes ecclesiastical (*c, i, p*); how it refers in the preamble to the Act of Parliament under which it is set forth (*d*); how, further, it recites the very words of the Proviso (*e*); how it refers to these "our letters" being warrant (*n*); how it is "given under our signet, at our Palace of Westminster" (*o*).

Before pointing out the bearing of this document [h] upon the question at issue, let me remind your Lordship that (*q*) is found preserved amongst the State Papers [1] of Elizabeth's reign (now in the Record Office), with additions in the handwriting of Cecil, the Queen's Secretary [j]; and (*r*) a fair copy exists amongst the Archbishop's papers, bequeathed to his college at Cambridge [k]; while still a third copy occupies the whole of the first page of fol. 215 in Archbishop Parker's Register, preserved in the Library of the Palace at Lambeth.

Lastly, let me remind your Lordship that so far as any change was involved in rubrical directions, (*s*) *alterations* were then made in all the authorized Prayer-Books. No Prayer-Book that I have seen with a date later than 1559 has the old order of Lessons; and one book, with the date in the title-page of

---

[h] It should be added that the document after notifying that there should be uniformity in arrangement, though Cathedral and Collegiate Churches may be more costly (which is given above in substance), provides for the supply of a Translation of the Service into Latin for use in Collegiate Churches. Letters Patent, it may be added, had been issued April 6th, the previous year (1560), on the subject of this Latin version.

[1] State Papers, Domestic Series, Elizabeth, vol. xvi. art. 7.

[j] The paragraphs marked (*g*) and (*h*) are amongst Cecil's additions, as also paragraph (*m*).

[k] Parker MSS., C. C. C., Cambridge, vol. cxxi. art. 31.

1559, preserved in the British Museum [1], has the Cancel, which was evidently printed to be inserted in Prayer-Books already in use. This Cancel, consisting of ten leaves, shews by the date of the Almanack to have been issued *at once*, namely, in 1561. Hence every effort was made to make all Prayer-Books conformable to the "further order taken."

III. ARCHBISHOP PARKER'S ADVERTISEMENTS OF 1566 CONTRASTED WITH QUEEN ELIZABETH'S "FURTHER ORDER."

Another document exists, entitled *ADVERTISEMENTS*, and your Lordship contends — indeed several pages of the NOTES are taken up with the contention — that this *also* is a taking of "further order" within the meaning of the Act.

A priori, I presume it would be admitted that two formal proceedings of the same nature, under the same sovereign, and taking place within four or five years of one another, would have some similarity in style; if totally different in style, there would be some ground for doubting if they were of the same nature.

Let me give here the title, and then such extracts as will present the purport and nature of this other document described by your Lordship as representing the "taking other order:"—

---

[1] The book is by **Jugge and Cawood**, folio, 1559; press-mark, **C. 25. l. 6.** The first twelve leaves include Title, Contents, Act of Uniformity, Preface, Of Ceremonies, Table and Kalendar expressing the order of Psalms and Lessons, Order how the Rest of Holy Scripture, and the Proper Lessons and Psalms according to the *old* arrangement, the last page of which is backed by an Almanack beginning with the year 1559. Here is inserted a *Cancel*, beginning with a fresh series of signatures, A i, The Order how, &c., and then The Proper Lessons according to the *new* arrangement, and running on A iij, A iv, &c., and so on to the end of the months of the year. The Almanack in the cancel-sheet, it will be observed, begins with **1561** instead of **1559**.

THE ADVERTISEMENTS OF 1566.

(a.) "ADVERTISEMENTS partly for *due order* in the public administration of Common prayers, and using the holy Sacraments;

(β.) "and partly for the *apparel* of all persons Ecclesiasticall

(γ.) "by vertue of the Queenes Majesties letters commaunding the same, the xxvth day of January, in the seventh yere of the raigne of our Sovereigne, &c.

"(δ) *The Preface.*

(ε.) "The Queenes Majestye of her godly zeale, calling to remembraunce howe necessary it is to the avauncement of gods glorye, and the establishmente of Christes pure religion for all her lovinge subjectes, especially the state ecclesiastical to bee knitte togeather in one perfecte unitye of doctrine, and to be conjoined in one *uniformity of Rites and manners* in the ministration of Gods holy word, in open prayer, and ministration of Sacraments,

(ζ.) "as also to be of one decent behavioure in their *outwarde apparell*, to be knowne partly by their distinct habits to be of that vocation whereunto they be called . . . .

(η.) "hathe, by her letters directed unto the Archebishop of Canterbury and Metropolitane, required, enjoyned and straightly charged, that with assistance and conference had with other byshops, namely suche as be in commission for causes ecclesiasticall.

(θ.) "*some orders* might bee taken whereby all *diversities* and *varieties* amonge them of the cleargie and the people (as breedinge nothing but contention, offence and breache of common charity, *and be agaynste the lawes*, good usage, *and ordinaunces of the realm*), might be *reformed*, and *repressed*, and brought to one maner of uniformity throughout the whole realme. . . .

(ι.) "Whereupon by diligent conference and communication in the same, and at laste, by assent and consent of the persons before sayd, these orders and rules ensuing have been thoughte *meete* and *convenient* to be used and followed;

nor yet prescribinge these rules as laws equivalent with the eternall worde of God, . . . but as temporall orders, meere ecclesiasticall, without any vayne superstition, and as rules, in some parte of discipline, concerning decency, distinction, and order, *for the time.*

(κ.) "*Articles for doctrine and preaching* [seven in number].

(λ.) "*Articles for Administration of prayer and Sacraments* [14 in number].

(μ.) "*Articles for certayne orders in ecclesiastical policy* [eight in number].

(ν.) "*Articles for outward apparel of persons ecclesiastical* [nine in number].

(ξ.) "*Protestations to be made, promised, and subscribed by them that shall hereafter be admitted to any office, room, or cure, &c.* [eight in number].

(ο.) "Agreed upon and subscribed by,

MATTHÆUS CANTUARIENSIS,
EDMUNDUS LONDINENSIS,
RICHARDUS ELIENSIS,
EDMUNDUS ROFFENSIS,
ROBERTUS WINTONIENSIS,
NICOLAUS LINCOLNIENSIS.
} Commissioners in Causes Ecclesiastical, with others."

And now let me compare, or I should rather say, contrast the two documents. We find, from the internal evidence of each, That the Order of 1561 is the Queen's personal act—by the Queen, and from the Queen—and addressed *to* her Archbishop and Bishops (*a, b, c,* &c.), while the Advertisements of **1566** are *not*. They are but " Articles agreed on and subscribed " *by* the Archbishop and five other Bishops (*o*).

That the Order of 1561 **refers to** the Act of Parliament by which it is issued, and recites in almost exact words the Clause authorizing it (*d, e*), while the Advertisements of 1566 refer to no Act of Parliament at all for their authority, recite no words directly or indirectly connected with that Act, or any other ; and, instead, refer only to a letter of the Queen [m], which does not, however, refer to any Act, or mention any 'further order.'

That the Order of 1561 represents itself as "a *royal warrant*" (*n*), while the Advertisements **of** 1566 represent themselves as *Advertisements* only issued by the Archbishop (*a*), **by virtue of** the Queen's letters (γ), directed to him (η).

That the Order of 1561 is "given *under our signet* at the Palace of Westminster," whereas the Advertisements imply that they are not given by the Queen at all, certainly not under her signet (*o*), but only agreed upon and signed by the Archbishop and Bishops (*o*).

That the original " further order " of 1561, engrossed in due form, and with additions **by her** Majesty's Secretary, is found filed amongst **the State** Papers in the Record Office (*q*)[n], while no copy of any kind, or even reference to their issue, can be found in the Record Office, nor, indeed, any engrossed **copy of** the Advertisements at all. The first draft of the same—the **only** MS. copy known and referred to by Strype—bore the very condemnatory words,—

"**Ordinances accorded** by the Archbishop **of** Canterbury, &c., *in his Province.* **These** were *not authorized* or published ; "

these important words being in the handwriting of Cecil, the

---

[m] Of this I **have to** speak presently, when dealing with the historical evidence bearing **on the Ad**vertisements. [n] See ante, p. 11.

Queen's Secretary. It is true that numerous printed copies exist, printed by the printer whom the Archbishop employed for other matters, but no known copy has any mark or sign to shew that it ever came beneath the Queen's eye.

That while a copy of the "further order" of 1561, addressed to Archbishop Parker from "THE QUEEN," finds a prominent place in his Register, preserved at Lambeth (*r*), no trace of any such order for the Advertisements of 1566 can there be found, nor is there any ground for thinking the Register imperfect in any way,—for it is in admirable condition, and foliated throughout,—or for suggesting any reason why so important a document, on which the Archbishop would have set so great store, if it had been forwarded to him by the Queen, would have been omitted.

And lastly, that while the alterations (*s*) involved in the Book of Common Prayer by the taking of the "further order" of 1561, find their place in *every* Prayer-Book printed from that time forward, and were even the cause of a "Cancel" being printed for Prayer-Books then in use ; not a single copy can be produced—neither throughout the various editions in that reign, nor in those of any other—with an alteration made in accordance with the Advertisements of 1566 ; and yet these are supposed to have taken a very definite "further order" in a Special Rubrick, and directly to over-ride the chief part of the enactment. On the contrary, the rubrick was repeated over and over again, and so directly contradicted the assumption, that any change of importance could have been made in its meaning.

But above and beyond these contrasts of outward form, the *internal evidence* derived from the wording *of* the two, as well as their direct purport, exhibit a still more striking contrast.

In the Order of 1561, we have in the preamble (*d*) the distinct mention of *"further order"* being the definite object of the document, and the matters on which the further orders are taken are clearly laid out. The wording of the clause is evidently a summarized form of what I have described as the *one* proviso, but which the Court in the Ridsdale Judgement had divided into two, and quoted only half; the words in the first half, "until *other order* shall be therein taken," and the words in the second half, "may ordain and publish such *further* ceremonies or rites [*]," are practically combined in the sentence, "whensoever we shall see cause to take *further order* in any rite or ceremony appointed in the Book of Common Prayer." I say practically, because the contents belong to the two parts of the proviso, as will be seen.

"Further, or other order" is there distinctly taken in *other* lessons (*f*, *k*) : the comely keeping of churches, and especially of the upper half, called the chancels (*g*, *h*, *l*), is perhaps not "other order," or indeed "further order," as the rubric already inserted in the Prayer-Book had, in a measure, restored the use of the *chancel*, by the substitution of the words, "accustomed place," instead of "in such place as the people may best hear;" and so, perhaps, the using of the chancels would involve their keeping them in a decent and comely state. But whether this paragraph, or rather the paragraphs (*g*, *h*, and *l*), are a taking of *further* order in themselves, or not, they lead up to the *other* order (*m*) of putting up the "Tables of the Ten Commandments," which, besides being for edification, were for a "comely *ornament*" of the church.

In fact, a great part of the order bears especially upon the ornamentation of churches, inveighing, as it does, against "unmeet and unseemly Tables, with foul cloths, for the Communion of the Sacraments." To *Further Order*, also, in rites and ceremonies belongs the appointment of an authorized Latin Service to be used in Collegiate Churches.

Now if we turn to the purport of the Advertisements, as derived from their internal evidence, we find no reference *whatever* to *further orders*. If they be a "further order," is not this in itself most strange? Note, too, the very first words of the title. They are *not* Advertisements for *further order*, but Advertisements for *due order* (a). The Preface speaks only of the neces-

[*] See the clauses of the Act, printed *ante*, p. 7.

sity of "*uniformity* of rites and manners," then **existing (ϵ),** nothing whatever of *further* rites to be ordained ; **and as the purport** is more fully explained, it **is** (θ) that "*some orders* **might be taken,** whereby all diversities and *varieties*" which " be against the laws . . . and ordinances of the realm, might **be reformed and** *repressed,* and brought to one manner of uniformity." Surely, my Lord, it is impossible **to conceive** that language such **as** this could **be intended to mean, or does mean, directly or in**directly, "**a taking of** *other* **order."** And when, again, we look into the nature **of the Contents, it is in the main a repetition of** Injunctions **or orders** previously issued, the principles **and** main features **of which may be** found in those issued **by** Queen Elizabeth, in the **first year of her** reign (1559), with **variations** and modifications suited **to the requirements of the time,** enforcing and explaining those Injunctions in which experience shewed there was especial negligence, and omitting **others where** enforcement **was** found impossible, or impolitic, **or** where, on **the** other hand, conformity had become **a** matter of custom, and **no** ecclesiastical pressure **was needed.**

It is not necessary **to go** through the thirty-eight Advertisements seriatim, of which I have given the subject‑headings (κ, λ, μ, ν); but **it may** be convenient, if I select two or three which bear **more directly upon the question** at issue, **to prove** what **I have said** respecting them, **namely, that** so far **from** taking "*further order,"* their **object** and practical result **was** simply to enforce *so much* of the existing laws **as** the Archbishop thought **expedient** or practicable; premising, however, that of the remainder **of the Advertisements no one militates** against the general character which these **quoted exemplify.**

In No. 3 of the Queen's Injunctions, issued in **1559,** it is ordered that—

"**The Parsons** . . . . shall preach in **their** churches, and every other cure **they have,** one Sermon *every month* of the year *at the least,* wherein they shall purely and sincerely declare the word of God . . . . and that the works devised **by man's fantasies, besides Scripture, (as** wandering of pilgrimages, &c., &c.)"

This, however, was followed in the same series of Injunctions by another :—

"The Parsons .... shall preach *in their own persons* once *in every quarter* of the year at least, one sermon, being licensed especially thereunto, as is specified hereafter."

In the Advertisements of 1566, amongst those for "Doctrine and Preaching" (κ), all order as to preaching once a-month is omitted, one rule only being given, involving preaching every quarter, and to this even important provisos are added. It runs thus :—

"*If the Parson be able* he shall preach in his own person every *three months*, *or else shall preach by another,* so that his absence be approved by the Ordinary of the diocese, in respect of sickness, service, or study at the Universities."

And to make it clear that the two Clauses of the Injunctions of 1559 are included under this one, it is added at the end,—

"Nevertheless yet for want of able preachers and parsons, to tolerate them without penalty, so that they preach in their own persons *or* by a learned substitute once in every three months of the year ᵖ."

Here, by giving the reason, and by reference to the "toleration without penalty" of a lesser obedience to the rules laid down, any one is prevented from interpreting this as a *limitation* of preaching; and elsewhere we must infer the same meaning where the words are doubtful. Should any one gloss the paragraph thus, "shall *only* preach in his own person every three months," you would, my Lord, at once condemn it as utterly unreasonable, since the object of the Advertisements, in their origin, in their profession, and in their effect, was, as will be seen, to enforce as much as possible, not to abrogate, the existing discipline.

To take another example. Amongst the "Articles for Administration of Prayer and Sacraments," (λ) No. 3 runs :—

"Item, that in Cathedral Churches and Colleges, the holy Communion be ministered upon the first or second Sunday of every month at the least. So that both Dean, Prebendaries, Priests, and Clerks do receive, and all other of discretion of the foundation do receive, *four times* in the year *at the least*."

ᵖ These are the very words used in the Archbishop's "Interpretation" of the Injunctions of 1559, preserved in his volume entitled *Synodalia*, and printed by Cardwell, Documentary Annals, vol. i. p. 236.

Now this has no counterpart in the Injunctions issued by Elizabeth, in 1559; but it derives its authority from the rubrick in the Communion, first introduced in the 1552 revision, but retained in 1559. It runs:—

"And in Cathedral and Collegiate Churches, where be many Priests and Deacons, they shall all receive the Communion with the Minister *every Sunday at the least*, except they have a reasonable cause to the contrary."

So here we find the stricter rule of the Prayer-Book allowed to be broken, so long as a less strict rule was adhered to. The whole rule could not be enforced; it was found impracticable; the Archbishop imposed a lower standard, which *he* would enforce. It would be to ignore utterly the purport of the Advertisements, to say that by that he meant to abrogate the higher standard, and to ignore the history of the Advertisements (of this I shall speak presently), if it is argued that he applied to her Majesty for authority to do so. But if the words necessarily involve a "taking of other order," it must mean this, or mean nothing. And if it was not abrogating the higher standard in this, why should it be so in the next three paragraphs, where, while the full Vestments are enjoined for Cathedrals, precisely as in the rubrick of the First Prayer-Book of Edward VI., the lower standard of the Surplice is all that the Archbishop and the Committee of Bishops think well to enforce in Parish Churches? The two are identical in principle; they agree with the general tenor of the whole series, viz., the desire to enforce as much of the discipline laid down in the Prayer-Book and Injunctions as the Archbishop considered feasible.

The three clauses next after the last quoted are as follow:—

"Item, In the ministration of the Holy Communion in cathedrall and collegiate churches, the principall minister shall use a cope, with gospeller and epistoler agreeably; and, at all other prayers to be sayde at that Communion-table, to use no copes, but surplesses.

"Item, That the dean and prebendaries weare a surplesse with a silke hoode in the quyer; and, when they preache in the Cathedrall or Collegiate Church, to weare theire hoode.

"Item, That every minister sayinge any public prayers, or ministringe the sacraments, or other rites of the churche, shall wear a comely surples with sleeves, *to be provided at the charges of the parishe.* And that the parish provide a *decente table* standinge on a frame for the Communion table."

In this it is very clear that these orders in respect of Vestments for the clergy are *all* excerpted from the rubricks of Edward the Sixth's Prayer-Book of 1549 [q]. They are directly opposed to the rubrick of the book of 1552; but so far as Cathedrals are concerned, the full Vestments are required; so far as the Parish is concerned, the Surplice will suffice. It must surely be a most unwarrantable interpolation to put in the word "*only*" before "a comely surpless," when the whole context (and more than that, the history, as will be presently shewn) of the Advertisements prove that the words "*at least*" are implied; for if there had been any intention to go back to the rubrick of 1552 for the order, instead of 1559 as enacted, the word '*only*' would certainly have been inserted, as that rubrick runs especially,—

"Shall use neither Alb, Vestment, nor Cope, but . . . being a Priest or Deacon, he shall have and wear a Surplice *only* [r]."

Further, had such a change been here intended, there was a formula in the previous paragraph which surely would have been adopted, i.e. *no* Copes, *but* Surplices. It is impossible to conceive that similar orders could have been so differently worded.

The expense of the Surplice, as of the Holy Table, was thrown on the Parish. This could scarcely be considered as involving "*other* order." The Surplice had been enacted by the Prayer-Book of 1549 to be worn at the ministration of Morning and Evening Prayer, Baptism, &c., and that or an Albe at the Holy Communion, *with* the Cope; all that Archbishop Parker does here, in ordering the Parish to provide it, is to direct what means are to be employed for enforcing the order already enacted.

---

[q] Rubricks Nos. § 2 and § **74,** of ed. 1549, in my edition of "Edward the Sixth's Prayer-Book," &c.

[r] Rubricks Nos. § 2, 3, of ed. 1552, in my edition of "Edward the Sixth's Prayer-Book," &c.

The Advertisements, however, are remarkable for the details which they enjoin as to "outward apparel," the nine last paragraphs being devoted to this subject. They order that the Archbishops and Bishops shall *continue* their customary apparel; Deans and other dignitaries shall wear in their common apparel certain gowns, &c., and tippets of sarsnet, *as is lawful* for them *by the Act of Parliament*, anno 24 Henry VIII.; and Doctors of Physic, and Prebendaries receiving twenty pounds and upwards, to wear the like apparel. And all Ecclesiastical persons to wear the Cap *appointed by the Injunctions*[*], and "no hattes but in their journeinge."

It must be remembered that the thirtieth Injunction of Queen Elizabeth, of 1559, ran thus:—

"Item, Her Majesty.... willeth and commandeth, that all.... that be called or admitted to preaching or ministry of the sacraments, ... shall use and wear *such seemly habits, garments, and such square caps*, as were most commonly and *orderly received in the latter year of the reign of king Edward the Sixth*."

Now, to many persons, the seemly habits and garments most commonly received in the sixth year of Edward VI., were unknown. The *explanation* of them in the eight or nine clauses of the Advertisements, was taking no *other*, or *further* order, but simply written with a view of aiding, or even enforcing, the uniformity already by law established. It is true, "and no hats but in their journeying," might be construed (on the principle applied by your Lordship to the clause as to surplices) to be *other* order; for it might be argued, I do not say reasonably, that they were bound then to wear their hats *only*. I conceive, however, that it was left optional to wear the "cap" or not in their "journeyings."

Before quitting the evidence to be derived from the contents of the Advertisements as to their being "the taking of other

---

[*] See Injunctions of Elizabeth, 1559, No. XXX. Cardwell, Documentary Annals, p. 225. So, again, in No. 3 of this series of Advertisements, Preachers are to command people to obey orders in the Common Prayer as "in the Queen's Majesty's Injunctions." Ibid., p. 324.

order by the Queen," I will ask your Lordship's attention to one more item, which stands No. 4 of the whole series :—

> "Item, that all licences for preaching granted out by the Archbishop and Bishops *within the Province of Canterbury*, bearing date before the *first day of March*, 1564 (= 1565 n. s.), be void and of none effect; and nevertheless all such as shall be thought meet for the office, to be admitted again without difficulty or charge, paying no more but fourpence for the writing, parchment, and wax."

Passing over for the present (as it belongs to the historical considerations) the particular mention of the date, 1564 *o. s.*, in the document which your Lordship contends (p. 16) was not issued or printed till 1566 *n. s.*, I would ask, Why should the Queen, if she intended to take *further order*, choose as a vehicle the Advertisements issued by her Archbishop, as it appears by this paragraph these were, to the *Province of Canterbury?* Were the Clergy of the Province of York still obliged to wear Copes, and those of the southern province forbidden? But such, my Lord, surely is the natural result of accepting these Advertisements of 1566 as her Majesty's "other order" upon this subject.

Up to this point, then, I have attempted to shew that the Advertisements of 1566, neither in their profession, purport, or nature, whether we regard their preamble or their contents, offer any grounds for considering them the taking of "other order," within the meaning of the Act, by her Majesty. And that, on the contrary, the general character of the contents, as well as many of the expressions which are used, are altogether inconsistent with that view. Incidentally to the argument I have shewn, how a few years before her Majesty *did take* further order, and how, in every detail, it fulfils the exact requirements of the Act.

I do not see amongst your Lordship's Notes any reference to the internal evidence of the document itself; for the argument as to its intent, seems to be wholly based upon external and historical grounds, and to this part of the subject I now turn.

IV. THE **HISTORY OF THE** QUEEN'S **LETTER OF** JANUARY, 1565, AND **WHY** ARCHBISHOP PARKER ISSUED HIS ADVERTISEMENTS **IN** 1566.

I feel a great difficulty in surveying, in **a few pages,** so vast an area as the history of the "Advertisements" covers. The data are so numerous, **and the** connecting links so intricate, that it is impossible to **do more than** sketch in an outline. But I believe that, **in a** case of this kind, an outline, however rough, if following the main **features, must convey** a more truthful notion of the events, than any intricate blending of passages, isolated from their context, or of facts separated from their surrounding circumstances, can possibly present. Many **of the data** which are referred to by your Lordship, **and more in full** by the Committee of the Privy Council in the Ridsdale Judgement, convey to my mind a very different interpretation **when** viewed with their immediate context, from that which **seems to** be put upon them in their isolation, and still more so when viewed as part of a general history. And first, let me venture **on a** few general remarks on the circumstances under which the events with which I have to deal occurred.

The ecclesiastical history of the early part of Elizabeth's reign was marked by lawlessness in discipline. It was not, perhaps, the active **lawlessness** of 1640-50, but rather **a** passive lawlessness,—a **deadness** and carelessness about all appearances; and it is much **to** be feared that this represented somewhat the **state** of religion actually. **Nor was it to be wondered at.**

The twelve years which preceded her accession to **the throne** had seen the death of Henry VIII., who **left the** Church with its constitution absolutely changed as regards externals, but its Services and internal **organization in a most unsettled** state. They had seen the new **Prayer-Book** of Edward—with its accompanying ritual,—after **it had been in use scarcely three years**[1] **superseded** by another, differing from **it in many** points of doc-

---

[1] The First Book was ordered to be used from and after the Feast of Pentecost [June 9], 1549. The Bill for the Second Book was finally returned to the House of Lords and agreed upon, April 14, 1552.

trine, and still more so in ritual. They had seen this in its turn, after being barely in use one year, again swept away, and an entirely new ritual taking its place, which in its turn had held its place barely five years and six months. And now Queen Elizabeth finds herself on the throne pledged to overthrow that, and substitute something else in its place. But it was not only with the Church Services and their accompanying rubricks that the Queen had to deal: there were also the Injunctions (which served the purpose of our Canons), and all else that belonged to Discipline; while all the acts of Edward VI., in this respect, had been swept away by Queen Mary. Out of the many changes in all these, Elizabeth had before her the task of evolving order.

A choice, as far as the new Prayer-Book was concerned, lay between that of 1549 and 1552. It is easy to understand her difficulty. New books would, at any rate, have to be printed, as both the 1549 and 1552 books had, in all the churches, been destroyed; though a few copies had, of course, been preserved in private houses. A new revision was at first proposed, and some few papers are preserved [a] relating to it, but whether by the Queen's command or not, or even with her sanction, is very uncertain. The Second Book of Edward VI. was, no doubt, pressed upon her by her advisers, on the ground of it being a compromise between the first book which she wished for, and the more radical changes desired by the Puritan party. Possibly she herself stipulated for certain changes. These were few in number; two or three very immaterial, but one most *material*. The doctrine of the Holy Sacrament had, by the words of delivery, been changed

---

[a] In the Paper, for instance, in the Cottonian collection, Julius F. 6, and printed by Strype, vol. i. pt. ii. p. 392, suggestions are made even as to what allowance 'those learned men' should have 'for the time they are about to review the Book of Common Prayer,' and where they should meet. Strype thinks it was drawn up by Sir Thomas Smith himself, and it was at his lodgings the writer of the paper proposes they should meet. Possibly the paper left behind by Guest (in Parker's volume of *Synodalia*, cccc.) represents some of the results of their deliberations. If so, it does not appear that they influenced the promoters of the Bill, which passed soon afterwards through Parliament.

in the Puritan revision. The words, "The Body of our Lord Jesus Christ, which was given for thee, preserve thy body and soul unto everlasting life," (which were the sole words of the 1549 book;) had been changed in the 1552 book to, "Take and eat this in remembrance that Christ died for thee, and feed on Him in thy heart with thanksgiving." Although, however, much else had been changed in the 1552 book, to bring into prominence the new doctrines respecting the Holy Sacrament, practically, nothing had been inserted absolutely to the exclusion of the old doctrine. Elizabeth simply ordered both forms of words to be retained, since they were not incompatible; and we have them still. It was not a policy of compromise which prompted this, but a policy of comprehension. The appointed Vestments followed naturally in the wake. The restoration of the older words, without the Vestments, would have been inconsistent, remembering the doctrine involved. The Puritan party, probably, accepted the words, because they could put their own interpretation upon them, and this practically they did; but to have the Vestments restored in the rubrick as a *necessary* adjunct to the due administration of the rite, would have evoked a more vigorous opposition. The most probable explanation of the singular circumstances attending the adoption of the Proviso (already referred to [1]), is that Queen Elizabeth, with somewhat of the spirit of her father, took the matter into her own hands, and made herself responsible for what might happen. Since, however, Parliament had enjoined a Prayer-Book with a certain rubrick, it was necessary that it should also authorise the deviation which the Queen made from it; and hence it appears in the form of a Proviso, and in effect in the Queen's name, or rather under her sole responsibility. At the same time, she extended her responsibility to the addition of other rites and ceremonies, which, of course, would be included with the ornaments of the Church and of the Minister, under the head of Ritual.

[1] See p. 6.

And so the Act passed. Besides, however, the Act of Uniformity, there were the Injunctions issued by her Majesty at about the same time. These were for general discipline of the Clergy, though they touch very closely, in one or two instances, upon the rubricks. They were chiefly a revival of the Injunctions of Edward VI.

That it would be very difficult to say exactly the status they had in law, that is, how far they might be proceeded on, and what were the pains and penalties involved by disobedience, I think will be seen by what occurred; and from the documents which have to be quoted, it will appear that the machinery of enforcing discipline generally was by no means as yet set in order. From one cause or other, much of the law was a dead letter.

From the moment of her accession to the throne, her Majesty's work of restraining the lawlessness had begun. Her first proclamation[?], viz. Dec. 27, 1558, had been to forbid *Preachers* who caused contention; and in the Injunctions[z], in order to prevent somewhat the robbery and pillage consequent on the second overthrow of the Roman Catholic Religion, a direction is inserted that inventories of the goods of churches should be taken.

Already "much zeal had been shewn," as Strype expresses it, by pulling down images without any public authority, and defacing the churches. Some of the cases were brought before the Queen's Council, e.g. at Shobury in Essex; Dover, in Kent; Haylesham, in Sussex; and Bow Church, in London[a].

In Parliament, early in 1559, attempts were made to bring in a Bill for "making ecclesiastical laws," but it appeared that as it had failed in Edward the Sixth's reign, so it failed now. As Strype says of it, "Men did not then care to be restrained by Church discipline[b]."

[?] Printed in Cardwell's Documentary Annals, vol. i. p. 208, from Strype's Annals, Appendix No. 3.

[z] Injunctions of Elizabeth, No. XLVII., Cardwell's Documentary Annals, vol. i. p. 228.

[a] Strype's Annals, vol. i. pt. i. p. 69, where an abstract of the cases is given.

[b] Strype's Annals, vol. i. pt. i. p. 85.

In September, 1560, the Queen found it necessary to issue a Royal Proclamation[c] against the defacing of **Monuments in Churches and stealing Bells**, beginning thus:—

"The Quenes Maiestie **understandyng** that by the meanes of sundry people, partly ignoraunt, partly malicious or *covetous*, there hath ben of late yeres spoyled and broken certayne auncient Monumentes, some of *metall*, some of stone. . . And where[as] the covetousness of certayn persons is such that as Patrones of Churches, or owners of the personages impropriated, or by some other **colour or pretence**, they do persuade with the person and parishioners **to take or throw** down the Belles of Churches and Chappels, and the leade of the same, converting the same to theyr **private gaynes**," &c.

And in the same year, disturbances at St. Paul's called forth another Proclamation[d] against fighting and quarrelling in churches, which was often excited by the language of the "Preachers."

In the year 1561, we find that "Further order[e]," to which I have already referred, was taken as to some minor details. The following incidental description shews to what a degree of apathy all respect for the decent state of Churches had sunk:—

"There is such negligence and lack of **convenient reverence used** towards the comely keeping and order of the **said Churches**, and especially of the upper part called the Chancels, that it breedeth no **small offence and** slander to see and consider, on the one part, the curiosity and cost bestowed by all sorts of men upon their private houses; and the other part, the unclean or negligent order, **or spare keeping of the House of Prayer**, by permitting open decays, and ruins of coverings, walls, and windows, and by appointing unmeet and unseemly tables with foul cloths for the Communion of the Sacraments, and generally leaving the place of prayers desolate of all cleanliness, and of meet ornaments for such a place, whereby it might be known a place provided for divine Service."

These and such-like *Public Documents*[f] present a fair notion of what state of things existed when Queen Elizabeth issued her letter of Jan. 25, 1564 = 1565. So much in the argument depends upon this letter, that I am obliged to print it entire.

[c] From an original printed copy (by Jugge and Cawood), which, with the first draft as corrected by Cecil, is preserved in the S. P. O., Elizabeth, vol. xiii. arts. 32, 33. Printed from Fuller's Church History, in Cardwell's Documentary Annals, vol. i. p. 289.

[d] Printed in Cardwell's Documentary Annals, vol. i. p. 310.

[e] See *ante*, p. 10.

[f] For evidence to be derived from correspondence and non-official papers, see *post*, cap. vi.

QUEEN ELIZABETH'S LETTER[a], *Jan.* 25, 1565.

"*To the Archbishop of Canterbury, from the* Queen's *Majesty, Jan.* 25, 1564 [= 1565].

"*Requiring him* to confer *with the Bishops of his province, and others having ecclesiastical jurisdiction;* for the redressing disorders in the *Church, occasioned by different doctrines* and rites; *and for the taking order to admit* none *into preferment, but those that are conformable.*

"Most reverend Father in God, &c. We greet you wel. Like as no one thing in the government and charge, committed unto us by the favourable goodnes of Almighty God, doth more profit and beautify the same to his pleasure and acception, to our comfort, and ease of our government, and finally to the universal weal and repose of our people and countries; than unity, quietnes, and concord, as wel amongst the public Ministers having charge under us, as in the multitude of the people by us and them ruled: so contrariwise, diversity, variety, contention, vain love of singularity, either in our Ministers or in the people, must needs provoke the displeasure of Almighty God, and bee to us, having the burden of government, discomfortable, heavy, and troublesome; and finally, must needs bring danger of ruine to our people and country.

"WHEREFORE, altho' our earnest care and inward desire hath always been, from the beginning of our reign, to provide, that by lawes and ordinances, agreeable to truth and justice, and consonant to good order, this our realm should be directed and governed, both in the ecclesiastical and civil policy, by public officers and Ministers, following, as near as possible might be, one rule, forme, and manner of order in al their actions, and directing our people to obey humbly, and live godly, according to their several callings, in unity and concord, without diversities of opinions or novelties of rites and maners, or without maintenance or breeding of any contentions about the same: yet we, to our no smal grief and discomfort, do hear, that where, of the two maner of governments, without which no maner of people is wel ruled, the ecclesiastical should be the more perfect, and should give example, and be as it were a light and guide, to allure, direct, and lead al officers in civil policy; yet in sundry places of our realm of late, for lack of regard given therto, in due time, by such superior and principal officers as you are, being the Primat, and *other the Bishops of your province*, with suffrance of sundry varieties and novelties, not only in opinions, but in external ceremonies and rites, there is crept and brought into the Church by some few persons, abounding more in their own senses than wisdome would, and delighting in singularities and changes, an open and manifest disorder, and offence to the godly, wise, and obedient persons, by diversitie of opinions, and specially in the external, decent, and leeful rites and ceremonies to bee used in the churches.

[a] Copied from Appendix to Strype's Life of Parker, vol. iii. p. 65, which appears to be taken from the contemporary copy preserved amongst the Burghley papers now in Lansdowne MSS., viii. art. 6. The first rough draft, with Cecil's corrections, is also preserved in the same collection, vol. cxv. art. 57, and it varies in some minor particulars from the above.

"So as except the same should bee spedily withstand, stayd, and reformed, the inconvenience therof were like to grow from place to place, as it were by an infection, to a great annoyance, trouble, and deformitie to the rest of the whole body of the realm: and therby empaire, deface, and disturb Christian charity, unity, and concord, being the very bands of our religion. Which wee do so much desire to encrease and continue amongst our people; and by and with which our Lord God, being the God of peace, and not of dissension, will continue his blessings and graces over us and his people.

"And altho' wee have now a good while heard, to our grief, sundry reports hereof, hoping that al cannot bee true, but rather mistrusting that the adversaries of truth might, of their evil disposition, encrease the reports of the same: yet we thought, until this present, that by the regard which you, being the Primat and Metropolitan, would have had hereto, according to your office, with the assistance of the Bishops, your brethren, in their several diocesses, (having also received of us heretofore charge for the same purpose,) these errors, tending to breed some schism or deformity in the Church, should have been stayed and appeased. But perceiving very lately, and also certainly, that the same doth rather begin to encrease, then to stay or diminish; we, considering the authority given to us of Almighty God for defence of the publick peace, concord, and truth of this his Church, and how wee are answerable for the same to the seat of his high justice, mean not to endure or suffer any longer these evils thus to proceed, spread, and encrease in our realm; *but have certainly determined to have all such diversities,* varieties, and novelties amongst them of the Clergy and our people, as breed nothing but contention, offence, and breach of common charitie, *and are also against the laws, good usages, and ordinances of our realm, to bee reformed and repressed,* and brought to one manner of uniformitie through our whole realm and dominions. That our people may thereby quietly honour and serve Almighty God in truth, concord, peace, and quietness: and therby also avoyd the slaunders that are spred abroad hereupon in foraign countries.

"And therfore wee do by these our present letters require, enjoyn, and straitly charge you, being the Metropolitan, according to the power and authority which you have under us over *this province of Canterbury,* (as the like wee wil order for the province of York,) to confer with the Bishops, your brethren, namely, such as be in commission for causes ecclesiastical, and also al other head officers and persons having jurisdiction ecclesiastical, as wel in both our Universities, as in any other places collegiat, cathedral, or whatsoever the same bee, exempt or not exempt, either by calling to you from thence whom you shal think meet to have assistance or conference, or by message, process, or letters, as you shal see most convenient: and cause to bee truly understand, what varieties, novelties, and diversities there are in our Clergy, or among our people, within every of the said jurisdictions, either in doctrin or in ceremonies and rites of the Church, or in the maners, usages, and behaviour of the Clergy themselves, by what name soever any of them bee called. And thereupon, as the several cases shal appear to require reformation, so to proceed by order, injunction, **or censure**, according to **the** order and appointment of such laws and ordinances **as** are provided by act of Parliament, and the true meaning therof. **So as** uniformity of order may bee kept in every church, and without variety and **contention**.

"And for the time to come, wee wil and straitly charge you to provide and enjoin **in our name**, in al and every places of your province, as wel in places exempt **as otherwise**, that none bee hereafter admitted **or** allowed to **any office, room, or cure**, or place ecclesiastical, either having **cure** of souls, **or** without cure, but such as shal be found disposed and **wel** and advisedly given to common order; and shal also, before their admittance **to** the same, orderly and formally promise to use and exercise the same office, room, or place, to the honour of God, the edification of our people under their charge, in truth, concord, and unity; and also to observe, keep, and maintain *such order and uniformity in al the external rites and ceremonies, both for the Church, and for their own persons, as by laws, good usages, and orders, are already allowed, wel provided, and established.* And if any superior officers shal bee found hereto disagreeable, if otherwise your discretion or authority shal not serve to reform them, we wil, that you shal duly inform us thereof, to the end wee may give in delayed order for the same. For wee intend to have no dissension or variety grow, by suffering of persons, which maintain the same, to remain in authority. For so the sovereign authority, which wee have under Almighty God, should bee violate and made frustrate. And wee might bee wel thought to bear the sword in vain.

"And in the execution hereof, we require you to use all expedition, that to such a cause as this is shal seem necessary: that hereafter we bee not occasioned, for lack of your diligence, to provide such further remedy, by **some** other *sharp proceedings*, as shal percase not bee easie to bee born by such as shal be disordered: and therewith also wee shal impute to you the cause thereof."

It **will be** observed that in this letter of Queen Elizabeth there is no allusion, directly or indirectly, to her desire to **change any** order **or** rubrick, **or to her** wish or expectation that Archbishop Parker would change any.

The account given by your Lordship of Queen Elizabeth's letter is as follows (NOTES, p. **13**):—

"In 1564 the attention of the Queen **was directed to** the disorder and in**consistency** of practice on this subject [i.e. **of Copes**, &c.] then prevailing in the Church, and **her** determination to *establish*, by the use of all legal means, *such a rule for the future* **as** might secure **uniformity**, was declared in her celebrated letter **to** Archbishop Parker of the 25th January, 1564-5.

"The Advertisements issued under it rather more than **a year later** (i.e. soon after the 28th **March, 1566**) were the result."

Whether or not there is any evidence that Queen Elizabeth's attention was drawn to the question of "Copes and Vestments," which your Lordship asserts [b], all I can say is, I have not found it. There is no reference in the letter to them, and though negligence in wearing them might possibly be included in the direction to "maintain such order .... in all the external rites for their own persons as by laws .... are already allowed," this would not justify your Lordship's statement. But when your Lordship says her determination "was to *establish* such a rule for the future," I would fain ask whether this at all represents her charging the Archbishop "to *maintain* such order and uniformity as by laws, good usages, and orders are *already established;*" or her determination to have "all diversities .... which *are* against the laws .... and ordinances of our realm, to be reformed and repressed."

If I understand your Lordship's words and argument aright, they mean that Queen Elizabeth was determined to establish some *new rule*, and it is intimated by the context (p. 12), to which I have before referred, that this new rule was to be a compromise, i.e. something between what, on the one hand, "Archbishop Parker and Bishop Cox had drawn up in their Paper entitled 'Interpretations' (i.e. of the Queen's Injunctions)," in which the Cope was proposed to be ordered only [i]; and, on the other, what were hereafter to be proposed in the Convocation in 1562, where, under the influence of Dean Nowell, Vestments, Copes, *and Surplices*, were all to be done away with. In a word, that the Cope was to be *ordered* for the Cathedral and Collegiate Churches to please the one side, and forbidden for the Parish Churches to please the other.

But so far from finding any hint of, or ground for, such in Elizabeth's letter, I find exactly the contrary. As the language is very verbose, and the sentences very complicated,

---

[b] The words, "This subject," can only refer to the one subject of the preceding paragraph.

[i] i.e. instead of some using Chasubles and some Copes. See Cardwell, Documentary Annals, vol. i. p. 238.

I will attempt to give the substance of the letter in a condensed form :—

"*The Queen to the Archbishop, requiring him to confer with the other bishops for redressing Disorders, and for taking order to admit none into preferment who are not conformable.*

"As nothing doth profit more than unity and concord,
"amongst ministers as well as amongst the people, our desire
"has been to provide by laws and ordinances this uniformity
"through our realm. In sundry places, however, of our realm
"of late, you the Primate and other Bishops have suffered
"sundry varieties and novelties to creep in, not only in opi-
"nions, but in external ceremonies and rites, which we thought
"that you, with the assistance of the Bishops, would have
"stayed and appeased. Perceiving that they begin to increase
"rather than diminish, we mean that they shall no longer do
"so, but have determined to have all diversities and novelties
"*against the laws and good usages* repressed.

"Therefore we require you to confer with your brethren of
"the province *of Canterbury*, and enquire what varieties exist
"in doctrine, or in ceremonies, or in rites ; and as cases oc-
"cur, to proceed by order, injunction, or censure, according to
"the order and appointment of such laws and ordinances as
"are provided by Act of Parliament.

"And we enjoin you not to admit to the Cure of souls any
"but such as shall be disposed to maintain such order and
"uniformity in all the external rights and ceremonies, both for
"the Church (i.e. vestments) and for their persons (i.e. apparel),
"*as by the laws* are **already established**.

"And in the execution we require you to use all expedition,
"so that we shall not have to use other sharp proceedings."

Nothing can be plainer. Novelties against the laws had been introduced, and were to be repressed. How can this be construed into anything meaning "establishing a rule for the future," which in itself would be contrary to the laws already established.

It appears to me that the expression of opinion upon this letter in the Ridsdale JUDGEMENT is even less guarded than in your Lordship's NOTES. It runs,—

"The Queen had, in the most *formal manner*, by her royal letters commanded the Metropolitan and other Prelates TO PREPARE THESE ADVERTISEMENTS [k]."

I confess, my Lord, to have been startled at this passage, and thought that I could not have read correctly. But it is there; and where there is anything about *preparing Advertisements* in the Queen's letter, I must beg to leave to your Lordship or others to point out; especially as the Advertisements which it is contended were so prepared at the Queen's desire, are elsewhere defined to be "taking of *other* order," than that *existing* law so specially named in the letter.

And if for a moment it be argued that, although the Queen did not require or intend her Archbishop and Bishops to issue "other order," but that, contrary to her instructions, the Archbishop and Bishops did so issue it, and that, therefore, any sanction she might afterwards give to the document would involve her sanctioning that other order, and so amount to taking further order, let me refer your Lordship again to the preface of the said Advertisements, in the consideration of which I have before shewn [l] that in itself it absolutely negatives "other order" being taken. I would, however, here point out how exactly this preface, as it stands in all the printed editions, proves what her Majesty required to be done, using in places identically the same words. With such testimony, even had there been passages which appeared clearly to abrogate and supersede an existing law, or to enact a new one, we should have been rather justified in doubting that they were intended to, or virtually did so; but when no instance occurs of a "further, or other order," beyond or beside what had been previously enacted by Act of Parliament or ruled by injunction, it seems

---

[k] Ridsdale Judgement, off. copy, p. 9.
[l] When speaking of the internal evidence of the Advertisements themselves. See *ante*, p. 17.

to me to be unjustifiable to take one clause from the whole series, and by inserting the word "*only*," make it by such insertion [m], and by such insertion alone, to appear a new law; and then to argue from this appearance that "other order was taken," while the historical evidence shews that the whole purport of the printing of the Advertisements was to enforce existing laws.

We possess, however, considerable evidence as to the circumstance of the drawing-up of these Advertisements. Although, as Archbishop Parker states in the preamble, they were " by virtue of her Majesty's letter of Jan. 25, 1565 *n. s.*, it does not seem that they were the immediate result of that letter. Indeed, these words seem to have been inserted in March, 1566, as an afterthought. For we find preserved in his Register the copy of a letter he wrote five days after, i.e. January 30, 1565, to the Bishop of London [n], beginning,—

"After my hartie commendacions..... Where[as] the Quenes Maiestie, the xxviijth daye of this present monethe, addressed *unto me her* Letteres, verie seriouslie and at great lengthe discorsed, in her godlie zeale, moche desyrouse to see unitie, quietnes, and concorde, [&c.] ... and that nowe of late for lacke of regarde of us the Bisshoppes ... sundrie varieties and novelties ... be crepte in.... Whereuppon her Maiestie hathe streyghtlie charged me, accordinge to *suche powre and authoritie as I have* under her, to have consideration of the same.... And further her commandement is, that none hereafter be admytted to any office [o], &c....

"Thes things thus considered .... I do by theise my letteres desyere yo[r] L[ordship], and in her name streytlie charge you to expende and execute the premisses. And also to signifie the same w[th] charge to the rest of o[r] bretheren in my province, that they inviolablye *see the Lawes and ordinances alreadie stablished* to be w[t]houte delaye and colore *executed* in theyr particular Jurisdictions, w[th] proceadinge agaynst the offenders by the censures of the Church, etc. And suche as be incorrigible to send uppe hether the causes and demerites of those persons; as they the said Bisshoppes to charge there inferiors havinge any jurisdiction to do the same."

Let me here pause a moment, to ask your Lordship's attention to the definite manner in which he interprets her Majesty's letter to him. How, may I ask, is it possible with those words which

---

[m] See *ante*, p. 20.

[n] From Parker's Register at Lambeth, vol. i. folio 253 a. It is printed in the Parker Correspondence, pp. 227—230, to which book I observe your Lordship refers.

[o] Almost verbatim, as in the Queen's letter itself.

I have put in italics,—and I assure you, my Lord, I have quoted all the material part of the letter,—that Archbishop Parker understood the Queen to take " other order," or to desire " other order" to be taken? or that the Archbishop himself meant to take " other order?"

The concluding part of the letter is material to the history :—

" And also, that youe and they severallie callinge the most apte grave men to conferre w^thin your and there Dioces, to certifie me *what varieties* and discorde there be either in doctrine *or in Ceremonies* of the churche, and behavio^r of the clergie themselves, by what name soever they be called ; whiche certificate to be returned by the *laste daye of Februarie* next to come at the furthest. And that you and they thereof fayle not, as ye and they will answere to the contrarie at your and their perill. From my House at Lambehith, the xxxth daye of Januarie, 1564 [= 1565 *n.s.*]

" Your lovinge brother,
" MATTHEU CANTUR."

One may reasonably suppose that some Bishops at least of his province complied with his instructions, and that before a month was over he obtained some lists of the varieties and novelties which chiefly required redress in his diocese. And he was expeditious in setting them in order, for on March 3 we find that he has arranged them (taking several from the " Resolutions and Orders taken by Common Consent of the Bishops," *c.* 1561)^p, and sends them to Secretary Cecil (with whom he was in consultation), together with a letter ^q which begins,—

" SIR,—I send yor honor a boke of Articles, partly of olde agreed on AMONGST US, and partly of late these iij or iiij days considered, which be eyther in papirs fasted on as ye see, or new written bi secretary hand. because it is the first vewe, not fully digested, I thought good to send it to yor honor to peruse, to know yor jugement, & so to retorne yt, that it may be fayr wryten *and presented.* THE DEVYSERS WER only the b[ishops] of London, Wynchester, Ely, Lyncolne, and myself."

The Queen's Secretary evidently returns the rough copy " fasted" together, and the Archbishop has a fair copy made and signed by certain Bishops. He writes^r, March 8, 1565 (that is, four days after),—

^p In the C.C.C. MS., Cambridge, vol. cvi. p. 423.

^q From Lansdowne MSS., viii. art. 1. Printed in Parker Correspondence, p. 233.

^r From Lansdowne MSS., viii. art. 2. Printed in Parker Correspondence, p. 234.

"SIR,—I send your honor OUR *boke* wch is subscribed to bi the byshops conferers, wch I kepe by myself. I trust yor honor *wil present it upon oportunitie* wch ye can take, in removing offenses that mygt growe by myne imprudent talke.

"Yf the Q. M^ie *wil not authoryse* them, **the most part be like to lye in the dust for execution of o^r parties,** *Lawes be so moche agaynst o^r privat doyngs,* 'The Q. M^ie, wth consent,' &c., I trust, shal be obeyd."

And later on in the same letter, referring to the same difficulty of enforcing laws for uniformity, but with special reference to the cases of Sampson and Humphrey, he writes :—

"Yf this ball shalbe tossed unto us, & then have *no* **authorytie** by the Q. M^ies hande, we wil set stil. I marvel that not vi wordes wer spoken fr^m the Q. M^ie to my L. of London, for unyform'ty of his London, as hymself told me; yf ye remedye is not bi letter, I wil no more stryve against the streme, fume or chide who will. Thus the Lord be with yow . . . .

"This 8th of March [1565]. "Your honour's,

"MATTH. CANT."

In a letter* of March 24, 1565, he complains to Cecil :—

"I wold ye had not have styred *istam camerinam*, or else to have set on yt, to som order at the begynnyng."

And again, on the 7th of April†, he explains his position as regards the enforcing uniformity. He writes to Cecil :—

"Sir, The talk, as I am enformed, is moche Increased : and onrestfull thei be, and I alone, they saye, am in fawt. For as for the Q[ueen's] M^ties part : in my expostulation wth many of them, I signifie there disobedience ; wherein, because thei see the daunger, they ceast to impute yt to her M^tie, for thei saye, but for my callyng on, she is Indifferent."

It follows from all this that Archbishop Parker could not obtain royal sanction to his Advertisements, the object of which, I trust, I have proved to be, to name particularly, and so enforce those existing laws, in which carelessness was either very serious, very general, or very reprehensible. I say *his* Advertisements, because up to this point there can be no pretence for saying the Queen had anything to do with them. One would gather, by the correspondence, that she had not even seen them ; and it is probably at about this time (i.e. March,

---

* From **Lansdowne** MSS., viii. art. 4. Printed in **Parker** Correspondence, p. 236.

† From Lansdowne MSS., **xix.** No. 1. Printed in Parker Correspondence, p. 237.

1565) that the fair copy, **duly** signed **by himself and the other** Bishops, was returned to **him** by Cecil, with Cecil's very distinct and expressive remarks on the outside :—

"*Ordinances accorded by the Archbishop of Canterbury, &c., in his Province. These were not authorized or published.*"

And these words, "Ordinances **accorded by** the Archbishop in his Province," shew exactly **how they were** regarded by the Queen's Secretary; **and render it** impossible to reconcile with his view of **them, the view that they were, in any sense,** "other Orders" issued " **by the Queen**" to the Church at large ".

And why should the Queen refuse to authorize them as Parker wished? It seems to me, their rejection was not due to any Puritan influence in the Court, which would probably, if it existed, have had but little influence on her Majesty; nor, on the other hand, to the Queen's own bias in regard to any question touched upon. We know her feelings as regarded ritual, by what she "retained" herself, and her absolute refusal to have the "ornaments of the chapel" interfered with, when Archbishop Parker, and **other Bishops, pressed** her to remove "the offendicle ᵛ;" it is evident, **too,** in the Injunctions, **that** one or two concessions had **to** be **wrung** from her, e.g. for Tables instead of Altars ˣ. On the other hand, though the Advertisements **did not enforce the full ritual which** she had ordered, **she** would **naturally have been glad to** have seen even so **much** carried out, rather **than none.** Any reason, therefore, derived from the supposition that they enforced too much ritual, or **too** little, is not likely to have affected Queen Elizabeth's decision.

ᵘ See *post*, pp. 40—42, **where I** speak of the difference between the printed and the MS. copies.

ᵛ It is supposed that it was a Crucifix which especially gave offence, **and** which is here referred to, though **in some** letters it is called simply a silver cross, e. g. Jewel writing to Peter Martyr Nov. 16, 1559, calls it "that little silver Cross of ill-omened origin!" but **later,** Feb. **4, 1**560, he calls it a Crucifix. It is **to this** that probably **Bishop** Cox alludes, writing about the same time : "We are only constrained, **to** our great distress of mind, to tolerate in our churches the image of the Cross and Him who was crucified."

ˣ "In the order whereof, saving for an uniformity, there seemeth no matter of great moment." Cardwell's Documentary Annals, vol. i. **p. 234.**

Of course it is difficult to judge of motives, but it appears to me that **one motive, at least, which** prompted her was that of **policy.** The Queen, by her letter, had ordered **the** Archbishop and Bishops to enforce the ritual of the Church; they **were, so** to speak, to bear the brunt of the opposition. **She did** not think it policy to have proceedings taken in her own name, and I gather rather that Cecil thought the same.

It is true the Injunctions **of** 1559 had been issued by her, but, as I have pointed out, there appeared to be a difficulty **in** enforcing them, just as **much** as there had been in enforcing the rubrick.

In the letters which **I have** already quoted, and there are others in **the same vein, from** Archbishop Parker, it appears **to** me he was as **anxious to** shift the responsibility of enforcing order upon the Queen, as she **was to throw the** responsibility on him, and herein lay the secret **of his anxiety.** The state of discipline into which the **Church had lapsed, as I** have shewn at the beginning of these remarks, required little less than a crusade to restore it. "Give me your Majesty's order under seal," **the** Archbishop seems to say, "dated this year, and I shall be **able to** go about with it as a weapon, and either terrify or slay. Otherwise I can do nothing; my own weapons are not sufficient."

But it is clear that the Queen made no response. The general letter of Jan. 25, 1565, is as much a complaint that the Bishops have not been doing their duty, as any very definite instruction to shew how they are to do it; though there is evidence that in its first draft Archbishop Parker had a hand [y]. But the Queen, at the same time, seems to have made it her own, for at the end there is a reference to some other "sharp proceedings," which bear the impress of her own mind, and by them she implies that she means the Bishops to set to work [z].

---

[y] See Sir William Cecil's letter to Abp. Parker, Jan. 15, 1565. Parker Correspondence, p. 223.

[z] See the concluding paragraph of the letter printed *ante*, p. 30.

This letter was, therefore, practically all the Archbishop had to work with; i.e. his only authority. He carried out her Majesty's orders so far as she gave definite directions, that is, he wrote to the Bishop of London, and through him to other Bishops, not to ordain any clergy who would not conform, and also to send him notes of the chief varieties and novelties which they met with. Purely on his own account, and so far as appears, *proprio motu*, he codified these latter, with the assistance of three Bishops, in order to restrain offenders in those particulars; but it was probably an after-thought that, having thus got them in order, so as directly to fit the chief cases, he would get them issued under the Queen's hand. In this we see he failed.

Your Lordship remarks (NOTES, p. 16),—

"That the Advertisements were never published in their rejected form (in which the *preamble was different*, and there were eight additional articles afterwards omitted) we know from Cecil's endorsement, *These were not authorized or published.*

"That they were not printed before 1566 in the form which they finally assumed, we know from Archbishop Parker's two letters, both dated the 28th of March."

No doubt this was so, but the important point to observe is the nature of the difference in what is called the preamble, between the two editions, as it is very material to the argument. Further, also, I think it suggests another motive why the Queen at this stage would not allow Archbishop Parker to issue his Advertisements.

As the Advertisements were originally drawn, i.e. in the MS. of 1565, they had no title. The title of "Ordinances accorded by the Archbishop in his Province," was, I suspect, given to them by Cecil: Archbishop Parker had hoped that they would be issued in the Queen's name, i.e. beginning "the Queen's Majesty, with consent," &c., as he writes in his letter of March 8, 1565, already quoted*; or "with assent," as appears in the draft itself. Having failed in this, as a last resource to give them the

* See p. 36.

appearance of authority, he prefixed to the printed edition of 1566 the new title,—

"ADVERTISEMENTS partly for [a] *due Order* in the public *administration* of Common Prayers and using **the holy** Sacraments, and partly for [b] the *apparel* of all persons ecclesiastical, by virtue of the Queen's Majestie's letters Commanding the same [i.e. commanding **due** order in administration &c. **and** apparel of persons ecclesiastical]*, Jan. **25.**"

No doubt this was better **than** Cecil's title, and the inser**tion of the** reference **to the** Queen's title no doubt gave additional strength, though it did not make them **any** the more the Queen's own orders.

I here put in parallel **columns** the preamble, or preface, as **at** first drawn, i.e. in **the MS. of 1565, and as** it was afterwards revised for the printed editions **of 1566** :—

MS. of 1565.	Printed Editions, 1566.
The Queen's Majesty of her godly state, calling **to** remembrance . . . [similar to that printed **at p.** 13] to whereunto they **be** called ;	The Queen's Majesty of her godly zeal, calling **to** remembrance . . . [similar to that printed at p. 13] to whereunto they be called ;
(η) Hath, by the assent **of the** Metropolitane, and with **certain** other her Commissioners in Causes Ecclesiastical, *decreed certain rules* and *orders* **to be** used as hereafter followeth.	(η) **Hath by** her letters directed **unto the** Archbishop, required, enjoyned, ... &c. [and **continued** as at p. 13,] to 'used and followed.'
Not yet prescribing these rules, &c. [See opposite page].	Nor yet prescribing these rules, &c. [as at p. 13].

It will be observed that the MS. of 1565 would at least amount **to** "*taking* **order**" **in** accordance with the Act of Parliament, whether "*other* **or** *further* order" would depend upon what followed.

And **hence**, perhaps, the words of the Ridsdale Judgement might **have been** derived, viz.—

"That the Advertisements . . . were a 'taking of order' within the Act of Parliament *by* the Queen."

And, indeed, your Lordship's argument throughout, that the Advertisements were authorized *by* Elizabeth, would be fully

---

b **I think** I detect in some writings **the idea that** the words "the same" **are to be referred** to "The Advertisements." Apart from the question of grammatical construction, there is the simple fact that the Queen's letter does not command the Advertisements, but does command order and uniformity to be enforced among the ministers, "both in the Church and in their own persons (i.e. apparel)." See p. 30.

borne out and proved had these words been left standing. But when we find these very important words were crossed out, and others implying something very different put in their place *before* publication, your Lordship not only loses a good argument, but gains in its stead one presenting many difficulties, as I have already pointed out when treating of the purport of this preamble[c]; and unless the purport can be explained away by some theory such as accident, or that the change was for some independent purpose, the difficulties are insuperable, and the argument becomes decisive the other way.

Towards the end of the preamble, Archbishop Parker had to make another slight change (possibly by Cecil's direction) before his 1566 copies were printed. In the MS. of 1565 the words stand,—

"Not yet prescribing these rules as laws equivalent with the eternal word of God . . . but as *constitutions*, meere ecclesiastical, without any vain superstition; *as positive laws in* discipline, concerning decency, distinction, and order for the time."

These words were of too legislative a character for an Archbishop to use, so before they passed into print in 1566 they became,—

"Not yet prescribing these rules as laws as equivalent with the eternal word of God . . . but as *temporall orders*, mere ecclesiastical, without any vain superstition; and as *rules in some part of* discipline, concerning decency, distinction, and order for the time[d]."

In the original MS. copy of 1565, too, it was ordered that the Articles agreed on at the last Convocation should stand in full strength, and that every parson and preacher should read the book of Articles and also a certain Declaration. All these three clauses were struck out before they came to be printed, as they were beyond the power of the Archbishop to order.

Next, I would call attention to a very small change, but it has a great deal of meaning; indeed, it is as important as the change in the title itself. In the sixth Article, in the MS. of 1565, the words run,—

[c] See *ante*, pp. 14–17, especially with reference to δ, ε, ζ, η, θ.

[d] For the context of these extracts, see *ante*, p. 13.

"And that all licences to preach graunted before the first day of March, 1564, to be voyde, **and such as shal be new admytted,**" &c.

Here the Archbishop **was** interfering with what did not come within his jurisdiction. He could not order anything respecting **the licences in** the Province of York, and so we find when **the** Advertisements came to be printed that the clause [e] runs,—

"Item, that all licenses for preaching granted out by the Archebyshop and byshopes *within the province of Canterbury*, bearing date before the first day of March, M.D.LXIV., be voyde, and of none effect; and nevertheless, all such, as shalbe," &c.

It is a very slight change, but very expressive, and it is to be remembered that it is in this edition—not in the former MS.—that your Lordship bids us to look for her Majesty's "other order." So that the argument derived from the comparison of the two, on your Lordship's assumption of the Advertisements being 'other order,' would run thus: in their former state, when they were practically addressed to the Church at large, they were not authorized by the Queen: but when addressed to the Province of Canterbury, then, and not *till then*, did her Majesty the Queen condescend to make that "other order" in accordance with the clause of the Act of Uniformity. Such is the result of the argument used by your Lordship, and found more fully expanded in the Ridsdale Judgement!

It would be beside the purpose to go through all the variations. Some are simply variations of wording, others are the addition of *authorities*, e.g. the "Table of degrees set forth by the Archbishop," referred to in the MS. of 1565, becomes in the printed copy of 1566, "... by the Archbishop, Anno Domini MDLXIII." In the rule respecting Deans, Doctors of Divinity, &c., "to wear a typet of silke" in the MS. of 1565, becomes in the printed copies of 1566 "to wear typpets of sarcenet, as is lawfull for them by thAct of Parliament, anno xxiv. Hen. Octavi." There are also some clauses omitted, which touched upon questions beyond the Archbishop's jurisdiction.

[e] Already referred to. See p. 22.

From the comparison of the MS. of 1565 with the edition of 1566, which has somewhat broken the sequence of events, I now return to the history.

The last letter quoted was that of the 7th of April, 1565. I do not find any reference to the Advertisements, or to matters directly connected with them which bear upon the argument, till March 12, 1566, and at this date I find Archbishop Parker still fuming, if I may use the expression, at his failure in enforcing discipline. Apart from the evidence which it affords of the little progress which he had made with respect to obtaining obedience to the Queen's commands, the letter provides some valuable information upon the object which the Archbishop had in view in drawing-up the Advertisements. I have italicised one or two passages (as I have done throughout these letters) for calling attention to such as bear on the questions at issue. The letter [f], as usual, is addressed to Sir William Cecil :—

"Sir,—I am moche astonyed, and in grete perplexitie to thinke what event this cause wil have in the proceding to an ende. **Where I have endevored** myself to enforce the Q[ueen's] Ma[ties] pleasure upon all my bretherne, and have desired that others shulde not hinder such procedinges bi secret aydyng **and** comforting, I see my service but defeated ; and then agayne otherwhiles dulled by variable considerations of the state of tymes, and of doutfulnes in discoraging som good protestantes yf this order shuld be vehemently prosquuted. *I have stayed upon such* **advertisements** *;* but I alwaye perceyved moche hurt might com of such tolerations (the partyes hardened in ther di*s*obedience) ; and at the last the Q[ueen's] M[ties] displeasure, to see howe hir commandement take little effect, where yet order for all other men's apparell, and Laws for abstinence, so moche forced and wel set to, maye induce an obedience, howsoever **a** grete nombre may be offended ; and therfor thei who thinke **that** di*s*ordre of o[r] state wer as sone reformed yf we had like helps, seame to me to speke reasonably [g].

"I have wryten to the Q[ueen's] M[tie], as youe **see. I praye** yo[r] honor use yo[r] opportunytie. And where onys this last yere CERTEN OF US consulted & agreed *upon som particularyties in apparell* [= to the last division of the

---

[f] From the Lansdowne MSS., viii. art. 83. Parker Correspondence, p. 262.

[g] This proclamation by the Queen, against the excess of apparel, was dated Oct. 21, 1559. The Act referred to is, 5 El. cap. 5, passed 1562, sections 14—23. The disorder of "our state" refers to the want of order in apparel amongst ecclesiastical persons.

Advertisements] (*wher the Q[ueen's] M^tie^ lettres* [i.e. of Jan. 25, 1565] *wer very genral*), and for that bi statute *we be inhibited* to set out any constitutions w^t^hout lycence obteyned of the prince, *I sent them to y*o^r^ *honor to be presented* [i.e. Mar. 4, 1565]; thei could not be alowed *then*, I cannot tell of what meaninge; wch I nowe send *agayn*, humbly prayeng that yf not all *yet so many as be thought good*, maye be retorned wth som authorytie, at the lest waye for *particular apparell:* or elles we shal not be able to do so moche as the Q[ueen's] Matie expecteth for, of us to be done," ...

On March 20, 1566, Archbishop Parker and Bishop Grindal (of London) join together in a letter [h] to Cecil, and they propose a plan of proceeding to enforce the "apparel." They wrote—

"After our ryht hertie Commendacions to your honour. This is to signyfie that we have consulted howe to procede, wherby we may have yor allowance or dysallowance. We have conferred withe some learned in the lawe, in what degrees to treate this matter.

"1. First, we meane to caule all manner of pasto^rs^ and Curats w^t^hin the Citie of London, to appear before us at Lambith in the Chapell there, and to propounde the cause, and saie somethinge to move them to conformitie, with intimacion of the penalty whiche necessarilye must ensue against the recusants.

"2. Item, after the generall propositions made (as afore) to the whole number, we entende particulerly to examyne every of them, whether they will promyse *conformytie in there* [a] *mynistracions* and [b] *outwarde apparell, stablyshed by lawe and Iniunction*, and testyfie the same by subscripcions of there handes.

"3. Item, it is entended presently to suspende all suche as refuse to promyse conformytie in the premyses; And also to pronounce sequestracion of their Ecclesiasticall livings from after the daie of our Ladie next, beinge nowe at hande. And after suche sequestracion, yf they be not reconciled w^t^hin three monethes, to procede to deprivacion of their lyvinges by due forme of lawe.

"4. Item, we may make an infymacion for the Sarcenet typpet, to suche as may were yt by act of Parlyament, anno 24 H. 8, and to none other, yf this shalbe thought good.

"5. In fine, we think verie many Churches wilbe destitute for Service this Easter, and that many will forsake there lyvinges, and lyve at prynting, teaching Children, or otherwise as they can.

"What tumult may follow, what speaches and talkes be like to rise in the realme, and presently in the whole Citie by this: we leave it to y^r^ wysdom to consider. We trust that the Quenes Matie will sende some Honourable to joyne w^t^hus two, to authorize the rather her commandement and pleasure, as yor honor signified unto me was purposed. And thus, praienge y^r^ H^r^ to

[h] From the original, with the actual signatures, preserved amongst the Lansdowne MSS., viii. art. 86. Printed in Parker Correspondence, p. 267.

consult wth whome yo[r] wysdome shall think most meet, that we may be resolvid ; and that on Fridaie, the parties summoned for there apperance on Saterdaie followenge at one of the clocke, order may be taken. Or els after those two holy daies [Sunday, March 24, and Lady-Day, March 25] on Tuesdaie at afternoone, at the furthest. And thus we byd yo[r] H[onour] well to fare, from my house at Lambith, the xxth of Marche, 1565.

"Your loving friends,
"Matthue Cantuar.
"Edm. London."

I have printed the above because it appears to carry on the history of the Advertisements, and to shew how the Archbishop proceeded to enforce uniformity *on his own authority.* By the clergy promising "conformity in their ministrations and outward apparel," is meant their agreeing to obey that "interpretation" of the stablished law and Injunctions which the Archbishop had set out in these Advertisements.

And now I reach the letters of March 28, 1566, two of which are laid stress upon by your Lordship (p. 16) as shewing the date when the Advertisements were first printed and issued.

The first letter[1], addressed to Sir William Cecil, runs thus :—

"I praye yo[r] honor to peruse this draught of letters, and the boke of advertisments wth your pen, w[ch] I mean to send to my Lord of London. *This form is but nuly prynted*, and yet stayed tyl I maye heare your advise. *I am nowe* fully bent to prosequute this order, and to delaye no longer, and I have *weded out* of these articles all such of doctryne, &c., w[ch] peradventure stayed the boke from the Q[ueen's] Ma[ties] approbation, AND HAVE PUT IN BUT THINGES ADVOUCHEABLE, AND, AS I TAKE THEM, AGAYNST NO LAWE OF THE REALME.

"And wher[eas] the Q[ueen's] Highnes will nedes have me assaye WITH MINE OWN AUTORYTIE what I can do for order, I trust I shal not be steyed herafter, saving that I wolde pray yo[r] h[onour] to have yo[r] advice to do that more prudently in this comon cause which must nedes be done.

. From my house at Lambith, this xxviijth of Marche, 1566.

"Your h[onour's] assueredly,
"Matthue Cantuar."

Nothing can be more important than these words, when we compare the first draft with the second. It is argued by your

---

[1] From the Lansdowne MSS., ix. art. 36. Printed in Parker Correspondence, p. 271.

Lordship that Queen Elizabeth "took *other* order" than the law of the realm (i.e. 1 Eliz. cap. ii. § 25) in these very Advertisements, in which Archbishop Parker so distinctly states he has inserted nothing *against the law* of the realm. How can it be so? Was Archbishop Parker entirely ignorant of what he was doing, and Queen Elizabeth equally ignorant of what he had done? Some such solution, my Lord, it appears to me, is absolutely necessary, to reconcile your Lordship's view with the evidence which I have adduced.

Your Lordship does not, in referring to these letters, notice these points, but in the Ridsdale JUDGEMENT, not only is the letter quoted, but there is what I must call the following remarkable comment [k]:—

"They could only be 'against no law of the realm' if they were issued by the Queen's authority. For what purpose were they sent to Cecil, except to obtain that authority for their promulgation in the form and manner proposed?"

I confess I cannot discover in the least what their Lordships mean. How can the fact of Archbishop Parker's putting into his book things "against no law of the realm" prove that they — i.e. his Advertisements — were, either before or afterwards, issued by the Queen's authority? If they *had been* so issued, i.e. before March 28, why is Parker sending them to Cecil *now* to "peruse them with his pen?" Perusing [l] with the pen, I take it, would mean that he was to strike out what he did not approve; and if so, how is this to be reconciled with their being already the Queen's orders. If they were to be authorized by the Queen afterwards, it surely could not have been worth Archbishop Parker's while to select only what was already authorized. Either reasoning is beyond me, and yet some explanation is needed.

---

[k] Ridsdale Judgement, official copy, p. 12.

[l] So in the preparation of the Queen's letters for the preservation of ancient writings, July 4, 1568, Abp. Parker writes to Sir William Cecil, "I pray your honour to *peruse* and correct these letters." S. P. O. Dom. Eliz., Parker Correspondence, p. 327.

The plain and obvious meaning, I contend, **is** simply this : The Archbishop, having failed **to** obtain the **Queen's approba-**tion of his Advertisements (or perhaps, to speak more accurately, her Secretary's approbation) in the form in which he had originally drafted them, had now altered them. Matters were **in** them before which touched doctrine, &c., **and,** as we have seen, details which were **not within the power of the** Archbishop to order ; but **he had struck out** *everything which was against the law of the realm.* **He therefore hopes the** Queen will not object to his **issuing his Advertisements,** *because* there is now nothing in **them against the** law of the **realm,** i.e. he had authority for every clause ; some were based upon rubricks, others upon **the Injunctions of 1559 ;** one upon the Queen's "further order" of 1561, **and the like, all of which were** established by law, either by Act of **Parliament or by the Queen's** authority. But mark, besides this, **he was to essay** *on his own authority,* and not on the Queen's.

The next letter appears to me **to** be equally decisive as to the nature of the Advertisements, and this the Committee of the **Privy** Council **in the** Ridsdale Judgement omits to notice, while your **Lordship only refers to** it incidentally.

The letter [m] to Bishop Grindal runs thus, so far as it relates to the Advertisements :—

> " Right welbeloved Brother, After my Right hartie commendacions in **our** Savio[r] **Christe.** Whereas you do well knowe what offence is taken, for that diverse and sundrie **of** the state ecclesiasticall be so hardely induced **to** conformitie in *administracion* of publique prayers and Sacraments, and **in** outward *apparel* agreable, in regarde of ordre, for them to weare, notwithstandinge established and other orders and ordinances prescribed in the same ; **in** whiche disorder appeareth (as is commonly interpreted) a manifest violacion *and contempt of the Quenes Ma[jes][ties] authoritie,* and abusinge her princely clemencie, in so longe bering w[th] the same w[t]hout execucion of condigne **severitie** for there due correction, **yf** the Lawes were extended uppon them ; and **whereas** the whole state of the Realme, by Acte of Parliament openly **published, dothe most** earnestly in goddes name requier us all to endever **our selves, to the uttermost** of our knowledge, duely and truly to execute *the*

[m] From Parker's Register at Lambeth, into which it has **been copied,** vol. i. fol. 256 b. Printed **in** Parker Correspondence, p. 272.

said Laws, as we will answer before god. By the wh^{ch} Acte also wee have full powre and authoritie to reforme, and punishe by censures of the churche, all and singuler persons wh^{ch} shall offende.

"And whereas also the Quenes most excellent Matie, *now a yere past* and more, addressed her highnes Lettres enforcinge the same charge, the contents whereof I sent unto your L[ordship] *in her name and authorite*, to admonishe them to obedience, and so I dowt not but your L[ordship] have distributed the same unto others of oure Bretherne w^thin this Province of Canterbury; whereuppon hath ensued in the most parte of the Realme an humble and obedient confirmitie, and yet some fewe persons, I feare more scrupulous then godly prudent, have not conformed them selves; peradventure some of them *for lacke of particuler description* of orders to be followed, which as your L[ordship] dothe knowe, were agreed upon *amonge us* Long agoe, and yet in certeyne respects *not publisshed*.

"Nowe for the spedie reformacion of the same, as the Quenes Highnes hath expresselye charged bothe youe and me, of Late beinge therefore *cauled to her presence*, to see her Lawes executed, and good orders decreed and observed, I can no less do of my obedience to Almyghtie Gode, of my alleageance to her princely estate, and of syncere zele to the truthe and promocion of Christian Religion nowe establisshed. But require and charge you, as you will answere to god, and to her maestie, *to see her* Ma[jes]ty's *Laws and injunctions* duely observid w^thin your dioc[ese]: *and also theis* OUR CONVENIENT ORDERS *described in theis Books at this presente sent unto your* L[ordship]. And furthermore, to transmite the same *books* wth your Lettres (according as hath been heretofore used) unto all others of our brethren within this province, to cause the same to be performid in their severall Jurisdictions and charges."

In the second letter, then, written also on March 28, 1566, addressed by Archbishop Parker to the Bishop of London (apparently without waiting for Cecil's answer), we gain a still further insight into the history of the issue of the Advertisements. In substance it runs as follows, since for convenience I again attempt an abstract:—

"You know what offence is taken by the disregard paid to conformity in ritual and outward apparel, so that there has been an absolute contempt for her Majesty's authority. You know also that we Bishops were required by Act of Parliament, duly to execute the said laws ourselves; and by the same Act we have authority to punish others for not obeying the laws.

"Now as the Queen herself wrote letters to me a year ago

[Jan. 25, 1565], which I duly forwarded to you in her name and authority[n] [Jan. 30, 1565], to admonish obedience to those laws, I have no doubt you duly distributed them. Much conformity has ensued, but still some persons, more scrupulous than godly-prudent, have not conformed: of these, some, perhaps, because they did not know exactly what was to be followed: and because of this, as you may remember, we drew up and agreed upon a summary of these laws[o] [i.e. the first draft of the Advertisements], which, however, we have never published. But the Queen has again of late charged us, 'being called to her presence,' to see her laws executed, and good orders [in accordance with these laws] decreed and observed. I therefore cannot do less than charge you to see her Majesty's laws and her Injunctions duly observed, and [in order to effect this] MY CONVENIENT ORDERS described in these books sent herewith [and entitled Advertisements, partly for due order in ritual, partly in apparel]."

A third letter was also written on this memorable March 28, 1566, and I beg to call your Lordship's especial attention to it, as it is not even mentioned, directly or indirectly, either by your Lordship, or the Judges in the Ridsdale case; but from the clear way in which it narrates, so to speak, the circumstances of *the publication*, it will be found as important as any which precede it. So far as I know, it has never been printed.

The side-note runs:—

"A copie of my L[ord] grace his L[et]tres written to Mr. D[r]. Cole, Deane of Bockinge."

The letter[p] runs as follows:—

"I commende me hartely unto you, And whereas I am informid that diuerse parsons, vicares and curats, w[t]hin my peculiar Jurisdiction of the deanrie of Bockinge (beinge as I feare more scrupulouse then godly prudente) have not conformed them selves to the Quenes Mat[ies] Lawes and Injunctions in *thadministracion* of publike prayers and Sacraments, and in outwarde *apparell* agreable in Regarde of order for them to weare, notwithstanding the said

[n] See *ante*, p. 34.   [o] See *ante*, p. 35.   [p] From Parker's Register at Lambeth, vol. i. fol. 257.

Lawes iniunctions and ordinances prescribed *for the same*. In which disorder appeareth (as yt ys commonly interpreted) a manifest violation and contempte of the Quenes Mat^ie authoritie and abusinge her princely clemencye in so longe bearinge wth the same w^thowte execution of condigne severitie for there due correction, yf the Lawes weare extended uppon them. I have sente you herewith *a booke of certeine orders agreed uppon* BY ME AND OTHER OF MY BRETHERNE OF MY PROVINCE OF CANTURBURIE, and hitherto *not published*, wyllinge and requiringe you wth all spede to call before you all and singler the parsons vicars and curats of my said peculier Jurisdiction of Bockinge, *to publishe* to them the said orders prescribed *in this boke*, and also to move persuade and commaunde them and euery of them as they will answer at there peril, duely to observe as well her Maties said Lawes and iniunctions in thadministracion of publique prayer and the Sacramentes and in there externe apparell, *as also* these orders sente unto you herewith, and such as will obstinately refuse to conforme themselves to the said Lawes iniunctions and orders that you do forthwith suspende them and euerie of them from there publique ministracions whatsoever, and also do sequester all the fructe of there benefice, &c.

"From my manno^r of Lambehethe this xxviij of March 1566."

We then have in the Register the following notes, written at the end in the same hand :—

"A like letter was written to Mr. Denne, Commissarie of Canturbery.

"Another like Letter to the Busshoppe of Chichester, Commissarie of the peculiar jurisdiction of Sowth Mallinge Pagh[a]m and Terringe.

"An other like letter to M^r. Doct^r. Weston, Dean of Tharches, Shoreh[a]m and Croyden, with severall *bookes above mentioned inclosed* severally in the same L[ett]res."

Here, then, we may be said to have the proof of the actual *publication* of the Advertisements, and the date of such publication; and after what I have said of the previous letter, it will be scarcely necessary to do more than to draw attention to the repetition of the orders in the Queen's letter, for enforcement of conformity in (*a*) *ministration*, and (*b*) *apparel;* and that it is with a view of obtaining conformity to her Majesty's existing laws, that he sends the "book of certain orders," which he says were agreed upon "*by me* and others of my *Province of Canterbury.*"

There is here no reference whatever to the Queen's authority in the Advertisements. He sends "*his* orders," and he desires obedience to them, because their purport is to enforce the Queen's established laws, **injunctions,** and ordinances, **and not to** take new or other orders.

Did the Queen ever go so far as even to sanction their issue? Possibly she **did**; but the **evidence** mainly rests upon the **two** **or** three words in the Archbishop's letter to the Bishop **of** London, viz. "hath charged us, *being called to her presence*, **to see** *her laws executed*." While, on the other hand, it is difficult to reconcile such a circumstance **with** the tenor of the Archbishop's letter to Cecil written the very same day.

I have little doubt **but that** the Queen was advised, with respect to what she did, by Cecil: he *might* have assured **her, as** the Archbishop had assured him when he requested **Cecil** to submit them, that the book contained no *new or other* **orders,** but only a repetition of such of the **laws,** derived from rubrics **and** such previous Injunctions, as were found to be most **in** abeyance. Then it was, and then only, she *might* have expressed, at the interview to which he refers, her satisfaction **with** what he proposed to do. But of this, as is said, the evidence is of the very slightest description. It is not at all certain that he ever shewed the book to her Majesty, but it is clear that she gave no formal assent in writing, or by attachment of signature, to any such document or book. It was *at most* her sanction, verbally given, to the Archbishop issuing *his own* Advertisements, as his letter to Cecil proves, when he writes, "the Queen would have me *assaye with mine own autorytie*."

Then, comes the question; Could this in any way **be a taking** "other order" **by** the Queen within the meaning of the Act?

Surely a verbal sanction (*supposing* such was given) **to** proceedings taken by her Archbishop, in order to carrying out **her** Majesty's *existing* Injunctions and the Parliament's enactments, cannot be reasonably construed into the Queen *herself* taking *other* orders. And further, it appears to me, that to say this **was the manner** which **Queen Elizabeth** chose for taking "**other order**" is little short **of a charge** against her of carelessness **in** conducting **the business of the realm;** nor is it **less a charge** against her **council of** culpable neglect, in permitting such a strange proceeding in so important a **matter,** especially, **as** in a previous taking of order, the utmost **formality** had been exercised in every detail.

I have said nothing upon the *à priori* improbability of Elizabeth **having** taken "other order" on this special subject. **It is not as if** history was silent upon her views on ritual; and to suppose **that** she would do this, unless very evident motives were **recorded, or** could be suggested, would be to ignore that history, **or, to** use your Lordship's own words (p. 4), "relevant facts." Nor is there again, from the mass of correspondence which we possess of Archbishop **Parker** (though it is much scattered), the slightest **ground for** supposing that he would have wished the change **to have been made** himself, **or** ventured **to** suggest it **to the Queen.** In the many private communications to the **Queen's** Secretary, **some** word here or there must have been dropped, pointing **in the direction of some** change being needed, or thought good, if it had **been so.**

The Advertisements themselves **we see** were not ordered, signed, nor even authorized by **the Queen**; and no words in them, as shewn in the previous chapter, involve **any** "other **order."** The theory of "other order" being taken **rests,** therefore, **upon a** "gratuitous" conjecture of a direct though unrecorded sanction given by the Queen to the issue of the Advertisements, combined with a "gratuitous" insertion of the word "only" in a **particular place** (as shewn in the previous chapter), and one inconsistent with the context.

I have now completed the evidence **as to** the object of **the** Advertisements **of** 1566, so **far as it** may be derived, firstly, from a consideration of the nature and contents of the document itself; and secondly, from the circumstances attending its origin, composition, correction, and publication.

V. THE LIGHT IN WHICH THE ADVERTISEMENTS WERE REGARDED, AS SHEWN BY OFFICIAL DOCUMENTS, 1566—1576.

I have still to deal with a large mass of evidence, relating to the way in which the Advertisements were regarded *in after years*. In the Ridsdale Judgement, I find that it is chiefly derived from Visitation Articles, and such-like official documents, which are adduced to shew the way in which Bishops quoted and made use of the Advertisements; in your own NOTES, my Lord, I find that the evidence is partly derived from incidental mention of the Advertisements in private correspondence, and partly from what historical writers thought of them. The first division is the most important, and to that evidence I now turn.

Although I cannot in the space of a pamphlet, and could not perhaps, even in a volume, deal thoroughly with this extent of circumstantial evidence, I propose again to attempt, as I did in the last section, to draw rough outlines of the main features. Incidentally, however, I propose here and there to pass in review some of the evidence adduced by your Lordship in the NOTES, and by others (with your Lordship) in the Ridsdale JUDGEMENT; and to point out what a different aspect such evidence presents when viewed in relation with other circumstances, than when isolated, or with interpretations put upon it which only that isolation would sanction.

The history of the actual growth and issue of the Advertisements closes with the letter of the 28th of March, 1566, when Archbishop Parker sent the printed copies to Edmund Grindal, Bishop of London.

First, as to the judicial proceedings resulting from the issue of these Advertisements. Neither in your Lordship's "NOTES," nor in the Ridsdale Judgement, are any cases referred to specially of prosecutions for wearing, or for not wearing, the Cope. I will not stop now to speak of the value of this negative evidence,—I presume, of course, that such reports of proceedings in ecclesiastical courts as we possess, have been duly searched; that what we have preserved to us are sufficient to serve as types of the rest; and that they go to prove there were *no proceedings* taken either way.

But I may note here the result of Archbishop Parker's and Bishop Grindal's proceedings of March 20 already referred to [q]. The day fixed for the ministers to promise conformity, in (*a*) "their ministrations, and (*b*) outward apparell stablished by law and injunction," was March 25, 1566.

On March 26, the day after, Archbishop Parker writes to Cecil as follows [r]:—

"Sir,—I must signifie to yo[r] honor what this daye we have done in the examination of London ministres. lxi promysed conformytie; ix or x were absent; xxxvii denyed, of wh[ch] nombre were the beste, and som preachers; vi or vii convenyent sober men, pretending a conscyence, dyverse of them but zelous, and of litle lerning and jugement. In fine, we dyd suspend them, and sequester ther frutys, and from all man[ner] mynisetrye, with signification that yf thei wold not reconcile them selfs w[th]in iij monethes, than to be deprived. They shewed reasonable qyetnes and modesty, otherwise than I loked for. I thinke som of them wil com in when thei shall feale ther want; specially such as but in a spiced fancie holde out; som of them no dout wer moved in a conscyence, wh[ch] I labored by some advertisements to pacifie, but the wound is yet grene; it is not felt as I think it wil hereafter.". . . .

Your Lordship may perhaps take exception to this being produced as the result of enforcement of the Advertisements, on the ground that the proceedings were not taken under them, since the Queen had not authorized them before March 20, when the proceedings were commenced. On the other hand, it will be observed that it was on the question of (*a*) ministration, and (*b*) apparel, the chief subjects of the Advertisements, and precisely the subjects on which, in order to obtain uniformity, the Advertisements were issued. Your Lordship so carefully avoids giving any date for the "taking of the further order," that I cannot tell what view your Lordship would

---

[q] See *ante*, p. 44.
[r] From the Lansdowne MSS., ix. art. 35. Printed in Parker Correspondence, p. 269.

hold on this question. All I find stated by your **Lordship** in
the NOTES is, that the Advertisements were *issued* **soon after**[*]
March 28, 1566 (p. 13), and they were not printed before **1566**
(p. 16). The nearest evidence of date I get in the JUDGEMENT
is, that "immediately after their **issue, an** event happened,
which event **takes** place **on May 21**, 1556;" this is, perhaps,
a little vaguer still. But **these vague dates of issue** tell nothing
of the date when "**the order was** taken;" yet I submit, my
Lord, that in **such a matter there must be a date when the** one
law ceased and the "**other**" began, and that that date ought
to be shewn. This passage **is important, then, as shewing the
action of the Archbishop of** Canterbury **and the Bishop of
London in dealing with the** questions touched **on by the Advertisements, at the very time when the laws on the subject**, according to your Lordship's view (not according to **mine), were
in** a process of change, **as** "other" or "further **order**" undoubtedly implies. The dilemma, however, is **this.** If they became the law *after* March **20, what need of them, when uni-**
formity was being enforced **without them?** if *before*, why are
the ministers not required to promise **conformity in** their ministrations and outward apparel "according to the new order taken
in the Advertisements," **instead** of that "**stablished by** law and
injunction?" There are many other difficulties which will
strike some perhaps in reading these letters, but this represents,
I think, the chief dilemma which **your** Lordship's theory **of the**
Advertisements involves.

I observe your Lordship puts in the forefront of the *Official*
testimony (with which **I am** now dealing) Bishop Grindal's letters
mandatory, as Bishop of London, to the **Dean and Chapter of**
St. Paul's, dated May 21, **1566** ("NOTES," p. 24), a complete
copy of which is printed in your Appendix (p. 74).

Before I quote this passage, **let me observe** that the question
at **issue is not so** much the abstract *question* of authority, as the
nature of the *authority*[†] of these Advertisements. What was

---

[*] I have shewn that they were issued on Mar. **28.** See p. **50.**   [†] See *ante*, p. 47.

their inherent force? I hold that it lay in the "established" laws and injunctions, of which they were only a repetition, or at the very most an explanation. Now Bishop Grindal's letter[u] in no way militates against this; on the contrary, he especially avoids saying the Advertisements are ordained by the "Queen's Majesties authority." What it says is,—

"After my hartie commendacyons, these are to require.... that you enjoyne everie [minister, &c.] upon payne of deprivacion to prepare forthw[th] and to weare *such* habitt and *apparell as is ordeyned by the Queenes Maiesties authoritie*, EXPRESSED in the treaty intituled the advertisem[ts], &c., which I send heerein inclosed unto yo[u], and in like to inioyne every of them under the said payne of deprivacion as well to observe the order of [a] mynistracion in the Church w[th] *surples*, and in such forme as is sett forth in the saide treatie, as alsoe to require the subscription of every of them to the said Advertism[nts]....

"from my House in London this xxi[th] of Maie 1566.

"Yo[rs] in Christ,
"EDM. LONDON.

" Indorsed to the right worshippful the Deane and Chapter of Powles (give theise)."

It is clear that it is "the habit and apparel" which "are ordeyned by the Queen's Majesties Authoritie;" and the ministers are to wear them, *as expressed*, that is, set forth and explained, in the book of Advertisements, which was sent with the letters, so that there might be no misunderstanding.

It will be remembered, as I have already[x] pointed out, that the Injunctions had ordered "that ministers and members of the University," or of other learned bodies, should "use and wear such seemly habits, garments, and such square caps" as were commonly received in the reign of Edward VI.; while the Advertisements give some *detailed* account of what these were, specifying what doctors should wear, and what other superior ecclesiastical persons should wear in their journeying, i.e.—

[u] State Papers, Domestic, Elizabeth, vol. xxxix. No. 76. The document itself is a clerk's copy, not in the Bishop's handwriting. The signature, however, is similar to his signature. The words "Indorsed to the," &c., are written at the foot of the page.

In all probability, it was the official copy filed by the Bishop for judicial purposes.

The "docket" date on the back is misleading, as it refers to the first of the three letters folded up together, one of which was Sept. 31, 1561.

[x] See *ante*, p. 21.

"Theire clokes with sleeves put on, and lyke in fashion to their gounes without gards, welts or cuts."

Hence, while obedience to the law is enjoyned on the ground of her "*Majesties Authority*," the direct reference is given to where that law can be found "*expressed*," namely, to the Advertisements.

The paragraph, when read with the history, amounts only to a further illustration of what I have already insisted on, namely, that the Queen had required a general conformity to the Rubrick and Injunctions, &c.; while the Archbishop of Canterbury, with some Bishops of his province, had chosen from them certain orders "which they had thought most *meet* and *convenient* to be followed^y, and these they had *expressed* in the Advertisements. It will be noted that they put outward "apparel" first, as the most important; but to this point I have to refer presently.

As in a previous case, however, your Lordship's caution in pointing out in so many words the implied drift of the passages quoted, seems not to be shared by the Judges in the Ridsdale case. They state what interpretation they put upon the clause, but, I venture to submit, somewhat rashly^z. They say:—

"Immediately after their issue, on the 21st of May, 1566, Grindal, Bishop of London, writes to the Dean of St. Paul's, requiring him to put them in force; and *stating* that THEY WERE ISSUED BY THE QUEEN'S AUTHORITY, and that he (Grindal) would proceed to deprive any who should disobey them."

The statement that the habit and apparel were ordained by the Queen's Majesty's authority (i.e. in the Injunctions of 1559), is perverted into the statement that the "Advertisements" were " ordeyned by the Queen's Majesty's authority," which is a very different assertion, and one wholly unwarranted.

It is obvious that the most important document towards the interpretation of these Advertisements of 1566, would be Archbishop Parker's first series of Visitation Articles, issued after

---

^y See p. 13, paragraph (*t*).   ^z Ridsdale Judgement, official copy, p. 9.

them; and it so happens the Archbishop held a Metropolitan Visitation the following year, 1567. To this, neither your Lordship, nor the Judges of the Privy Council, make the slightest reference whatever, although the Articles are duly printed in Dr. Cardwell's volume [a]. But the importance of the negative evidence to be deduced from these is very great.

The questions he asks are:—

"I. .... Whether they use **semely or** priestly garments, according as they are commanded by the *quenes majesties* INJUNCTIONS to **doe?**"

"III. Whether your divine service be used, and your sacraments **ministred** in manner and forme **prescribed by the** *quenes majesties* INJUNCTIONS, **and none** other way? whether it be said or songe in due time? whether in al points according to the statutes of your church, not being repugnant to any of the *quenes majesties* LAWS *or* INJUNCTIONS?"

Although referring to precisely the cases on which the Advertisements touch, he does not name them as enforcing the obedience to his monitions, but if they had the Queen's authority, he *would* naturally have done so: if they contained "other order," he *must* have done so.

Passing over the Visitation Articles of 1567, their Lordships, in their process of selection, fasten upon a line of Archbishop Parker's Articles in his ordinary Diocesan Visitation of 1569; while your Lordship makes a still greater jump (p. 24) to those of Archbishop Whitgift, of 1583, to find something which may tend to support the idea of the Queen's authority being given to the Advertisements.

And first, as to the Articles issued by Archbishop **Parker** 1569. The words of the JUDGEMENT are [b]:—

"The Articles of Archbishop Parker speak of them as Advertisements set forth by *public authority* [c]."

The Judges very distinctly imply—following, as the passage does, another relating to the taking of order by the Queen—that

---

[a] Cardwell, Documentary Annals, No. lxviii. vol. i. p. 337. Also printed in Strype's Life of Parker, Appendix, No. LIII.

[b] Ridsdale Judgement, official copy, p. 9.

[c] The reference to this is 1 Card. Doc. An. 320, which in the edition of 1839 I find refers to—

"Articles to be enquired of within the Diocese of Canterbury, in the ordinarie visitation, &c. ... MDLXIX."

the expression, "*public authority*," necessarily involves "the *Queen's* authority." When, however, the words on which they rely are read *with their context*, it will be seen a different meaning belongs to them. The words and context are as follow :—

"Imprimis whether divine service be sayde or songe by youre minister or ministers in your severall churches duely and reverently as it is set forth *by the laws of this realme* without any kinde of variations.

"And whether the holy Sacramentes be likewise ministred reverently in such manner as [a] by *the lawes of this* realm, and [b] by the *Queen's Majesties injunctions*, and [c] by *thadvertisements* set forthe by *publike authority*, is appointed and prescribed."

Hence there appears to be a distinction drawn between the Injunctions issued "by the Queen," and the Advertisements issued "by publique authority." It is the more difficult to account for the Judges isolating the six words from the rest of the paragraph, which gives so different a colour to them, when it is remembered that Dr. Cardwell, to whose book such frequent references are made in the NOTES, and several also in the JUDGEMENT, thus lays stress upon the passage: in describing the Advertisements, he says [d],—

"Their title and preface certainly do not claim for them the highest degree of authority; and although Strype inferred from certain evidence which he mentions, that they afterwards received the royal sanction, and recovered their original title of Articles and ordinances, it seems more probable that they owed their force to the indefinite nature of episcopal jurisdiction, supported, as in this instance was known to be the case, by the personal approval of the sovereign. The way in which the Archbishop speaks of them in his Articles of enquiry, issued in the year 1569, certainly assigns to them '*public authority*,'' but clearly distinct from *that of the Crown;* and in the year 1584, Archbishop Whitgift refers to them as having authority, but still calls them simply the book of Advertisements."

I call attention to the passage quoted in the Ridsdale JUDGEMENT for another reason. No mention is there made, either in text or note, as to the date of the "Articles" in question, though a large number were issued by the Archbishop: the only reference is to Cardwell's "Documentary Annals," but

---

[d] Cardwell's Documentary Annals, note, p. 321.

the page is that of an *old* edition[e], though a little further on the references are to the 1844 edition[f]. So that the note gave me, as it might others, a good deal of trouble before getting at the rights of the case, and the real import of the passage.

Later on in the same series of Articles of 1569, we find the distinction of the two authorities made still clearer:—

"XVI. Item, Whether there be in your quarters any . . . that speake to the derogation of the *queen's majesties aucthority* and power, or of the lawes set out by *publike aucthority*."

It surely is perfectly clear from such a passage that the "publique authority" is precisely other than the Queen's authority. And the words on which the Judges rely, so far from proving that Articles issued under publique authority were *therefore* issued by the Queen, prove, if anything, exactly the reverse, viz. that they were *not*.

If we look still a little further in these Articles, we find several questions asked with reference to the Queen's Injunctions. The Advertisements are only once mentioned, and that incidentally:—

"II. A comely and decent table for the holy Communion, covered decently, and set in place prescribed by the *quene's majesties* injunctions[g]."

"III. Whether youre prestes, curates, or ministers, do use, in the time of the celebration of Divine Service, to weare a surples prescribed by the *quenes majesties injunctions*, and the boke of Common Prayer[h]."

---

[e] The first edition of Cardwell's Annals bears date 1839, the second, 1844.

[f] There are in the Ridsdale Judgement six references to Cardwell's Annals. The first to 1839 ed., the next two to the 1844 ed., then one with a wrong reference altogether, and then two more to 1839 ed. All your Lordship's references, I observe, are to the 1844 edition, and to this edition I have myself referred throughout what I have written.

[g] See Injunctions "for Tables in Churches," Cardwell, Documentary Annals, vol. i. p. 234.

[h] This reference to the Injunctions *as well* as to the Book of Common Prayer (unless an error on Archbishop Parker's part), affords *à priori* evidence that the "Interpretations and further Considerations" were considered by him as part of the Injunctions. For the Injunctions themselves contain no reference to the Surplice, the Considerations do. The same formula occurs in his Articles of Enquiry as early as 1563.

"IV. Whether your Curates ... do ... reade in manner appointed (*a*) the *quene's majesties* injunctions¹, (*b*) and homelies ; (*c*) the *Advertisementes* lately sette forthe by '*publique authoritie.*'"

"V. Whether they do use to minister the holye Communion in Waferbread, according to the *quenes majesties* injunctions ᵏ, or els in common bread."

"VIII. Whether they ... releave the poore charitably ... according to the *queen's* injunctions ˡ."

"Whether they pray for the prosperous estate of the Queenes Majestye, as is prescribed in her *graces* Injunctions ᵐ."

"XIV. Whether they make their ordinarye sermons according to the *Queen's Majesties* Injunctions ⁿ."

"XXII. Whether they teach any other grammar then such as is appointed by the *Queenes Majesties* injunction º annexed to the same or not."

Surely, if the Advertisements had an equal authority with that of the Injunctions (which your Lordship's theory implies), Archbishop Parker would have referred to them. If not (as I venture to contend was the case) it is easy to understand why reference was made to the Injunctions as representing the source whence the several orders named, derived their authority.

Thus far, then, the two earliest examples of official evidence which your Lordship and the Judges adduce — to prove that the Advertisements were issued by the Queen — depend the one on the interpretation of a sentence, the other on the meaning of a special phrase. I trust I shall not be considered too bold in saying that the construction in one case, and the context in the other, absolutely upsets the interpretation so relied upon. I propose now to quote other examples of official evidence which bear upon the status of the Advertisements, still following, as far as possible, a chronological order.

Together with the Articles of Visitation by Archbishop Parker

---

¹ See Injunctions, Nos. XIV. and XXVII., Cardwell, Documentary Annals, pp. 217 and 224.

ᵏ See Injunctions "for Tables in Churches," Cardwell, Documentary Annals, p. 234.

ˡ See Injunction XI., Cardwell, Documentary Annals, p. 216.

ᵐ See Injunctions, "Form of bidding the Prayers," Cardwell, Documentary Annals, p. 235.

ⁿ See Injunctions III. and IV., Cardwell, Documentary Annals, p. 212.

º See Injunction XXXIX., Cardwell, Documentary Annals, p. 227.

in 1569, ought to be mentioned the "Injunctions" by Parkhurst [p], Bishop of Norwich, of the same date. He enjoins,—

> "Finally, ye shall diligently observe, and put in ure, all such Orders and Injunctions as have been appointed you beforetyme as well (a) by the Injunctions of the *Queen's Majestie*, as (b) by the *Archbishop* of Canterbury's grace, and (c) the Bishop of the Diocese."

If the Advertisements are referred to at all, they must be included in the second series (b). I may perhaps add the first of the "Articles to be enquired of," which are printed with, and are evidently of the same authority as, these Injunctions.

> "Imprimis, whether your Divine Service be sayde or song in due tyme, and reverently, and the Sacraments duely mynisterd in such decent apparel as is appoynted by (a) the laws, (b) the *Queen's Majesties* injunctions, and (c) other orders set forth by *Public Authoritie* in that behalfe."

Here, again, we have a clear distinction laid down between "the Queen's Injunctions" and "orders by public authority." I do not see that the Advertisements are referred to *by name* at all throughout the Articles as an authority.

The Injunctions of Bishop Cox [q], of Ely, were issued about 1571. One of them names the Advertisements with regard to the apparel:—

> "Item, that every Parson, Vicar, and Curate, shall use in the tyme of the celebration of Divine Service, to weare a surplesse prescribed by the *Queen's Majesties* Injunctions, and the booke of Common Prayer, and shall kepe and observe all other rightes and orders prescribed in the same booke of Common Prayer and *Injunctions*; as well about the celebration of the Sacramentes, as also in their comely and priestlyke apparell to be worne accordyng to the precept set foorth *in the booke called* the Advertisements."

Here the way in which the Book of Advertisements is spoken of adds an additional illustration, if such were needed, how it was regarded by the Bishops as distinct from the order of the Crown, or of the Parliament. Besides, surely the words "in the book called" is a way of speaking of her Majesty's commands, which no loyal Bishop could possibly employ. There

---

[p] These will be found reprinted in the Second Report of the Ritual Commission (1868), p. 404.

[q] Second Rit. Com. Report, p. 406.

are other details in the passage worthy of comment, but I must keep to my definite line of argument.

The next documents in order of date to which I have access, are the Articles of Grindal, at his first Metropolitical Visitation [1]. Here, as one might expect, the Advertisements *are not once mentioned*, nor any authority mentioned, which could by any possibility be considered to represent them. Why? The answer is very simple,—the Advertisements issued by the Archbishop of Canterbury could not affect the Province of *York*, to which see Bishop Grindal had been translated. Had they been issued by the Queen, they would probably have been here named, because it must be remembered that Grindal, when he was Bishop of London, had had a hand in drawing them up, and had been very energetic in enforcing that Uniformity, to aid which the Advertisements had been printed. The marked omission by him of any reference to them, though negative testimony, is still valuable under the circumstance, to shew that they were not issued by the Queen.

And when we examine the series of Injunctions [2] which the Archbishop issued about the same time, we see in them no reference, even incidentally, to the Advertisements, though more than one to the Queen's Majesty's Injunctions; also to the Book of Homilies, "set forth by the Queenes Majesties' Authoritie," and by implication to her Majesty's 'further order,' (taken Jan. 1561) inasmuch as they are to have "all things requisite for common prayer, and Administration of the holy Sacramentes, before the 20 of April next ensuing, specially the book of Common Prayer, *with the newe Kalendar.*"

In 1575, Archbishop Parker held a Metropolitical Visitation within the diocese of Winchester. His Articles issued on this occasion are very similar to those issued on previous occasions. The way in which he uses the term "Advertisements" is some-

---

[1] He had been Bishop of London till 1570, when he was translated to York. His primary Visitation began May 15, 1571, and the Articles are printed in Cardwell's Documentary Annals, No. LXXVI.

[2] These are reprinted in the Second Ritual Commission Report, p. 411.

what different, but it is equally distinguished from the Queen's Injunctions, as in the previous Articles issued by him. The first passage runs as follows :—

9. "Whether your Preachers set out in their Sermons the Queens Majesties Authorities over all her subjectes, and in all Causes, and exhort their hearers to due obedience under the same, to the folowyng of her Majesties Injunctions, and other lawes, statutes, orders, *advertisements*, and decrees, set forth by *common authority*."

This expression, "*common authority*," I presume may fairly be said to be synonymous with the "*public authority*," which the Archbishop employed in the Articles at his previous Visitation, to distinguish them from the Injunctions issued by the " Queen's Majesty." Later on in the same series he again mentions the Advertisements :—

"16. Item, whether they . . . minister the Sacraments reverently in such sort as it is set forth by [a] the lawes of this Realm, [b] the Queenes Majesties Injunctions, and [c] the advertisements."

Whether or not, in either of the above instances, he is by the term referring to the Advertisements of 1566, may be questioned; but when we come to No. 38 of the series, we may safely say that he is not. The Article is as follows :—

"38. Item . . . whether your Churches and Churchyards be well repayred, adorned, and fenced; whether the Roode loftes be pulled downe, *and a **partition** made*, and kept betwixt the Chancil and the Church, *according to* THE ADVERTISEMENTS."

I need not remind your Lordship that there is not a word in the Advertisements of 1566 about a partition between the Church and the Chancel. To what then is he referring? I do not insist upon this theory, but I throw it out for want of a better: viz. that the Archbishop had already issued some Diocesan or Metropolitan Injunctions, which he here styles "Advertisements," containing a clause with respect to the keeping of chancels separate. There is no doubt whatever that our collections are very imperfect of the Articles issued at different times by the Archbishops and Bishops, as they would be papers that would be considered of no value after another Visitation had been held; and therefore it is quite possible that such a document may have been issued, and no copy in existence. My reason for putting it to a somewhat early date is, that at his Visitation in 1563, he makes the enquiry

"Whether the rood loft be pulled down according to *the order prescribed*, and of [*sic*] the partition between the Chancell and the Church be kept."

I feel that in making a suggestion of this kind, I am laying myself open to another charge of "gratuitous conjecture[1];" but whether it be this, or something else, it is clear that there are more than one series of Advertisements in the field; and so the assumption that Advertisements referred to by the Archbishop are necessarily *authoritative* in the sense of being issued by her Majesty will scarcely hold; unless it could be shewn that this unknown series also was issued by the Queen.

What I have attempted has been to gather up all the passages which appear to refer to the Advertisements in the *official* documents for the ten years or so after their issue, i.e. from 1566 to 1576. Taken together, there can be no doubt of the meaning they impose upon the much-disputed book; a meaning, I venture to say, consistent in every way with what the contents, when read as a whole, exhibit; as well as with the history of their origin, purport, and actual status, as shewn in Archbishop Parker's papers. They were the means employed by the Archbishop, in conjunction with his fellow Bishops, to carry out the established laws; they were not laws in themselves; and I have already spoken of the improbability that the Queen would have chosen such a vehicle for promulgating "other order," or to speak plainly, "*a new* law." But when we see how the Bishops regarded them; how they contrast them, so to speak, with all that is known to be issued by her Majesty, I cannot express the wonder that I feel that any now should regard them in the light of the Queen's "other order in accordance with the twenty-fifth clause of the Act of Uniformity."

[1] "And even if so *gratuitous* conjecture could be accepted." NOTES, p. 10.

It is, perhaps, true that *in after years* the Advertisements came to be more and more mistaken for the laws themselves, instead of what I may call the reflection of those laws. They had been printed several times, probably at intervals, though with the same colophon. Amongst the copies in the British Museum, there are those of at least three different editions presumably anterior to 1570, and two after.

    C. 25. c. 6. i.e. one copy, Reginald Wolfe, London, 4to. n. d.
    3505. e, T 1014, two copies,   ,,   ,,   ,,   ,, ,, ,,
    T 775, 3475 aa., two copies,   ,,   ,,   ,,   ,, ,, ,,
    T 1013   one copy,   ,,   ,,   ,,   ,, 1571.
    T 1014   one copy, Thomas Dawson,   ,,   ,, 1584.

These being kept in print, while the Injunctions of Elizabeth became scarce, gradually came to be looked upon as their substitute; and when I look through the Visitation Articles and Injunctions issued by Bishops and Archdeacons, as we approach towards the end of Elizabeth's reign, I admit the Advertisements seem to be more directly referred to as authoritative; but even with all this, I find no instance in which that authority is claimed for them, on the ground of their being issued by the Queen herself.

Take, for instance, the example which your Lordship adduces (p. 24), and which, with the letter of Bishop Grindal, constitute the chief additions of official documents made by your Lordship to those already quoted in the Ridsdale JUDGEMENT. The passage is from the Articles presented to the Queen in the year 1583, by Whitgift, Archbishop of Canterbury, and Piers, Bishop of Salisbury, in the name of other Bishops[n]:—

    "That all preachers and others in Ecclesiastical Orders doo at all tymes weare and use such kind of apparell as is prescribed unto them *by the book of* Advertisements. That is, cloke with sleeves, square capp, goune, tippett."

This, to begin with, is against the theory that the Advertisements are the Queen's orders; for the expression "by the book of" is, as said before, most unlikely to have been used if they

---

[n] State Papers, Domestic Series, vol. clxiii. No. 31.

had been issued by her **Majesty**. Two glosses are, however, to be noticed,—both of which are duly recorded (NOTES, p. 24, and Appendix, p. 77), although **not commented on, by your** Lordship, and go far to weaken the testimony which the passage may be thought **to** afford towards proving the Queen's having "taken order" in that book. First, to the Articles thus prepared by **the Archbishop and Bishop to be** presented to her Majesty, this gloss has been added:—

"The last wordes, viz. **Cloak with Sleeves, &c., may be leaft out,** *yf it bee thought* good. But the article is *warranted* **both by the Advertisements sett** out by her Maties **authoritie, and** *also* by the Q. Injunctions anno primo Elzab."

The distinction here **between the Queen's Injunctions and** the Advertisements "set out by her authority," is not, it **is** true, demonstrated so clearly **as in** the earlier documents, and **I** believe I have stated the true reason, viz. that the Advertisements came gradually to be looked upon as taking the place of the Injunctions; moreover, being always issued with the title, " by virtue of the Queen's letters," they were in process of time, **as** their history was forgotten, looked upon as having an authority which they did not really possess. I would observe also that a great deal in this case depends upon the use of the word "authoritie:" **set out** by the Queen's authority may well mean no more than that **she** was supposed, from the **title, to have** sanctioned* Archbishop Parker's proceeding, in explaining the laws established by the Prayer-Book, and the Injunctions by issuing his Advertisements. But if we look at the context, this consideration suggests itself. Supposing that on **this** question, viz. the order of the clerical apparel, the Advertisements had the Queen's *direct* authority, why was the order for the cloak to be left **out,** if "*it be thought good;*" and why were the Articles said to be warranted "also" **by** the Injunctions, if the Advertisements were the Queen's warrant? As the Injunctions were

* See *ante*, p. 47.

the authoritative order, though general in their character, and the Advertisements only explanatory, the reason for the double reference is clear.

The second gloss to be noted is to the same effect, namely, that to the rough draft of these Articles we find that after the word "Advertisements," when they were *presented*, were added the words[x],—

"And her Majesty's Injunctions anno primo."

I do not discuss here how far the Queen gave her sanction to Archbishop Whitgift's Articles of 1584, or compare that sanction with what she is supposed to have given to Archbishop Parker's Advertisements of 1566, since no one has proposed to argue that she took "further order" in the latter.

One of the peculiarities of the reference to the Advertisements in later *official* documents is but very slightly noticed by your Lordship (p. 16); I mean their being called the Advertisements of the year 1564, instead of the year 1566, but I venture to think it is of some importance. It is obvious, as your Lordship observes, that it is an error, and that the error is to be traced to the fact that the year 1564, and that year alone, occurs in the title[y]. Now it is Elizabeth's name, and Elizabeth's name alone, that occurs in the title; and I venture to submit that your Lordship's argument as regards the one must equally apply as regards the other. The *error* of their being issued in 1564, and the *error* of their being Elizabeth's, can be traced to a common source. Had the date 1566, and Archbishop Parker's name appeared there instead, neither error would ever in after years have arisen. I have already explained how it came about that in order, as far as possible, to add to the weight of his Advertisements, Archbishop Parker made reference to the Queen's letter. He could not foresee the effect of his title.

[x] Appendix to your Lordship's Notes, p. 77. fourth Article, as I have shewn. See *ante*, p. 21.
[y] It occurs also in the text in the

VI. THE **LIGHT IN WHICH** THE ADVERTISEMENTS WERE **REGARDED, AS** SHEWN BY UNOFFICIAL WRITINGS.

I find that my pages are extending to a length beyond what I at all calculated **upon** at the outset, and I therefore cannot deal so fully as I would wish with the next **class of** evidence, namely, that derived from **ordinary Letters, and** other *unofficial* sources.

Again I **say** what I have said **of previous evidence,**—a line here and a **line there, a paragraph here** and a paragraph **there,** joined by what I must perforce **term imaginary** links instead of their historical context, cannot result **in a truthful picture.**

Your Lordship brings to **bear extracts from what is** usually known as the Zurich Correspondence: **but I should observe,** a different question appears to be more prominently raised in these from that in the *official* documents.

In all the official evidence **the question has turned chiefly upon** (1) whether the Queen took "order" **in the Advertise**ments, and **only** incidentally **(2), whether any** order taken in them was "*other*" than the established law.

In the Correspondence, the evidence tends especially to prove **what was the** understanding **at** this time as to the legality of **wearing the Cope, and therefore** whether there had been "*other* order" **as to the law,** that **is,** *change* of law, **on the subject:** the question **whether** the Queen issued the Advertisements can only be said **to be raised** incidentally.

The use **here and there** of the expression "edictum regium," on which your Lordship **relies (NOTES, p. 19), is comparatively of** little or no value **as** evidence **on this latter point, since the terms used in** unofficial **documents are of no** moment, even **when the** facts recorded may **be of** importance. Still, so that **I should not incur** the suspicion **of** evading it, because I was afraid that **this argument** told against me, I will touch upon it before I begin **my survey.**

The references given by your Lordship (p. 19) to the use of the word are two. The first is to Bullinger's letter [a] of May 1, 1566, where he is replying to questions put to him by Laurence Humphrey, but the fact is, he simply repeats Humphrey's question almost word for word, that question being,—

"An qui hactenus in libertate sua acquieverunt, vi *regii edicti* hac servitute implicare se et ecclesiam salva conscientia possint?"

I have to add, that Humphrey's letter [a], where the question is asked, is dated Feb. 9, 1566, which is surely too early for it to contain any reference to prove that Advertisements which were not issued till March 28 following were "her Majesty's edict."

In the other reference, namely, to the letter [b] written by Gualter to Beza, Sept. 11, 1566, we are met also by the fact that in the first instance, where he speaks of the *regium edictum*, he evidently does not refer to the Advertisements at all, but to Elizabeth's Injunctions of 1559. These are the words:—

"Quia enim de solo habitu ministrorum lis erat, quos regina a laicis distingui voluit, et *in edicto regio* conscientiis infirmorum diserte cavebatur ne quis in illo vel ministerii vel Sacramentorum *dignitatem* sitam existimaret. . . . &c."

which appears to me to refer very *distinctly* to the sentence at the end of the XXXth Injunction,—

"not then by meaning to attribute any holiness, or special *worthiness*, to the said garments."

This Injunction relates especially to apparel (the subject on which he is writing), and I find no words at all to which they can be applied in the Advertisements.

Your Lordship also, besides the two references, quotes an extract from another letter where the words *decretum tuum* occur, in a letter from Humphrey to the Queen [c]. As it is

---

[a] Strype's Annals, Appendix, vol. i. No. XXIV.
[a] Epistolæ Tigurinæ, First Series, Ep. LXVIII. p. 90.
[b] Epistolæ Tigurinæ, Second Series, Ep. I.VII. p. 85.

[c] The MS. from which Strype took his copy is preserved in the British Museum, Harleian MSS., vol. ccccxvii. art. 93. He prints it in Appendix to Annals, vol. i. No. XXVII.

without date, and your Lordship gives no reason for assigning the date *after* the issue of the Advertisements, it can scarcely be accepted as evidence on them. As I observe, too, that Humphrey writes to the Bishop against the Apparel *now* ordered to be adopted, as early as May, 1565[d], I should fix this also to a date *before* the issue of the Advertisements, and make it refer *wholly* to the Queen's letter.

On the whole, then, the evidence derived from the expression, "Regium Edictum," is of no great value. The fact is, the cap and surplice were understood, though not quite accurately, to have been ordained by the Queen's Injunctions of 1559; e.g. Gualter, writing to Humphrey[e] in Aug., 1565, says,—

"Yt troblyth me not a lytle that the *Quenes M*^{es} *Ordynaunce*[f] for ye weryng of the surplisse and Prests cappe, wheras ther had bene greater nede of the reformacyon and amendment of other thinges at this tyme then to sett up agayne such Ordnances."

And the authorities generally in this matter were very confused, as a letter written by the Bishop of Winchester to Gualter, July 17, 1565, (that is nine months before the Advertisements were issued) shews. We find the following[g]:—

"This calumny has gained strength from the *Act of Parliament for repressing the impiety of the Papists*, which passed before our return[h], by which, though the other habits were taken away, the wearing of square caps and surplices was yet continued to the clergy, though without any superstitious conceit, which was expressly guarded against *by the terms of the Act.*"

The last line shews that Bishop Horne was referring to No. XXX. of Queen Elizabeth's Injunctions, which he appears to confuse with the Act of Parliament.

Only once do I find the Advertisements named in the numerous letters which passed just at the time between the leaders of the Puritan party in England and their sympathizers on the

---

[d] State Papers, Domestic, Elizabeth, XXXVI. art. 64.

[e] From the Lansdowne MSS., IX. Art. 1. Referred to also in Strype's Annals, vol. i. part ii. p. 135.

[f] No doubt this refers more directly to the Queen's letter of Jan. 25, 1565, ordering the Injunctions to be enforced.

[g] Zurich Letters, First Series, lxiv.

[h] Horne was back in time for the Westminster Conference towards the end of March, 1559, and took an active part in it.

Continent, and that is in the letter[1] written by George Withers and John Barthelot to Henry Bullinger and Rodolph Gualter, and dated August, 1567. Amongst several details which belong to general history, they write—

"How true is this denial of theirs appears from the form of Baptism which we gave you, and is also evident from THE ADVERTISEMENTS OF THE BISHOPS [*ex monitis Episcoporum*], Article XVI., where THEY THEMSELVES require that no infant be baptized otherwise than in the manner prescribed[k]."

But surely the Zurich letters, my Lord, do something more than shew that before 1566, and probably after that as well, writers refer to the Injunctions of Elizabeth under the title of "Edictum Regium;" while others, possibly misled by the title, might call the Advertisements an "Edictum Regium" also.

Surely, my Lord, they have much more to say *directly* upon whether the Advertisements affected the law as to the Cope, and not only the minor point, whether the Queen issued them or not. They tell us very distinctly, if not of the origin, at least of the early stages of the controversy in connection with which the Advertisements were issued, and how those were understood in regard to enforcing or repealing the "Ornaments rubrick."

Others have gone over this ground, but as your Lordship has for some half-dozen pages [pp. 18—24] referred so frequently to the Zurich letters, I must briefly go over it again, in order to make my argument complete.

I think the first intimation we get of the controversy is in Bishop Horne's letter[l], already referred to, namely, in July, 1565[m]; and later on, the series of letters from the old English exiles after their return to England, and who were most of them advanced to high offices here, addressed to their old

---

[1] Zurich Letters, Second Series, lviii. p. 146.

[k] It is No. 16 of the Advertisements of 1566 (and of no other document with which I am acquainted) which refers to Baptism, and it contains the words, "nor in any other form than is already prescribed."

[l] Zurich Letters, First Series, lxiv. p. 141.

[m] The earliest document is, perhaps, that of May, 1565, in which Dr. Laurence Humphrey petitioned against the Apparel *now* ordered to be adopted, (i.e. I presume by the Queen, Jan. 25, 1565).

friends and acquaintances left on the Continent, constantly refer to the "Vestiarian Controversy," as they term it.

I feel a few preliminary words, however, are necessary, not for your Lordship, but for those who may read this.

The chief controversy was as to the ordinary dress of the Clergy, i.e. the "apparel," as it was termed, which included the square cap. The lesser controversy was as to the special dress for Ministration, viz. the surplice and cope. The cope is mentioned but rarely: it appears to be included under the surplice, just as the "*habit*" was included under the cap.

Though both the "apparel" and the "vestments" were objected to by the same party, and on the same grounds, viz. that there should be no distinction between priest and people, the Puritans in their writings used the term "Apparell" for the ordinary dress of the clergy out of doors, and as quite distinct from the vestments used for ministration.

There could not be, my Lord, any ground for the following hypothesis, which you put forward in the NOTES (p. 12):—

"The Alb and the Chasuble seem to have then found no advocates; there is reason to suppose that the 30th Royal Injunction of 1559 was practically interpreted as excluding them, without much enquiry into the sufficiency of that authority for such a purpose."

The 30th Injunction, to which I have more than once had occasion to refer[a], relates wholly to the "apparel," including a special order for wearing the square cap; and if it related, as your Lordship would imply, either directly or indirectly to the "vestments" for the administration of the Holy Communion, then it would afford very strong grounds for the use of the foreign cap, only very lately introduced amongst us, and for which the authority seems to be somewhat doubtful. If your Lordship were right in your conjecture, it would not only be lawful, but by a complicated chain of reasoning, similar to that which makes the cope illegal on the ground of the Advertisements, this "ornament of the minister" might be argued

---

[a] See especially p. 21.

to be absolutely *enjoined* by reason of the Injunctions. But it is not so. The "apparel" and "vestments" are distinct.

The first note, then, which the Zurich Correspondence gives us of the controversy is in the letter sent by Horne, Bishop of Winchester, to Gualter at Zurich, on July 17, 1565, as follows :—

> "The heads of that party [the papists] are in public custody; the rest ... are endeavouring ... to bring themselves into power and us into odium, having obtained a handle of this kind (small enough indeed) through the controversy lately arisen among us about [a] *square caps* and [b] *Surplices*[o]. ... *It was enjoined* us (who had not then any authority either to make laws or repeal them) either to wear the *Caps* and *Surplices*, or to give place to others. We complied with this *injunction*, lest our enemies should take possession of the places deserted by ourselves."

Perhaps, in order to shew the connection between these letters and the history of the Advertisements, I may call attention to the word "*enjoined*," which refers, no doubt, to the issue in the preceding January [1565] of the Queen's "letter," which he here calls an "injunction."

I do not find the answer from Gualter to Bishop Horne, but later in the year (Nov. 3, 1565) I find in a letter from Bullinger to Bishop Horne[p], a reply to some other letter which the latter had written, probably much in the same strain as the one quoted. John Abel had also written. Bullinger here recommends, as he consistently recommends throughout, prudence :—

> "On the other hand I also recommend prudence, who do not think that Churches are to be forsaken because of the Vestments."

The Zurich letters, with which I am now dealing, do not give any more references during that year to the controversy. From other documents, however, more may be found. It was in the December of this year that the disorder as to apparel and surplice came to a climax, so to speak, at St. John's College, Cambridge. The Letter[q] sent to Cecil gives a striking ex-

---

[o] A continuation of this paragraph has already been given. See *ante*, p. 71 ; Zurich Letters, 1st S. lxiv.

[p] Zurich Letters, First Series, App. II.

[q] State Paper Office, Domestic Series, Elizabeth, vol. xxxviii. art. 7. See also art. 1 and 2 in the same volume, on the same proceedings.

ample of the unsettled state of mind in the country on religious questions, and the difficulties with which the Queen, Sir William Cecil, and Archbishop Parker had to deal. I therefore give an abstract of it which I made from the original :—

[Dec. 8, 1565.] "*Certaine Articles truly declairinge howe the dysorder concerninge* [a] *Apparell and* [b] *Surplesses hathe sprong, increased, and grown into suche an extremytie in St. Jhon's Colledge.*

"Fyrst, one Mr. Fulke sometimes of the Innes of the Courte, about three yere last past left his place there and came into Cambridge. . . . .

"2. Also the said Mr. Fulke, sone after the said election, lefte of wearinge a *square cappe* and used a hatt, and then also insinuatinge him self into the familiarytie of certaine yonge divines, amonge whome he perswaded Mr. Johnson and Buckley to reiecte theyre cappes, gounes, and surplesses, and in the same pointe in lyke sorte hath misseled up his and theyre youths.

"3. Also, that he shortly after in St. Maries pulpyt did wthe vehement words (ut est in eo genere causarum disertus) invehe against suche popyshe trumpery as he then termed yt, dehorting all men from the use of the same when as in no good sense they might be used amonge Chrystian men, and that the users thereof were reprobates and damd.

"4. Also, he hathe in the Colledge privatly in dyvers Sermons in lyke sort reasoned agaynst dyuers ceremonies and ordres of the Churche allowed by the *Quenes Maiesties Iniunctions*, wthe most Bytter words, viz. in one against the unleavened Bread, calling it starche for past. In another, against the knelinge at the receavinge of ye Communyon. In the thyrd, against the minystringe of the same in *Cope* or *surples*. And in the fourth, against the use of *surplesses* generally, whiche Sermons of his have bread dysorders as folowythe.

"His fyrst of these four sermons so wrought withe the M[aste]r that presently he commanded common breade to be brought in the Communyon then in hande.

"His second had this effect, that some standing some syttinge in theyre stalles, very fewe knelinge, receaved the Communyon. At another time The Minyster goinge all alonge in his goune, scantly withe suche reverence as holly breade was delt in the popishe time, to the greate offense of many there present, and withdrawinge of them from communycatinge at the same time.

"His third Collation caused the Communyon to be ministred for a time eather the prest or deacon havinge *no surples*, but in fine they waxed so whot [= hot] that they could abide no suche garment uppon them. And further, his mencioninge of *Copes* at that time moved some so greatly, that rather then they shuld any longer abide amongst us they made Robin hoodes penyworthes of them, beinge amongest them them selves bothe marchauntes and chapmen, wherby the Colledge was so endamaged as the losse of fortie pounds comythe to, the which was longe before offered but reiected by Mr. Pilkinton, then M[aste]r as to lytle [too little]."

These Puritan excesses were, I am afraid, very common; besides others at Cambridge, there were the cases of Humphrey and Sampson at Oxford, which I have not space to describe here; but in spite of them, as I have shewn when treating of the history of the Advertisements and in Archbishop Parker's letters, there was no yielding on the part of Elizabeth, such as the abrogation of Copes would imply. The Puritans fought hard, but the Government firmly resisted. Had they once given way to the lawlessness of the Puritan party, there would have been such an antipathy created amongst the steadier folk, that they would have welcomed back the Roman priests, and they, regaining popularity, would soon have paved the way for the return of the Papal power.

The ultra-Puritan party was therefore as dangerous to the State as the Roman party, and we see how firmly they were repressed in high quarters. It is instructive to watch even in this one instance, and at a single College, how the members of the College gradually came to follow the Queen's Injunctions in wearing the surplice (they had no copes left); yet we find on Dec. 18, the Master of St. John's (Dr. Longworth) writing humbly to Cecil (who was Chancellor of Cambridge), to know whether common bread *may be* used at the Communion, and if, when he preaches in Chapel to the House [i.e. to members of the College only], he *may* do so *without a surplice.*

I may also perhaps (while on this subject) refer to a letter from Cecil's chaplain (who was at Cambridge, Cecil being Chancellor of the University), a copy of which I find amongst my notes, and dated about this time, viz. Jan. 20, 1566 :—

"I have done your honour's commandement, to Mr. Vice Chancellor. . . . The Bysshope of Ely had stayed his jornye before my cominge, and sent your honour for a present a doo, the which his keper, understanding *I was your honour's chaplayne*, would need leve to my disposition. . . . It is demanded of Mr. D. Beaumont [r], who is very diligent in observing the order prescribed by your honour, by *what authoritie* he can, for not wearing of a *surplis*, deprive any man of his lyvinge [s]."

[r] This, I presume, is Dr. Robert Beaumont, the Head of Trin. Coll.

[s] State Papers, Domestic Series, Elizabeth, vol. xxxix. art. 14.

Here we see the enforcement of even the Surplice presenting a difficulty, and the Queen's Secretary asked for his advice as to the mode of proceeding.

The year 1566—the year of the publication of the Advertisements—finds the controversy perhaps at its height, and the position I propose to establish is, that the issue of the Advertisements did not change the aspect of the controversy; and on the special argument, namely, that the Advertisements in ordering the Surplice *thereby* abrogated the Cope, I shall shew that the correspondence in question—first by negative testimony, secondly, by positive statements—affords as strong a proof as it is reasonable to expect in any such matter, that the Cope was *not* abrogated.

To Henry Bullinger, of Zurich, the returned exiles appear to look as to a father for advice, if one may judge by their letters. They are not the terms of ordinary courtesy, but association with him had evidently excited in them feelings of great admiration for his ability and learning. To Horne's first intimation of the controversy, Bullinger, under date of Nov. 3, 1565, had replied that he "commended the prudence of those who did not think that Churches were to be forsaken because of the Vestments." He, however, prefaces this remark: "As, however, I am most probably unacquainted with all the circumstances, I hesitate to pronounce any opinion on the subject."

On Jan. 3, 1566, Edwin Sandys, then Bishop of Worcester, in writing to him, mentions incidentally [1]—

> "The true religion of Christ is settled among us, the Gospel is not bound, but is free and faithfully preached. As to other matters, there is not much cause for anxiety. There is some little dispute about using or not using the Popish habits, but God will put an end to these things also.
> "[*Signed*], EDWIN WORCESTER."

The next month, that is, Feb. 8, John Jewel, then Bishop of Salisbury, writes somewhat in the same strain to him [a]:—

---

[1] Zurich Letters, Parker Society, First Series, 1842, No. LXVI.

[a] Ibid., No. LXVII. The letter is addressed to Henry Bullinger.

"The contest respecting the *linen Surplice*, about which I doubt not but you have heard either from our friend Abel or Parkhurst, is not yet at rest; that matter still **somewhat** disturbs weak minds. And I wish that all, even the slightest vestiges **of** popery, **might** be removed from our churches, and above all from our minds. But **the** queen at this time is *unable to endure the least alteration* in matters of religion [!].

"[*Signed*], JOHN JEWEL, ANGLUS."

It will be observed he lays stress upon the question as to the " Vestments," viz. the Surplice; he does not refer to the " Apparel."

But Bullinger's letter to Bishop Horne, above mentioned, inviting further information as to how matters stood exactly, is taken up by the English leaders of the ultra section of the Puritan party, namely, Humphrey and Sampson. Humphrey had been elected Professor of Divinity at Oxford in 1560, and President of Magdalen College in 1561; Sampson had been elected Dean of Christ Church, but was now deposed. Both the one and the other had given considerable trouble in their resentment to conformity.

Laurence Humphrey writes from Oxford*, Feb. 9, 1566, to Bullinger; and, speaking of the Commentary on Isaiah which Bullinger was writing, he says,—

"In the third chapter, where the prophet is discoursing about ornaments, and female attire, should you think fit to insert anything respecting *this affair* of the habits, it would, in my opinion, be worth your while.

"I am not ignorant of what you have already written, but you seem to have expressed your sentiments too briefly, and without sufficient perspicuity. Wherefore, I again and again entreat your piety to reply in few words to those little questions of mine :

" 1st. whether laws respecting habits may properly be prescribed to Churchmen, so as to distinguish them from the laity in shape, colour?

" 2nd. whether the ceremonial worship of the Levitical priesthood is to be re-introduced into the Church of Christ?

" 3rd. whether, in respect of habits and external rites, it is allowable to have anything in common with the papists, and whether Christians may borrow ceremonies from any counterfeit and hostile Church. . . . . &c.

"[*Signed*], LAURENCE HUMPHREY."

* Zurich Letters, Parker Society, First Series, No. LXVIII.

In all he asks seven questions, the seventh perhaps being the most practical, viz. "whether the habit is to be worn rather than the Office deserted?"

Thomas Sampson, who, after his deprivation, seems to be living in London, may have seen Humphrey's letter of the 9th. But in his letter of the 16th*, also written to Bullinger, he does not say so, and leaves one rather to infer he had not. He goes over much the same ground.

"Our Church remains in the same condition as was long since reported to you. For after the expiration of seven years in the profession of the Gospel, there has now been revived that contest about *habits* in which Cranmer, Ridley, and Hooper, most holy martyrs of Christ, were formerly wont to skirmish. The state of the question, however, is not in all respects the same, but the determination of those in power is more inflexible. But that you may more readily understand the matter in controversy, I have thought it best to reduce it into certain questions, which are these:

"I. Whether a peculiar habit, distinct from that of the laity, were ever assigned to the ministers of the Gospel in better times, and whether it ought now to be assigned to them in the reformed Church?

"II. Whether the prescribing habits of this kind be consistent with ecclesiastical and Christian liberty?

"VI. Whether it be expedient to borrow rites from idolaters or heretics, and to transfer such as are especially dedicated to their sect and religion to the use of the reformed Church?

"XI. Whether a man ought thus to obey *the decrees* of the Church, or on account of non-compliance, supposing there is no alternative, to be cast out of the ministry?"

And after twelve questions (of which the above four are characteristic), he says, "Here you have, most esteemed Sir, our difficulties."

"Here many pious men are hesitating, for the sake of whom I again ask it as a favour from you, that, having well considered the matter with Master Gualter, and the rest of your colleagues, with your wonted piety you will plainly state your opinion, and send a written answer to each of the above questions. . . . ."

"[*Signed*], THOMAS SAMPSON."

The reply comes, dated from Zurich, May 1, 1566. It was not what was expected. In spite of his association with the

* Zurich Letters, First Series, No. LXIX.

new continental school, Henry Bullinger writes temperately and wisely. He in a previous letter had said, "I approve the zeal of those persons who would have the Church purged from all the dregs of popery;" but he does not write with that virulent hatred to everything that was old, and the wild infatuation for the modern doctrines, systems, and fashions, to which his party were wedded. The questions had been framed with a view to obtaining from their master (whom those who differed from him respected), a full and clear justification of their non-conformity; but in this they were grievously disappointed. If I had space, I would quote the letter entire, but I must content myself with selecting a passage or so which appears to bear most directly upon the question at issue. He writes [1],—

"And to repeat my sentiments in few words, I could never approve of your officiating, if so commanded, at an altar *laden* rather than adorned with the image of him that was crucified, and in the appropriate dress of the mass, that is, in the alb and cope, *on the back part of which also the same image is represented.*

"But as far as I can understand by a letter from England, there is now no dispute concerning habits of this kind; but the question is, whether it be lawful for the ministers of the gospel to wear a round or square cap, and a white garment *which they call* a surplice, by the wearing of which the minister may be distinguished from the people? And whether it be a duty rather to relinquish the ministry or sacred office, than to wear vestments of this kind? . . . .

"1. To the question, whether laws respecting habits, &c. . . . . I reply that there is an ambiguity in the word *ought*. If it is taken as implying what is necessary . . . . to salvation, I do not think that even the authors of the laws themselves intend such an interpretation. But if it is asserted that for the sake of decency and comeliness of appearance, or dignity and order, some such regulation may be made . . . I do not see how he is to blame, who either adopts a habit of this sort himself, or who commands it to be worn by others.

"2. Whether the ceremonial of the Levitical priesthood is to be re-introduced into the Church. I reply, if a *cap* and *habit* not unbecoming a minister, and free from superstition, are commanded to be used by the clergy, no one can reasonably assert that Judaism is revived. . . . . You see, then, that all the Levitical rites are not to be so abrogated as that none of them may be lawfully retained. Thus far Peter Martyr.

[1] Zurich Letters, First Series, Appendix, No. III.; and Strype, Annals, vol. ii. pt. ii. p. 505.

" 3. *Whether it is allowable to have a habit in common with Papists.*

" I answer, it is not yet proved that the pope introduced a distinction of *habits* into the Church; so far from it, that it is clear that such distinction is long anterior to popery.

"Nor do I see why it should be unlawful to use, in common with papists, a vestment, not superstitious, but pertaining to civil regulation and good order. If it were not allowable to have anything in common with them, it would be necessary to desert all the churches, to decline the receipt of stipend, to abstain from baptism, and the reciting of the Apostles' and Nicene Creed, and even to reject the Lord's Prayer. But after all you do not *borrow* any ceremonies from them; for the use of the habits was never set aside from the beginning of the Reformation; and it is still *retained*, not by any popish enactment, but by virtue of the ROYAL EDICT, as a matter of indifference, and of civil order.

" 11, 12. The last two questions come more closely to the point : ' Whether it is more expedient thus to obey . . . or be cast out.'. . . I answer, if in these ceremonies there is no superstition, no impiety, but yet they are imposed upon godly pastors, who would rather that they should not be imposed upon them. I will certainly allow, and that most fully, that a burden and bondage is imposed on them; but I will not allow, and this for most just reasons, that their station or ministry is on that account to be deserted, and place given to wolves, as was before observed, or to ministers less qualified than themselves."

In reading the whole of the two letters of Humphrey and of Sampson, and also of that of Bullinger (in which he replies categorically to the questions put by both his correspondents), it becomes clear that he considers the authority for the "apparel" to rest precisely upon the same grounds as the authority for the "Vestments." And when, in the reply to the third question of Humphrey's, following as it does immediately after the question relating to the *ceremonial worship* of the Levitical priesthood, and no distinction whatever suggested, it clearly implies that the Surplice and Cope, as much as the Cap and Habit, were " by virtue of the ROYAL EDICT [7]."

It may be, perhaps, well to mention, though it does not affect the argument, that Bullinger considered this a public letter. He

---

[7] Whether the words " Royal Edict" refer to the Injunctions of 1559 or the Advertisements of 1566 just issued, makes no difference to the argument, provided that they enact the same. But if the Advertisements imposed a different law to that of the Injunctions, it is necessary to determine which is meant, and to compare with subsequent letters.

did not send it direct to Humphrey and Sampson, but enclosed it to Bishop Horne, of Winchester; and in the letter [2] which accompanied it, dated May 3, 1566, he writes:—

"We send our letter on the *vestiarian controversy*, written by us to the learned men and our honoured godly brethren N. and M. And we send it to you on this account, that ye may understand that we would not have any *private* communication with the brethren without the knowledge of you the principal ministers. . . . Prevail upon her Majesty to grant that these worthy brethren may be reconciled and restored.

"We entreat likewise that you, Master Horne, our honoured Lord and very dear brother, to whom this letter will first be presented, will forthwith take care that it may be forwarded to the Bishop of Norwich, and that you will communicate it to Masters Jewel [Salisbury], Sandys [Worcester], and Pilkington [Durham]. . . . We pray you, reverend Master Horne, to communicate this letter also to the illustrious personage Edmund Grindal, Bishop of London, whom, although he is not personally known to us as you are, we love and desire to be loved by him in return."

The letter did not perhaps, therefore, reach Sampson and Humphrey for some weeks after it arrived in England. It reached London early in June, as on the 6th, John Abel, writing to Bullinger, says he has already forwarded it.

In July, 1566 (the letter gives the month and the year, but not the day), Laurence Humphrey and Thomas Sampson make their reply [a] to Bullinger's letter. They are evidently, as already said, much disappointed. They write:—

"We sent your reverence some questions upon which the force, and as it were the hinge, of the whole controversy seemed to turn. To these your reverence has accurately replied; but if we may be permitted to say so, *not entirely to our satisfaction.*"

Their objection to the answer to the second question concerns the present argument most, and it is as follows:—

"In the second place you answer hypothetically that, if a cap and a habit not unseemly and without superstition be prescribed to the clergy, Judaism is not on this account brought back. But how can that habit be thought consistent with the simple ministry of Christ, which used to set off the theatrical pomp of the popish priesthood. For not only (as our people wish to persuade your reverence) are the square cap and gown required in

---

[1] Zurich Letters, First Series, Appendix IV., p. 356.

[2] Zurich Letters, First Series, No. LXXI. p. 157.

public, but the *sacred garments* are used in divine service ; **and the surplice or white dress** of the choir and the *COPE are re-introduced.*"

They then go on to answer the objection which Bullinger had made, that the vestments were not "borrowed from" popery :—

"As to your adding that the use of the habits was not abolished at the beginning of the Reformation, your informants have again stated what is by no means the fact. For in the time of the most serene King Edward VI. the Lord's Supper was celebrated in simplicity in many places *without the surplice*[b]*;* and the COPE, which was then abrogated by law[c], *is now restored* by a *Public Ordinance* [*Publico decreto*]. This is not to extirpate popery, but to replant it ; not to advance in religion, but to recede."

There can, therefore, be little doubt as to the fact that, in July, 1566, that is, some four months after the Advertisements were issued, the Cope was considered by the Puritan party to be ordered ; not, be it remarked, with any reservation, e.g. as to Parish Churches, &c., but as a general fact. It may be worth while, however, to ask what is here meant by the *Public Ordinance.* If it is solely another name for the Advertisements, and your Lordship's theory as to their purport is right, then your Lordship has to explain how it is that these Puritans, ready to take advantage of every liberty which the law allowed, failed to discover that it *abrogated* the use of the *Cope,* instead of *restored* it ; if the name refers to the Injunctions only, then it still remains to be explained how it was that Humphrey and Sampson were ignorant of the Advertisements.

The explanation I should give myself would be that it refers to the Queen's letter as well as to the "Advertisements ;" and that "restoration" means, that by the clause in the Act of Parliament the Surplice and Cope were made the *law;* but by the issue of the Advertisements, that law was to be enforced. So that, while the law in this respect was before probably allowed to be a dead letter, no one could henceforth, so far as the particulars named, break it with the same impunity.

[b] They ought to have added, "though against the law," even if his facts were true.

[c] They ought to have added, "though not till just at the close of his reign, up to which time it was ordered."

At the end of their letter they sum up with a list which they entitle,—

"*Some blemishes which still attach to the Church of England.*

"1. In the public prayers, although there is nothing impure, there is, however, a kind of popish superstition, which may not only be seen in the Morning and Evening Service, but also in the Lord's Supper.

"2. In addition to the exquisite[d] singing in parts [*Præter musicæ sonos fractos et exquisitissimos*], the use of organs is becoming more general in the churches.

"5. The *sacred* habits [*sacræ vestes*], namely, *the Cope and Surplice*, are used at the Lord's Supper. Kneeling is enjoined to those who communicate, and an unleavened cake (*placentula azyma*) is substituted for common bread.

"6. The *popish* habits [*vestes papisticæ*] are ordered to be worn out of Church, and by ministers in general; and the Bishops wear their linen garment, which they call a *rochet*, while both parties wear the square cap, tippets, and long gowns, borrowed from the papists.

"13. Lastly, the Article composed in the time of Edward the Sixth, respecting the spiritual eating, which expressly oppugned, and took away the Real Presence in the Eucharist, and contained a most clear explanation of the truth, is now set forth amongst us mutilated and imperfect."

We are not dependent on this one letter; we have another letter of about the same time[e], written by Miles Coverdale from London, in conjunction with Humphrey and Sampson. It is addressed to William Farrell, Peter Viret, Theodore Beza, and others, and again is written for the purpose of explaining to their sympathizers on the Continent the exact state of the Church in England. The Puritan party had, through the enforcement of discipline, met with a great reverse; and so the commencement of their letter exhibits their despondency.

They write :—

"The unhappy condition of our times and fresh troubles compel us to have recourse to you, not only that you may be informed more fully of the state of our affairs, and our own opinion respecting them, but that we also may more fully understand your sentiments. Our affairs are *not altered for the better*, but alas! are sadly deteriorated. For it is *now settled and determined*

---

[d] The word is used, of course, in the sense of the very elaborate mode of singing, which the Puritans would condemn.

[e] The letter is dated simply July, 1566, omitting, like the last, the day of the month, so that we cannot tell which has the priority. Zurich Letters, Second Series, No. L., p. 121.

[*Hæc enim acta et transacta sunt*] that an unleavened cake *must* be used in place of common bread; that the Communion *must* be received by the people on their bended knees; that out of doors *must* be worn the square cap, bands, a long gown and tippet; while the *white Surplice* and *COPE are to be retained* in divine service. . . . . Thus you have the image and representation, such as it is, of our Church."

Miles Coverdale had been once Bishop of Exeter, and Laurence Humphrey and Sampson I have already spoken of sufficiently to shew that they must be equally considered authorities on such matters.

To continue the history of the controversy will throw no more light on the subject. After this it appears to have cooled down somewhat; according to Bishop Grindal's letter [f] of June 11, 1568, it was again revived by "some more zealous than learned."

As I read letter after letter, I cannot but see that the question of habits and vestments were but the external symbols of the impatience of all authority. The actions of the dissenters—whom Bp. Grindal describes in this letter as holding meetings in London, and administering the Sacraments and ordaining ministers and deacons their own way, and excommunicating those who seceded from them—shew the spirit which animated them. Sampson and Humphrey would not unite with them, and they regarded these two, therefore, as semi-papists, and forbad their followers, as Bp. Grindal avers, to attend their preaching. Take also the letter of George Withers [g], who in writing to the Prince Elector Palatine (but without date), surveys the history of the Church, and it will be seen that the chief point in his complaint lies in the enforcement of the authority of the Queen and of the Bishops :—

"Under the auspices of Henry VIII.," he says, "England drove away the Roman Antichrist, but in such a manner as that his authority seemed not so much suppressed as transferred to the King;" and tracing the history to his own time, he says: "They "deprived Sampson, a most learned man, in the hope that the

[f] Zurich Letters, First Series, No. LXXXII., p. 201.

[g] Ibid., Second Series, No. LXII., p. 156.

"rest would be deterred. When, contrary to their expectations,
"they found **all prepared for resistance,** they made a second
"attempt, **and summoned all** the ministers of the Church in
"London [March 26, 1566[b]], and required them to promise
"obedience to all the commands of the Queen, and more than
"**thirty were** deprived in one and the self-same day. When
"**they** found this plan did not succeed, they devised another
"attack, by prohibiting any one to expound the Scripture in
"**his own** Parish, without a special licence under the Bishop's
"seal.

"You perceive, therefore," he goes on to say, "most excellent
"Prince, the wretched aspect of the Church of England. Upon
"doctrine I will not touch, which, though sound in most re-
"spects, is lame in others. In what way the Sacraments are
"*disfigured* by human invention, will easily appear from the
"public form of prayer,—'the ROYAL INJUNCTIONS *and the*
"ADMONITIONS, *or (as they call them)* the ADVERTISEMENTS, OF
"THE BISHOPS.' For those persons cannot be said to be minis-
"ters of Christ, but servants of men, who can do nothing accord-
"**ing to** the prescript of the word, but are obliged to act, in
"every respect, at the nod *of the Queen* and *of the Bishops*. . . . .
"What, lastly, when the sword of excommunication is taken
"out of the hands of the clergy and handed over to lawyers?"

With this abstract—pointing so clearly as it does to the nature of the Advertisements, as well as to the impatience of the obligation which they, together with the Injunctions, imposed—from an undated letter, probably written between 1568 and 1570, I conclude my survey of the *unofficial* evidence, so far as it is derived from correspondence. This evidence on the whole, I venture to contend, not only bears out fully the arguments which I have adduced from the *official* evidence, but offers additional **proof** of the enforcement, as far as possible, of the *established* **law,** and consequently dispels any notion that Queen Elizabeth could possibly **have so** far abrogated that law in the Bishops'

[b] See *ante*, p. 54.

Advertisements as to render the use of the Cope in any class of churches illegal. Such a change most certainly, on the one hand, would have been alluded to as a triumph for the Puritan party; and, on the other, they could not have written in such general terms as they did that the "Cope was by the Advertisements re-introduced or restored."

There still remains for me to say a few words upon the testimony of HISTORIANS, (on which your Lordship appears to rely for corroboration of the arguments adduced,) before I pass on from the *unofficial evidence* to other matters.

I cannot, however, undertake to give a summary of such testimony, or even to deal thoroughly with that of the ten or twelve authors selected by your Lordship. It is not that I fear that such testimony, when fully examined, would tell against my arguments, but solely because I have already extended my letter beyond reasonable limits.

I would first of all make this general remark upon such testimony. If we have to deal even with a contemporary historian, we have, in matters which he did not actually see or take part in, to test the value of his statements *very much* by the documents he quotes, or by the opportunities which he, in one way or another, shews himself to have possessed for acquiring information; but when we have to deal with historians of a century and more afterwards, we must test the worth of their statements as to facts *wholly* upon the documents to which they refer, or on which they may be presumed to rely.

Your Lordship remarks (p. 28) :—

"These passages in Cosin's Notes, &c., when published in 1710, became the fountain-head of *a new tradition*, afterwards carried on by several writers of the eighteenth and present centuries, by Nicholls, Gibson, Wheatley, John Johnson, Burn, Cardwell, and others, *reversing that* of Hooker, Sparke, L'Estrange, Wren, Heylyn, Sparrow, and every other earlier Churchman of views similar to Cosin's, except Cosin himself."

On this statement I have, first of all, to remark that I find nowhere explained what "the *new tradition*," as it is termed, is, much less what the *old tradition* was, as exhibited in the writers named. Hooker (quoted, NOTES, p. 13) neither implies that the Queen took "other order" as to the Cope, nor that she did not. All he does is to speak, and that incidentally, of the Advertisements as a "decree agreed upon by the Bishops, and confirmed by her Majesty's authority;" misled evidently by the circumstance of Queen Elizabeth's name appearing on the title. There is a clear but concise note in Mr. Keble's edition, to which edition I see your Lordship refers your readers, shewing the difference between the character of the Ordinances as originally drawn up, and the printed edition, issued after her Majesty's authority had been refused.

When we come to Sparke (NOTES, p. 13), the Puritan writer, he magnifies still more her Majesty's part, namely, that *she* appointed the *Surplice* instead of the *Albe*. He does not say a word about the Surplice being used *only*, or about the Cope being forbidden; but the special feature of his statement is, that he gives the grounds upon which he bases it, viz., "*as appears* by the Book of Advertisements, then [i.e. in the seventh year of her reign] *by authority published*." Here we have obviously the error of the "seventh" year, and "her Majesty's" authority derived from a common source, viz., the title.

Your Lordship next refers (p. 14) to a paragraph from L'Estrange[j], but as it is not given, I here quote it entire, as a characteristic example:—

"*The Minister shall use such Ornaments, &c.*] In the latter end of the Act for Uniformity, there was reserved to the queen a power to make some *further* order, with the advice of her Commissioners, &c., concerning ornaments for ministers; but *I do not find* that she made any use of that authority, or put her power into exercise further than is expressed in her Advertisements of the *seventh* year of her reign, by which it is ordered that 'in Cathedrals the chief minister officiating at the Communion shall wear a decent Cope, with Gospeller and Epistoler agreeable.'"

For the ornaments of the Church, the Queen took "further order," i.e. January, 1561, as I have shewn[k]. Whether he was

[j] Anglo-Catholic Library edition, p. 104. (Oxford, 1846.)
[k] See *ante*, p. 10.

ignorant of it or not, may be doubtful, but surely he is not to be trusted as an historian, when he thinks that the use of a Cope in Cathedrals, with a "Gospeller and Epistoler agreeable," constituted a taking of "*further* order."

Heylyn (who lived till Charles the Second's reign) gives us, in the passage quoted by your Lordship (p. 14), another variety of interpretation of the Queen's letter, namely, that—

> "To bring this quarrel to an end [i.e. of the Cap and Surplice] ... the Archbishop is required to consult together with such Bishops and Commissioners as were *next at hand*, upon *the making* of such rules and orders as they thought necessary, ... and that they might be known to have the stamp of royal authority, a Preface was prefixed before them, in which it was expressed .... that *in obedience to her commands* the said Metropolitan and the rest had agreed upon the rules and orders ensuing, which were *by her* thought meet to be used and followed."

With Heylyn it is not a question of the Surplice, instead of the Albe, as it was with Sparke; or the addition of the Cope, with Epistoler and Gospeller, according to L'Estrange; but the ordering of the Caps and Habits and Surplices. Hooker thought the Bishops agreed upon the Advertisements, and her Majesty *confirmed* them; Sparke thought her Majesty, with the consent of the Archbishop, *appointed* the Albe; while Heylyn thought that in order to bring the "*quarrel to an end*," the Queen commanded the Archbishop to *make* the order, ignoring altogether that the Queen's letter—the one which is quoted in the title, and the only shadow of any authority which could be found—was itself the cause and beginning of the quarrel to which he seems to refer. All this is worthless as history; it rests wholly upon guesses made from the title, which had been misunderstood.

The difference between Strype and most of the historians who preceded him is, that he takes the trouble to refer very frequently to his authorities, (I wish his references were fuller,) and from time to time to quote them entire. At the same time, his conclusions are not always drawn very clearly. He was a laborious writer, but he was not methodical, and he too readily argued from single documents, without taking sufficient pains to compare them with others which would illustrate and explain them.

But the passage quoted by **your** Lordship (p. 15) is, to my mind, an instance of his accuracy rather than otherwise, viz. :—

" The Archbishop thought it advisable to print them, under his and the rest of the Commissioners' hands, to signify at least what *their judgment and will* was, and to let *their authority go as far as it would*, which was probable to take some effect with the greater part of the clergy, especially considering their canonical obedience they had sworn to their diocesans. But because the book wanted the *Queen's authority*, they thought fit not to term the contents thereof Articles or Ordinances, by which name[s] they at first went, but by a modester denomination, ' Advertisements.'"

And your Lordship thus speaks of it (p. 15) :—

" There is one passage in Strype *avowedly conjectural*, which being itself *erroneous*, may not improbably be the principal source of the error of Collier and Neal."

Strype, when he speaks of the "Advertisements" having authority with the greater part of the clergy, is evidently referring to Archbishop Parker's letter[1] of March 28, 1566, i.e. written on their publication. I cannot think the first part of the passage deserves the sweeping condemnation of your Lordship (p. 15), that it is "*avowedly conjectural;*" or in itself *erroneous*. As to the second part, namely, the change from Ordinances to Advertisements, I will speak presently [m].

What, then, was the *old* tradition, and what the *new?* We have seen, by the one or two quotations already given, how varied were the ideas of historians respecting the Advertisements. It would be a difficult task to arrange the opinions of the many ecclesiastical writers who incidentally touch upon this question, in an exact chronological sequence ; but I do not think the result would be found to bear out the view put forward by your Lordship, that Cosin's remark had anything to do with what is supposed to be a change in the traditions, which **were** just as varied after 1710, as before. Surely the fact **of the** commencement of **the** publication of *original authorities* by Strype, in 1709, had a great deal more to do with the change in the general character

---

[1] See *ante*, p. 48, the following words : "**Hath ensued** in the most parte of **the Realme** an humble and obedient conformitie." **And com-**pare also with the Archbishop's proceedings at Lambeth on March 20.

[m] For remarks on this paragraph, see *post*, p. 93.

of these traditions, than a single line in Cosin's Notes. It is quite possible that Cosin, when he was writing those Notes (towards the middle of the seventeenth century), took the trouble to look to original authorities for himself (as his opportunities, when in London, during the early part of his career, were many); and hence the general agreement of his statement, that "no other order *so qualified* was taken as regards the ornaments of the minister," with what Strype afterwards wrote. But your Lordship's supposition, that Cosin made the *error*, and later writers followed it, seems to me, for reasons which I have given in the early part of this pamphlet, to be untenable.

The explanation of all this variety of opinion appears to me to be a very simple one, namely, that a reference to *authorities* scattered the old *traditions* of various kinds to the winds, and new ones naturally took their place, depending upon a more or less close attention to the evidence which these authorities supplied. There is, then, no reason to suppose that Nicholls, Gibson, or Wheatley (NOTES, p. 28), were copying Cosin, or that Collier and Neal were copying a particular passage of Strype (NOTES, p. 15); but much to suppose that all, and a great many more, had had their eyes opened through access to original authorities, for which, perhaps, some were more or less indebted to Strype. Hence the general character of the new series, of what your Lordship calls "traditions," but which are really opinions based upon accessible documents, varies from the general character of the statements based upon conjectures as to what the Title to the Advertisements meant.

Let me, in a concluding quotation, contrast with the vague statements of these older historians, the practical, matter-of-fact references, by a legal authority, highly esteemed for his learning,—I mean the Editor of the Sealed Book of 1662 [a], published under the auspices of the Ecclesiastical Society, with

---

[a] "The Book of Common Prayer, with Notes Legal and Historical. By Archibald John Stephens, Barrister-at-Law." 3 vols., London. For the Eccl. Hist. Soc., 1849.

very copious and valuable notes; and also of the "Statutes[o] relating to the Ecclesiastical Institutions of England," with the decisions thereon, in which the notes are most complete as to their references, I mean Mr. Archibald John Stephens.

In the latter book[p], to the Clause XXV. of the Act of Uniformity (i.e. respecting other order), occur the following concise notes :—

"1. *Ornaments of the Church :*—Pursuant to this clause, the Queen (Anno **Regni** 3) granted a commission to the Archbishop, Bishop of London, Dr. Bill, and Dr. Haddon, to reform the disorders of chancels, and to add to the ornament of them, by ordering the commandments to be placed at the east end.—Strype, Park. App. 28.

"2. *Until other order :*—Which *other* order (at least in the method prescribed by this Act) was never made; and therefore, legally, the *ornaments of ministers* in performing divine Service, are the same now as *they were in* the 2nd of Edward 6."

To Clause XXVI. (i.e. respecting further ceremonies),—

"3. *Ceremonies or rites :*—Pursuant **to this clause,** the queen granted a commission to the Archbishop, the Bishop of **London,** Dr. Bill, and Dr. Haddon, her ecclesiastical commissioners, to **peruse the** order of the lessons throughout the whole **year,** and to cause some new Kalendars to be imprinted. . . . . Which commission is stated at length in the Register of Archbishop Parker, and published by Mr. Strype, as is also the Archbishop's mandate to the Bishop of London, for publishing the alterations by them made.—Strype, Park. App. 29 ; Parker, Regist. 215 (*a*), 228 (*a*)."

Here we have the judgment of the lawyer, combined with the knowledge of the historian, and the exact references prove at once the dependence to be placed upon his statements; while they form a marked contrast to the vague assertions, with slovenly-copied extracts, and incomplete references (if any), which characterize the work of the historians on whom your Lordship would rely.

---

[o] "The STATUTES relating to the Ecclesiastical and Eleemosynary Institutions of England, Wales, Ireland, India, and the Colonies ; with the Decisions thereon. By Archibald John Stephens, Barrister-at-Law." In 2 vols. 2nd Edition. London, 1846.

[p] The Statutes, vol. i. p. 370.

VII. OBITER DICTA.

There are some points in the NOTES which have appeared to me scarcely to range themselves definitely under any especial date or fact recorded; but they involve considerations which are more or less connected with your Lordship's argument. I therefore throw them together in one section, giving (on account of my limited space) only a few lines to each.

I. THE NAME "ADVERTISEMENTS." Your Lordship quotes (pp. 15, 16) Strype's remarks[q] with respect to the title :—

> "But because the book wanted the Queen's authority, they thought fit not to term the contents thereof, 'Articles' or 'Ordinances,' by which name they at first went, but by a modester denomination, 'Advertisements.'"

and then follows this remark by your Lordship (p. 16), which I confess to being quite unable to understand :—

> "He [Strype] had evidently not compared with the rejected draft, or with Sparrow's reprint, the original text of the 'Advertisements,' as officially issued in 1566, which perhaps he never may have seen : and he may reasonably be supposed to have been misled by the date, A.D. 1564, at the foot of Bishop Sparrow's title-pages."

Sparrow's reprint is a fairly accurate copy of any one of the three original editions by Wolfe : the spelling, of course, agreeing with none. It is, therefore, *not* a reprint of the rejected draft, but *is* of the edition issued in 1566. Strype had *the* original draft of 1564-5, which he mentions "*penes me*," and he compares it with this. Sparrow's title-pages have *not* 1564 at the bottom of each, but "Printed for Blanch Powlet, MDCLXXXIV." It is true, there is a head-line with the words, "Articles Anno 1564," which of course arose from his believing the Articles were drawn up and issued because of, and immediately after, the letter; and had taken no more trouble to investigate the history, than many other writers both before and after his date. But this in no way militates against Strype's argument, or helps your Lordship's.

[q] For the first part of this paragraph, see *ante*, p. 90.

The fact therefore remains, first, that the word *Ordinances*[1] was used in the title, and that for some reason or another Archbishop Parker modified it into "Advertisements;" secondly, that Strype knew this, having the evidence before him.

While touching upon the question of "reprints" and their value, I may note that Cardwell's reprint — which appears to have been put in as evidence in the Ridsdale case, and accepted by the Judges as an *official* copy I suppose—also fairly agrees with the original copies. It is true this was printed from the preface to Hearne's edition of Camden's "Annals," and compared with the edition of 1584, printed by Thomas Dawson (which happened to be in the Selden collection). Why Cardwell should not have printed direct from an original copy then in the Rawlinson Collection in the Bodleian, instead of printing from it at second-hand, I must leave to others to guess, or explain. And they might perhaps explain, at the same time, why an original copy was not produced in so high a court as that of the Committee of her Majesty's Privy Council, instead of a reprint in 1839, or 1844 (both editions are referred to), of a portion of a Preface to a book printed by Hearne in 1717, which professed to be a reprint of a copy possibly printed in 1566.

One other "obiter dictum." The title "Advertisements," so far as I can find, was never applied to any commands or directions of any kind issued by the Queen. It was not unfrequently applied to Articles issued by Bishops, e.g. amongst the Articles[2] of Overton, Bishop of Lichfield, issued in 1584, are,—

"Certaine *Advertisementes* for a continval order to be observed inuiolably, without any alteration touching the pointes following, within the Diocesse of Cowentrie and Lichfield."

And to such several of the questions put in the Articles of Visitation evidently refer.

---

[1] See *ante*, pp. 40, 41. of the Ritual Commission (1868),
[2] Printed in the Second Report p. 429.

2. THE PRINTER OF THE ADVERTISEMENTS.—Your Lordship states :—

"At the foot of the title-page are the words, *Londini cum privilegio ad imprimendum solum.* .... At the end, after the names of the subscribing bishops, are the words, *Imprinted at London by Reginald Wolfe.*"

Whether, by bestowing half-a-page upon Wolfe's merits and position as a printer, your Lordship intends to imply any special authority to all the books which he printed, I cannot venture to say, but it appears to be so. No doubt certain printing-offices had their special character, as they have now; but because an office had printed one book, issued by "authority" of either Queen, Parliament, or Convocation, it would not follow that other books issued at the same office had the same authority[1].

I do not happen, however, to have found any documents issued by the Queen's direct authority printed by Wolfe, and I have looked through a long list. But what I do find is, I think, very much more to the purpose, namely, that he printed all the documents issued directly by the Archbishop's *own* authority.

The earliest document I have found printed for the Archbishop is in 1560, viz. :—

"An Admonition for the necessitie of the presente tyme, &c., set forth by the Most Reverend father in God, Matthew, Archbyshop, &c. Imprinted by Reginald Wolfe, anno 1560."

A little before 1566, I find :—

"Articles to be enquired of, in the Visitation of the Moste Reverend Father in God, Matthew, by the Suffraunce of God, Archebyshop of Canterbury, &c. MDLXIII.

"Imprinted at London by Reginald Wolfe, Anno Domini MDLXIII."

Again, a little after 1566, I find :—

"Articles to be enquired into in the Diocese of Canterbury by the Reverend Father in God Matthew, by the Providence of God Archbishop of Canterbury, MDLXIX.

"Imprinted at London by Reginald Wolfe, A.D. MDLXIX."

[1] For instance, the Queen's printers, Messrs. Spottiswoode and Co., print the Acts of Parliament by "Authority of *Parliament.*" They also print the "Saturday Review."

WERE ALBES AND CHASUBLES ORDERED, OR ONLY SURPLICES AND COPES?—This is a different question from those which have been discussed; but it enters into the argument, from the circumstance that while the evidence adduced, whether in official or unofficial documents, shews that the Surplices and Copes were understood to be ordered, rare mention is made of Albes, and none of Chasubles whatever.

In the Advertisements themselves also, when speaking of the Ritual to be enforced in the Cathedrals, the Albes and Chasubles are not mentioned, but the Cope only. It may well be asked, why was this? There is little doubt that in the rubrick of the First Prayer-Book of Edward VI., which chiefly governs the "ornaments of the minister" in the administration of the Holy Communion, the expression, "in a white Albe plain, with a Vestment or Cope," meant that a garment which is known by the name of Chasuble might be used, *or* a Cope, whichever, in fact, the Church possessed. Probably, as a rule, the Chasuble was not of so costly a nature as a Cope, or the "principal vestment," as it appears sometimes to have been termed [a], and that may be one reason; there were other reasons, no doubt, why the option was given, but such belong to *minutiæ* of Ritual, which it is not necessary here to touch upon.

To make the matter clearer, I may observe that on a comparison of the several rubricks in the Prayer-Book of 1549, which is undoubtedly the authority in this matter, it appears that the Albe or Surplice were optional, in fact, the difference was not great, both being white garments; but the Surplice is mentioned rather in connection with the Cope (though not excluding the use of the Albe), while the Albe only is (by implication) presumed to be used chiefly with the Vestment:—

[a] "Therefore that it may be known what the Rectors or Vicars are concerned to uphold and repair, and what things by the Parishioners. We ordain . . . the chalice, the principal mass vestment of the Church, 'missale vestimentum ipsius ecclesiæ principale,' with the Chesible, the Alb, the Amyt, the Stole, &c."—Abp. Gray's Constitutions, 1250; apud John Johnson's Canons, A.-C. L. ed., p. 176. Confer also Abp. Winchelsey's Constitutions, ibid., p. 318.

"§ 3. And whensoever the Bishop shall celebrate . . . he shall have upon him, beside his rochette, a *Surplice* or *Albe*, and a *Cope* or *Vestment*. . . .

"§ 74. The Priest that shall execute the ministry shall put upon him . . . . a white *Albe* plain, with a *Vestment* or *Cope*.

"§ 134. The Priest shall put upon him a plain *Albe* or *Surplice*, with a *Cope*.

"§ 447. After the Gospel . . . . . the elected Bishop having upon him a *Surplice* and a *Cope*, shall be presented by two Bishops, being also in *Surplices* and *Copes**. . . ."

In Queen Elizabeth's Injunctions of 1559 there are no definite orders respecting the Ornaments of the Ministers, nor is the evidence as to the exact date when those Injunctions were issued by any means clear; the only thing we know is, that Cecil had a hand in them, and it is quite possible that Sir Thomas Smith and the Divines had none whatever. But there appear to be some further regulations, called "RESOLUTIONS and Orders taken by comon consent of the Bishops," with a sub-heading of "Interpretations and furder Consideracions of Certen Iniunctions." A MS. copy is preserved amongst Archbishop Parker's Papers in Corpus Christi College, Cambridge ʷ. I have never seen a printed copy, though the paper follows on after similar Admonitions of the Bishops, which are printed.

In this document, amongst various explanations (in some cases modifications) of the Articles of the Injunctions, occur what may be best described as some explanations and modifications of the rubrics of the Prayer-Book. One of these directly refers to the Vestments, and it is thus :—

"Item, that there be used but *only one* apparell, as the *Cope* in the ministracion of the Lord's Supper, and the Surplesse at all other ministracions; and that there be none other manner and forme of ministringe the sacraments, but as *the Service boke* doth preciselie prescribe, and withe suche declaration as be in the Iniunctions, concernyng the forme of the Communion bread and placing of the common borde ˣ," &c.

ᵛ The numbers to these rubricks are those of the rubricks as printed in my edition of the "First Prayer-Book of Edward VI. compared with the Successive Revisions." § 3 is from the general rubricks: § 74 is the first rubrick but three, and § 134 is the last but seven in the Holy Communion : § 447 is the third in the Consecration of Bishops.

ʷ Parker MSS. C.C.C.C., vol. cvi. art. 141.

ˣ Dr. Cardwell prints the last lines erroneously, "with the declaration of the injunctions; as for example the common bread." D. A., i. p. 238.

These " Resolutions" were drawn up certainly after Jan., 1561, as they refer to matters enacted in Elizabeth's "further order" of that date, and the probability is, that they had no authority beyond that of Archbishop's Articles. In many particulars the rubricks were very general; on many questions they were silent. These " Resolutions," therefore, and " Interpretations," which as their title tells us " were orders taken by consent until a synode may be had," were employed as a means of promoting a general uniformity. How far they were successful or not is a question on which I need not enter, but that they were in some way or another accepted and understood to be *the law*, I have every reason to believe, though not emanating from the Crown. They are no doubt what Abp. Parker refers to in his letter [1] of Mar. 3, as forming the basis of the first draft of the Advertisements which he sent to Cecil. By "agreed on *amongst us*," he means the four bishops. Several of the articles seem to have been repeated verbatim in the Ordinances of 1565, and retained in the Advertisements of 1566.

I know of no other way to account for the mention only of the Surplice and Cope both before 1566 and after, as being the only Vestments for the Holy Communion, than that these Resolutions were considered to be authorized, and that the Albe and Chasuble, though not abrogated by any more definite authority than the Archbishop's paper implies, had gone out of use.

In arguing from the clause in the Advertisements on which the whole question hangs, and in order to shew that in ordering " a comely Surplice" the Article meant a comely Surplice *only*, the Judges say [2], after quoting the clause from the Advertisements,—

"It was not seriously contended that *Albs* or *Chasubles* could in any reasonable or practical sense, or according to any known usage, be worn, or could be meant to be worn *concurrently* with the Surplice. If, *therefore*, the use of the *Surplice*, at the administration of the Holy Communion, was rendered lawful and obligatory by these 'Advertisements,' the use of *Albs* or *Chasubles* at that administration was thereby rendered unlawful."

[1] See *ante*, p. 35. I do not think the papers preserved at Cambridge are the very ones which were "fasted" on, as there are no marks to shew it.

[2] Ridsdale Judgement, p. 13.

I need not go to the rubrics of the Missal to point out why this sentence will not bear examination. A consideration of the rubrics of the Prayer-Book of 1549, to which I have called attention above, is quite sufficient to shew that the Surplice and Cope were the corresponding vestments (practically) to the Alb and Chasuble; and therefore, to say that the Surplice was not used with the Albe or with the Chasuble seems to evade the question at issue, which is, whether a *special* Vestment was ordered for the Administration of the Holy Sacrament, different from that used in the rest of divine service. The rubrics quoted above shew distinctly that the Surplice does not displace the Cope, since the two are ordered together four times in the four rubrics. That a Cope *may* be put over the Albe is distinctly allowable by the second rubric named. That naturally an Albe, being a more closely-fitting form of white garment than a Surplice, would be associated with a Chasuble, which in its more modern form at least (what its ancient form was is a question of some difficulty) is a more closely-fitting vestment than a Cope. The first rubric does not forbid the *interchange*, but by implication it implies what was most convenient.

I venture to submit, then, that what at first may appear to be a strong argument, turns out, when examined, to be no argument at all. It is only begging the question. I cannot think for a moment this could have been intentional, but that some alterations or corrections must have been made accidentally in the paragraph before it was sent to the printers, which has deprived it of its original purport. For the argument suggested is, that the ordering the Surplice negatives the use of the Cope, and this clearly it does not.

This question also I would ask :—Why should Abp. Parker intend to exclude the Cope in this paragraph of the Advertisements, any more than in the preceding paragraph but one [a] he should intend to exclude the Surplice, where it is ordered that "the minister shall wear a Cope:" he is not there

---

[a] For the three paragraphs printed in full see *ante*, pp. 19, 20.

precluded from wearing both the one and the other, surely; or, again, in the second paragraph, when the dean or the prebendaries preach, they are ordered 'to use their hoods;' they are not surely to use their hoods *only*. Although your Lordship does not follow the Court in the Ridsdale Judgement, and imply that the clause does exclude the Cope, the whole of your Lordship's argument is based upon this theory. For if it was not that the Cope was excluded, in what particular did Queen Elizabeth take that "other order" in the Advertisements, which, if I may so say, it is the chief object of your Lordship's NOTES to prove?

But returning to the original question, although no "other order" was taken upon the question, there seems to have been an *understanding* in Elizabeth's reign that the Surplice and Cope only were to be used, and I can discover no other document which seems to supplant the Albe and Chasuble by the Surplice and Cope than the "Considerations" which I have quoted. Whether the agreement amongst the Bishops, and avowedly only that upon a special interpretation of the rubrick then, would in the least affect the law now, is quite another question.

NEED ORNAMENTS AUTHORIZED BE IMPERATIVE?—I observe that when your Lordship speaks (p. 11) of the bearing of Sandys' letter upon the way in which the act of legislation was interpreted, you say,

"Upon Sandys' 'gloss' it is unnecessary to dwell. It shews, however, that even in 1559 some of the divines of the school to which Sandys belonged were prepared (whether *reasonably* or otherwise) to interpret that proviso [i.e. XXV. of the Act] as leaving the 'Ornaments' of 1552 still in force, and as imposing no *legal obligation* to wear the Vestments of 1549."

The words of Sandys, to which, I take it, your Lordship refers, are:—

"Our gloss upon this text is that we shall *not be forced* to use them, but that others, in the meane tyme, shall not convey them away, but that thei may remayn for the quene."

By the remark, "whether *reasonably* or otherwise," it appears to me that your Lordship bestows a silent approval on the view that the proviso might *possibly* impose no *legal obligation* to wear the vestments of 1549, although their *legality*—that is, that those who had them *might* wear them—was unquestionable. Yet it is difficult to reconcile such a view with that laid down elsewhere[b], by others in common with your Lordship, that Vestments thus *authorized* are *imperative*. If this latter view is held by your Lordship to stand good in Elizabeth's reign, the interpretation of Sandys and others could scarcely be spoken of by you as "reasonable or otherwise;" it could only be as "otherwise." But which is the right one?

Historically, there can be no question that such a policy as Sandys interpreted the proviso to convey was the more probable one. Many were, like the Queen herself, loath to part with the ornate ritual which had been retained under the revision of 1549, and revived under Mary, and to adopt instead the Puritan fashion of the Continent. Many, on the other hand, including the active Puritan faction itself, excited by the overthrow of the Roman ceremonial, would have strongly resented the complete Vestments being forced upon them. The pressure of the Surplice was as much as they could bear, and even the gentle manner in which that was at first imposed was not sufficient to obtain uniformity.

Historically, too, I think it may be said (mainly from the absence of any proceedings being taken to enforce the Cope upon any who had conformed so far as to adopt the Surplice) that Sandys' "gloss" turned out to be true, that ministers were not "*forced* to use them." And this circumstance helps no doubt to explain why the use of Copes fell into disuse; not being enforced, advantage was of course taken to disuse them altogether. There were other reasons also, quite independent of any imaginary law against them, and to these I will next refer.

[b] In the Ridsdale Judgement, p. 5, "the use of the Vestments is not "merely authorized, it is enjoined. "If the Rubrick is taken alone, the "words in it are not optional, they "are imperative."

WERE COPES IN COMMON USE? I think not. There had been in Edward VI.'s reign more than one raid upon all church ornaments (of any monetary value), under the name of banishing superstition; and few persons can look at the actual records of this period without being struck with the outburst, at times, in most districts, of a rage for peculation of Church goods, which seems to have been permitted almost with impunity; it is difficult, indeed, to believe but that this was one important element in the popularity of the Puritan cause. The spoliation of lands by the Crown had probably suggested the spoliation of even the fabric of the Church, by Patrons (as the necessity of Queen Elizabeth's proclamation proves[c]); we could scarcely expect, therefore, those in a humbler sphere to be free from that "covetousness," in respect of the ornaments of the Church. I have given an illustration of the "zeal" shewn in S. John's College, Cambridge[d], where, by the preaching of Mr. Fulke, some were moved so greatly as to become amongst themselves both buyers and sellers in vestments, which were valued at £40, equal to about £400, at least, of our money.

At times, it is true, Commissioners, or Archdeacons, came down upon the depredators. I have only lately had an opportunity of examining some cases in the Register of the Archdeacon's Court for the Oxford Diocese. I here give one or two as a specimen:—

"9 *November*, 1583. *Officium domini contra Will'm Hawkins de Midleton, detect.*—Citat personaliter per Dasie die Lune ult' Comparuit, jurat ad billam detecc'onis respondet in vim jurament' prestit' that being churchwarden he had certayne churche goods w[ch] at the end of his yeare he delivered up, and at this present hath but one peece of a coape w[ch] he paid xij[d] for to William Nixon, and Will'm Capper, fatetur y[t] theare weare belonging to the churche copes, vestments, crosses, censers, and other churche goods.

"Monit est ad inducendum dicta bona eccl'ie."

"—— *Officium domini contra Will'm Nixson seniorem de eadem, detect.*—Citat personaliter per Dasie similiter ut supra comparuit jurat fatetur y[t] he

[c] See *ante*, p. 27. [d] See *ante*, p. 75.

hathe a peece of a coape and a peece of a crosse and noe other thing or churche goods, and hath payed nothing to the churche for yt as yet."

"—— *Officium domini contra Simonem Hawkins de eadem*, **detect**.—Citat personaliter per Dasie die Lune ult Comparuit, jurat, fatetur that he hath none of the churche goods but one peece of a coape et fatetur that he chaunged the chalece of the p'isshe into a communion cuppe of the valewe of iij^{li} what the valewe of the chalece was he knoweth not or howe manie ownces. Monit ad inducendum bona ecclesia in quindenam."

"—— *Officium domini contra Ric'um Smyth de eadem*, *detect*.—Citat personaliter per Dasie similiter ut supra, Comparuit jurat he hath a peece of a coape and noe other church goods, monit ad inducendum."

"—— *Officium **domini contra** Simonem Smyth de eadem, detect*.—Citat per Dasie similiter ut supra Comparuit, jurat fatetur he hath a peece of a coape as his neighbours have and a candlestick wch he solde awaye bye consent of his neighboar Carter for xij^d, and hath answered to the churche as yet nothing for yt."

"20 *March*, 1584. *Officium Domini* **contra** *Jacobum Browne de Sholdham.* —Reservata est pena contumacie in hunc diem, comparuit jurat ad articulum objectum fatetur that he hathe dwelte in Souldern 54 yeares, fatetur that he knewe certeyne churche goods in Mr Stutberies wiffe's hands, viz. candlesticks, a Bason, a crucifixe, other in her hands or Elizabeth Glidwell's hands, and in the same weomen's hands certeyne handbells and Banner clothes & crosse clothes and ye crosse & crucifixe & in Ihon Da.... ll's hands a palme clothe & one chalice w^{ea} Mr. Stuttsburie hathe in his hands for xl^s, but ye moneye he payed not yet & as he thinketh all the vestments be in good wiffe Gledwell's hands."

I take this opportunity of referring to these extracts, because it is from the series—I believe from the same volume—that the late Archdeacon of Oxford, in his last Charge , issued in June, 1877, took the passages to which he specially refers, as shewing that—

"In country parishes there had been before the year 1584 a removal or a destroying of Copes and Vestments, and that in the few instances in which these had escaped, *they were kept as a kind of sacred relique*, which in some cases resulted in their being kept, or detained, or treasured up for what appeared to have been *superstitious uses*."

I am afraid that few, if any, of the examples will bear this interpretation, but that they are of the character of those which

---

* "The Efficacy and Power of the Archdeacon's Court in former Centuries. A Charge to the Clergy and Churchwardens of the Archdeaconry of Oxford, in the year 1877. By the Ven. Charles C. Clerke, Archdeacon of Oxford." (Oxford, 1877, p. 15.)

I have quoted. **They do not,** I fear, illustrate the superstition so much as the **peculation which** was then so prevalent throughout our country villages, under the name of Religious Zeal.

This, and other causes, **had** made the Copes very scarce. When **once taken,** they **were too** expensive to replace, and the clergy of country parishes were, as a rule, **very** poor. I have sometimes been surprised, in looking at records **of** this period, at the illustrations of the comparative poverty of the clergy.

No doubt, too—I readily admit it—the Puritan influence was so strong, that Vestments were **unpopular;** and so they ceased to be used, except in the larger and wealthier **churches.** Public opinion effected the gradual sweeping away of vestments, though the law was certainly opposed to it. The fact does not tell one iota in favour of the view that the law was changed, but **it** does shew the difficulty which the Bishops must have had in enforcing the Cope **in country** parishes; and explains, therefore, why they **enforced** it **only in** cathedrals, **and those** endowed churches where robbery had, from different circumstances, been perhaps **less** general, and where, **if the** church **or** cathedral had been robbed, there were funds sufficient to replace the Vestments.

VIII. THE REVISION BY JAMES I., AND THE RESTORATION BY CHARLES II.

The chief feature which marks the opening of James the First's reign, in connection with the subject of Elizabeth's Advertisements, is that he took "further order," according to the Act, following exactly the precedent of Jan. 22, 1561, and so presenting a marked contrast with the supposed "other or further order" of March 28, 1566. The order was issued thus [e], (Pat. 1 Jac. I. 5. div.)

"James by the Grace of God . . . Whereas all such jurisdictions, rights, privileges, **superiorities and** pre-eminences, spiritual **and ecclesiastical** . . . . are for ever, by authority of Parliament of this our realme, united and annexed to the imperial crowne of the same.

"And whereas also by Act of Parliament it is provided and enacted, **that** whenever we shall cause to take *further* order, for or concerning any *ornament, rite*, or ceremony in the Book commonly called the Book **of Common** Prayer, . . . and our pleasure known therein, either to our **Commissioners** authorized under our great seal for causes ecclesiastical, **or for the** Metropolitan of this our Realme of England, **and thus** further **orders** should be taken therein accordingly.

"We, therefore, understanding that there were in the said booke certeyne things which might **require some** declaration **and** enlargement by way of explanation, and in that respect have required you our metropolitane, and you the Bishops of London and Chichester, **and some other** of our Commissioners, &c., according **to the intent and** meaning of the said statute, and some other statutes alsoe, and by our supreme authority and prerogative **royal, to take some** care and pains therein, have received from you the said **particular thinges in** the said booke declared and enlarged by way **of** explanation, made by **you** our metropolitan, and the rest of our said **Commis**sioners, in manner and form following. . . ."

I am well aware that this refers to "further" order **rather than** to "other" order, **but, as seen in the** previous **case, the** distinction is of no very **great importance**: except this. That "other" order, if taken, would necessitate **an** alteration to be made in the Prayer-Books far more than "further" order. By its **omission, the clergy** in following the Prayer-Book, would in one

---

[e] Printed **in Rymer's** *Fœdera*, vol. **vii.** p. 565, Lond. **1715**; and vol. vii. p. 105, Hagæ, **1742**.

case act absolutely wrong; in the other, although they might not do all that was required, whatever they did would be right as far as it went.

Now it is difficult, in the light which King James's actions throw upon this matter, to conceive how *no* alteration whatever was made after Elizabeth's "other order;" while after James's "further order," a royal proclamation was issued March 5, 1604, "to cause the *whole* book of Common Prayer, with the same explanations, *to be newly printed*." And how *every* detail in the order was duly adopted in all the printed books.

Your Lordship does not refer to this contrast, but only to the circumstance that James I. and his advisers *retained* the Ornaments Rubrick of Elizabeth intact. I had referred to this as an argument, that they could not have understood the rubrick to have been repealed, or that "other order" had been taken in one of its most essential provisions; else they would not have repeated it, because, while the opportunity was afforded by so many corrections being made, they would have seized it to make one in this.

Your Lordship writes (p. 30):—

"Mr. Parker observes that the 'Rubrics, as to the place of Morning Prayer and on Church Ornaments, introduced in Elizabeth's reign,' were at this time 'kept intact and totally uninfluenced by the "Advertisements" of 1564.' It could not be otherwise, unless some unauthorized person had then taken occasion of the King's directions to do what the King had not directed."

But the question at issue is, why did not the King direct the error to be set right? Surely the plea of oversight could not be urged. He had counsellors enough, and no small amount of petty fault-finding, with everything which could be seized hold of to urge alteration, was present amongst the Puritan section of those who were admitted to his presence.

It is inconceivable that any of them had any idea—I might say, had even dreamed—that Elizabeth had taken "other order," and abolished the COPE and other ornaments in parish churches, and not pressed the question on the King.

I take it, that the "myth" of this order having been taken had not yet started into life, or we should have heard something of it.

But your Lordship goes on to adduce an illustration (NOTES, p. 31):—

"The subsequent republication, therefore, of those Rubrics, did not alter their effect, or their relation to the law. An illustration sufficiently apposite, may be derived from a recent example *in which there might have been much greater reasons for changes,* which, nevertheless, were not made. In 1871 an Act of Parliament was passed, authorizing many deviations from the order of Divine Service prescribed by the present Rubrics. But the Rubrics themselves were, and have ever since been 'kept intact,' and totally uninfluenced by that Act of Parliament."

I am at a loss to understand the words which I have italicised. Surely a consideration of the five clauses of the Act of 1872 will shew how very different in principle is its effect from that of the supposed taking *other order* by the Queen.

The following is an abstract of the clauses[f]:—

"2. The *shortened form* (specified in the Schedule) *may be used* on certain days, in lieu of the Order prescribed by the Book of Common Prayer.

"3. Upon any special occasion there *may be used* a *special form* of service approved by the Ordinary.

"4. An *additional* form *may be used* on any Sunday or holyday, [under certain conditions].

"5. The Order for Morning Prayer, Litany, and Holy Communion, *may be used* together, or in varying order, as separate services.

"6. A Sermon *may be preached* without the Services appointed by the Book of Common Prayer, provided it is preceded by certain Collects, &c."

No rubrick is here done away with; nothing that any rubrick enjoins is rendered illegal.

All that is enacted is purely permissive, and above and beyond the Prayer-Book. Any one acting up to the strict rule of the rubricks of the Prayer-Book, cannot be complained against. One must remember that some few years ago not one church in a hundred had any daily service *at all* (Query, have more than one in ten

---

[f] Act 35 and 36 Victoria, cap. 35, (18 July, 1872). Clause 1. refers only to meaning of terms used. Clause 7 excludes the Universities. Clause 8 refers to the Schedule; and Clause 9, to the title of the Act. I have not thought it needful to add these to the abstract.

now), and the law was broken, and still *is broken* with impunity, for all that Bishops did or do to enforce it. The first and chief clause here amounts to this: If you will not do *all* that the law directs you to do, at least do some of it; If you will not read the three Psalms appointed, at least read one of them; If you will not read both lessons, at least read *either* the first or second. Three clauses *permit* extra services, and sermons, if approved of the ordinary; and the remaining clause *permits* having those services separate, which it would be difficult to say that the Prayer-Book ordered to be said together without pause.

Had Queen Elizabeth issued a "further" order of this kind, "that the Priest, if he have no Cope or Vestment, *may* administer the Holy Sacrament in his Surplice," the cases would have been parallel, so far as regards the first of these clauses. If it had been, "that the Priest, in addition to the Vestments ordered by the rubricks of the First Prayer-Book of Edward VI., *may* wear such and such;" or that, "instead of the Cope prescribed, he *may* wear something else," then we should have a parallel case to the other clauses. But, it will be observed, the case is very different; and the comparison which your Lordship here invites between the supposed result of Archbishop Parker's Advertisements, and the Act of Victoria, exhibits rather a contrast than analogy, and suggests that, while for obvious reasons in the latter case the change in the rubric would not be necessary, in the former case, for the same reasons, i.e. if that "other order" had been taken, Queen Elizabeth, to have been consistent, *must* have had the rubric itself changed; and if from any reason (to my mind, it is inconceivable that there could be any) she had omitted to have had this done, her successor, while revising the Prayer-Book, would certainly have repaired the error.

Your Lordship (pp. 31—42) next passes on to what was done by the Lords' Committee of 1641: but it bears so little upon the point at issue, that I cannot spare the space to discuss it. It opens up, practically, a totally different series of questions; and to treat the actions of the Puritan party of 1640 in a small space, would be a more difficult task than I found it to be in treating of them in the early part of Elizabeth's reign.

Possibly I have, in a measure, exaggerated the importance of the report of the [sub]-Committee of 1641, and its bearing upon the Savoy Conference,—nor rightly described it, in the few lines given to it; but no point in this question touches, so far as I can see, the argument with which I am now dealing, so I venture at once to pass on to the Revision of 1661.

I presume I may take it for granted that there is no question as to Cosin's own opinion upon the subject at issue, namely, that the Vestments of the First Prayer-Book of Edward VI. were the legal Vestments of the Church of England. The question is, how far his opinion was shared by the other Bishops who were responsible for the revision; and, secondly, how far, supposing there is any expression which is of doubtful meaning, their known intention may be allowed to weigh in the interpretation. If the words they used are plain and straightforward, as I contend they are, no evidence of that kind is either required, or legitimate.

The object, as I gather from your Lordship's opening paragraph is, as far as possible, to counteract any impressions which might arise from the statements which I had made respecting the active part which Cosin played in this revision; and though it leads me away from the subject, I must clear the ground, so to speak, before I deal with the main subject.

Your Lordship says (p. 43) :—

"Mr. Parker evidently thinks that the entries in 'Cosin's Book' had been accumulating for a long time before the restoration; and that in the state in which it stood before Sancroft's alterations, that book was the product of Cosin's individual mind, influenced, no doubt, by the authorities from which his 'Notes' had been compiled, but unaffected by anything which passed in 1661, at the Conference or elsewhere.

"To the present writer, on the contrary, there seems to be proof *approaching to demonstration*, that (although some entries may have been made in it by Cosin long before) it was made up and assumed the character which *alone* gives it importance, during the interval between the close of the Savoy Conference and the meeting of Convocation on the 21st of November in that year; and that it then represented the mind, not of Cosin only, but of others who were his fellow-labourers in the work.

"Mr. Parker takes notice of the impossibility that the work done by the Upper House of Convocation between the 21st and 27th of November, 1661, could have been got through in that time, without previous preparation; but he makes no reference to the positive statement of Lord Clarendon, which *places this point beyond the region of conjecture.*

"The Bishops, (says Clarendon), had spent the Vacation [July 30—Nov. 20] in making such alterations in the Book of Common Prayer as they thought would make it more grateful to the dissenting brethren, &c."

First, I should like to know if your Lordship had seen the book in question. The expression ("although *some* entries had been made long before"), I think, shews that your Lordship has not. There are a *great many* entries, in different styles of writing, and evidently at different times, though all undoubtedly by Cosin himself; and these constitute a great proportion of the whole of the corrections in the book. The rest are in one hand, apparently written at or about the same time, and sometimes over Cosin's writing, and all by Sancroft.

On the whole, I have come to the conclusion, that the Book was brought to the provisional Committee with none but Cosin's writing in it. And I am inclined to go a step further, and say, that all which was done by this Committee, was written in by Sancroft. I have not stated this in so many words in my book, but I have more than once implied it, e.g., "If, then, we assume that the Corrections in Sancroft's hand were made *by order of* the Committee [g];" again, "by his own hand, or by that of Sancroft, acting *under* the Committee [h]." Cosin's Book, with the title-page of 1619, with his corrections and Sancroft's further corrections, was the rough copy; the other, with the title-page of 1634, was the fair copy. No correction in the latter is in any handwriting but Sancroft's.

It is impossible so to describe a book as to give the reasons for conclusions, from varieties and dates of handwriting. I can only say that were your Lordship to handle the book for a short

[g] Introduction, p. 97   [h] Ibid., p. 385.

time, you would, I believe, arrive at much the same conclusion as myself.

Next, I come to your Lordship's supposition (based on Clarendon's statement) that Cosin had, with the other Bishops, spent the *Vacation* (i.e. from July 30 to November 20, as the note points out) in making these corrections.

In my Prayer-Book, I was unable to give the date when Cosin came up to London for the preparation necessary before Convocation met. Mr. Edward Scott of the British Museum, some short time ago, directed my attention to a letter in one of the collections of original papers—(I have not the reference at the moment at hand, or would give it)—proving that Cosin returned to London only on All-hallow-e'en, that is, on Thursday, Oct. 31. As Convocation met on Nov. 21st, there were just 20 days, including the Sundays, for this revision. I don't see why a *general* statement of Clarendon, in a matter *of this kind*, should place the point beyond the region of conjecture, when a *definite* statement, equally reliable, disproves it.

Then as to the other point; if Cosin had been making corrections *at the same time* as Sancroft, i.e. after October 31, the book would not, I think, have presented quite the appearance it does. It is, of course, impossible to say that Cosin made *no* corrections when he was away between July and November, i.e. after the Savoy Conference, which had closed July 25; or, again, that he made none after the Committee met; but I see no reason for the hypothesis. The only note, and perhaps the most important one of all, which is certainly of this latter date, namely, the one beginning, "My Lords the Bishops at Ely House ordered all in the old method," is certainly in Sancroft's hand, and corresponds with all the rest.

We have clear evidence that, at the provisional meetings of Bishops for these twenty days, or less, and afterwards at the Committee of Bishops, the Ornaments Rubrick was considered amongst others. The words adopted, instead of the words which were in the Prayer-Book, are those written by Cosin in the 1619 book, which it is clear was the rough draft on which the Bishops worked. The rubrick, or (as it afterwards became) schedule of an Act of Parliament, is *clear* and *complete*. There is no room in itself for any doubt as to the general meaning. There may be, perhaps, doubt as to *exactly* what "ornaments" were in the Church of England by the authority specified; but none as to the fact, that if any were known to be in the Church by that authority in 1549, then they were to be retained in the Church in 1662, and so long afterwards as the rubrick remained intact.

That Cosin knew of this theory about Elizabeth having taken "other order" in the matter of Vestments is clear; but that he knew better than to accept it is also clear, as your Lordship practically admits. It was not necessary to repeal anything which Elizabeth had done in this matter, because he knew she had done nothing, and he therefore proposed nothing. The attempt to fix exactly the Vestments which should be used, as he had himself desired[1], naturally fell through. Apart from awaking slumbering controversies, there were good reasons why it should be left somewhat general, and to legislate on the ornaments of the Church would have been productive of more harm than good. It is true that Elizabeth had ordered *all* churches to put up "The Ten Commandments" as a reredos (whether their previous ornamentation admitted it or not); but otherwise the ornaments of the Church, whether in the shape of those for use, or only for ornament, were to be kept *generally* similar to those in 1549. Wealthier churches would have costlier ornaments than others, and it would not be possible to adopt such a mean, which would not involve an appearance of poverty of decoration in large and rich town

---

[1] As shewn by his Considerations of 1641. Qy. was this the time when the rubrick with the words, "That is to say . . ." was written. He had some time before the rubrick was erased, inserted the word "all," but this probably was done when, as he tells us in the first year of Charles's reign (1625), he went to the printing-office, and had the matter looked to, the word "*all*" having been inadvertently left out.

churches, which would not be, if enforced, hard upon poorer and country churches. And so with ornaments of the minister. It is true the Bishops had, early in Elizabeth's reign, issued their Resolutions to reduce the *number* of Vestments, so as to obtain a certain amount of uniformity for all; and later, Archbishop Parker, in the Advertisements, had ordered that *all* cathedrals should have the full complement of such ornaments, the Gospeller and Epistoler being attired agreeably; but it would have been hard to apply this to *all* parish churches. And indeed, on the other hand, if we survey England now, there are some parish churches grander and wealthier than some collegiate churches, and to which the complete apparel would be more suitable.

No doubt also there were the two parties in the Committee. One would have been for restricting the order to too little; the other, perhaps, for enforcing too much. The obvious conclusion, therefore, was come to, of leaving matters as they were. Under the old law, the Bishops had enforced sufficient for decency and order, without pressing too hardly upon those who could not afford it. There was every reason why a law which had worked well should be left alone.

Had I space, I would willingly follow your Lordship through the numerous details which you refer to, touching the progress of the revision; and I feel I ought to say more upon the importance of the part which Cosin played in the undertaking, and which at the outset I had intended to do, but other matters have involved a more extended treatment than I calculated on. The greater part, however, of your Lordship's argument being based upon the hypothesis that the old Ornaments-rubrick had been in a great measure repealed; and being directed, as regards this question, against the view that the revisers reinstated the old rubrick entire, without reservation, loses all its force, if we take into consideration that the rubrick had never been repealed, and that Cosin, the chief of the revisers, *knew* this to be the case.

There are many criticisms also, which your Lordship bestows upon my INTRODUCTION in this part of your work, on which I should have liked to have taken the opportunity to have said a word; but they do not affect the definite argument which I have made the aim and purpose of this letter. Those criticisms which occurred in the early part of your Lordship's work I had an excuse to comment on; but on these I have none. I accept with thankfulness errata, such as *debate* for *delendum* (NOTES, p. 67), and here venture in a note[k] to offer a similar correction in return; also I am obliged for having pointed out (NOTES, p. 38) the repetition of the word "died," after Bishop Hacket, instead of "was not appointed before," which of course the context required, but which, by a slip in copying off my rough notes, was omitted.

Throughout my letter I have, as I have said, another object in view than to defend my work on the Prayer-Book, and it has been this :

To shew that the Advertisements of Elizabeth do not follow in the least degree the precedent which was set for taking "other order" in 1561.

To shew that in themselves they do not profess to be "other" or "further" order, but to be essentially for the purpose of enforcing existing order.

To shew that their history, read by the original communications of Archbishop Parker and others, coupled with the Queen's own letter, prove that whatever order was taken—if any by chance was taken in them—was so, not by the Queen, but by the Archbishop, and that he was not authorized to take any "other," or "further" order, but strictly commanded to enforce existing order.

To point out that your Lordship, and the Court in the Ridsdale Judgement, ignore all this strong evidence, both nega-

---

[k] In Sandys' letter, printed NOTES, p. 11, your Lordship writes : "we have *minuted* reasons to maintain that part." On looking at the original, I find it is "*ministred*."

tive and positive, and rely only upon incidental expressions in official documents, partly contemporary, partly of long-subsequent years.

To shew that of the contemporary documents of this class produced as evidence, not one, when the context is taken into account, supports the view that the Queen took order at all in the Advertisements, but that all imply the reverse; while of those of subsequent years, extending as they do to the end of Elizabeth's reign, and even beyond it, only very few admit of the interpretation of the Queen having taken order; while none, whether early or late, imply that she took *other* order, but on the contrary, all by implication negative the theory.

To shew that the Unofficial Correspondence of the time, from which your Lordship has here and there extracted a passage to prove that some persons thought the Advertisements to be issued with the Queen's authority, do not, when judged as a whole, bear that interpretation; but, on the other hand, that they do very distinctly and in a remarkable manner, prove that the supposed fact of the Queen having taken this " other order," was totally unknown to those who would have been most likely to know, had she done so.

To shew that of the Historians, those who give evidence of making use of original authorities, at once set aside as untenable the view that the Queen took this *other* order; while those only who copy one another, and follow so-called traditions, which can be traced more or less to a misunderstanding of the title, believe the Queen to have taken order at all, and of these, only a very few believe that she took special order in this other matter: in a word, that the theory has all the elements about it of the Historical myth. Such, for instance, as that of Alfred's founding the University of Oxford, which, unknown to all contemporary or nearly contemporary writers, finds its origin in some unrecorded fiction or error, and grows and increases in detail and circumstantial evidence with successive historians, and in proportion as they are further removed from the event.

Conclusion.

In the reign of Richard II., the myth of Alfred's foundation of University College came to be enshrined as an historical fact in the Rolls of Parliament; and our own day has seen the myth of Elizabeth's "Further Order" enshrined as an historical fact in the Records of a high Court of Justice. The one had gained for the members of University College an advantage to which, perhaps, they were not entitled[1]; the other has gained, perhaps, a temporary triumph for the Puritan party in our Church. Further, I dare not prophesy.

The case, too, supplies a good instance of what your Lordship describes (p. 31) as "the way in which, under the influence of controversy, historical errors may grow."

Of a few incidental matters I have spoken amongst the "Obiter dicta;" and while following your Lordship's book down to the revision of 1661, I have added one or two remarks upon matters connected with the later history of the Rubrick.

But throughout I have endeavoured to take an historical, not a polemical view. I have been obliged, it is true, here and there to refer to the Judgement in the Ridsdale Case, but it has arisen from your Lordship's NOTES appearing to be supplemental to the statements there put forward, and so scarcely to be judged fairly without reference to the Report of that Judgement.

And in taking my leave of the subject, which has occupied more of my time and thoughts than I anticipated when I put pen to paper, I conclude with the sincere hope and trust, that in anything I have here written to your Lordship, I have not overstepped the bounds of legitimate criticism.

Believe me, my Lord,
Your Lordship's most humble and obedient servant,
JAMES PARKER.

THE TURL, OXFORD,
March 28, 1878.

To the Rt. Hon. the Lord Selborne.

---

[1] See the Petition, and results given (p. 127), in Smith's "Annals of University College" (Newcastle-on-Tyne, 8vo., 1728). But the very confused account which he gives of the proceedings, renders it impossible to determine the exact rights of the case.

www.ingramcontent.com/pod-product-compliance
Lightning Source LLC
Chambersburg PA
CBHW031829230426
43669CB00009B/1285